EMPIRE BUILDERS

EMPIRE BUILDERS

*An Illustrated History of the Rise and Fall
of Cleveland's Van Sweringen Brothers*

LAUREN R. PACINI

Foreword by John J. Grabowski

INDIANA UNIVERSITY PRESS

This book is a publication of

Indiana University Press
Office of Scholarly Publishing
Herman B Wells Library 350
1320 East 10th Street
Bloomington, Indiana 47405 USA

iupress.org

© 2024 by Lauren R. Pacini

All rights reserved
No part of this book may be reproduced or utilized in any form or by any means, electronic or mechanical, including photocopying and recording, or by any information storage and retrieval system, without permission in writing from the publisher.

This book is printed on acid-free paper.

Manufactured in Canada

First Printing 2024

Library of Congress Cataloging-in-Publication Data

Names: Pacini, Lauren R., author.
Title: Empire builders : an illustrated history of the rise and fall of Cleveland's Van Sweringen brothers / Lauren R. Pacini ; foreword by John J. Grabowski.
Description: Bloomington, Indiana : Indiana University Press, [2024] | Includes bibliographical references and index.
Identifiers: LCCN 2023055988 (print) | LCCN 2023055989 (ebook) | ISBN 9780253069825 (hardback) | ISBN 9780253069832 (ebook)
Subjects: LCSH: Van Sweringen, Oris Paxton, 1879-1936. | Van Sweringen, Mantis James, 1881-1935. | Railroads—Ohio—History. | Businessmen—Ohio—Biography. | BISAC: HISTORY / United States / State & Local / Midwest (IA, IL, IN, KS, MI, MN, MO, ND, NE, OH, SD, WI) | TRANSPORTATION / Railroads / Pictorial
Classification: LCC HE2754.V25 P33 2024 (print) | LCC HE2754.V25 (ebook) | DDC 338.7092/277132—dc23/eng/20240214
LC record available at https://lccn.loc.gov/2023055988
LC ebook record available at https://lccn.loc.gov/2023055989

Unless otherwise indicated, all photographs are the property of Artography Studios and Press. Copyright © Lauren R. Pacini, Photographer. All rights reserved

In loving memory of
Philmore J. Hart, 1922–2022
Architect and Activist; Inspiration and Friend

CONTENTS

Foreword viii
Acknowledgments xi

Prologue   1
Introduction   4
ONE | Building a City   7
TWO | The Emergence of Eastern Suburbs   35
THREE | Building Shaker Heights   65
FOUR | Creating an Empire   129
FIVE | Building a Railroad Empire   155
SIX | The Dominoes Fall   173
SEVEN | After the Van Sweringens   191
EIGHT | Afterword   203

APPENDIX A   Population of the Western Reserve   245
APPENDIX B   Genealogy of the Van Sweringen Family   246
APPENDIX C   Real Estate Standards   248
APPENDIX D   Deed Restrictions   252
APPENDIX E   Van Sweringen Demonstration and Master Model Homes   256

Index   259

Links to online images appear on pages
5, 70, 86, 90, 101, 103, 105, 116, 117, 217, 225, 234

FOREWORD

THE TERMINAL TOWER, WHILE NO LONGER THE TALLEST BUILDing in Cleveland, remains, for many, as "the" symbol of the city. Perhaps, more importantly, it also stands as a reminder and, indeed, a monument to the business empire created by two brothers, Oris Paxton and Mantis James Sweringen.

Yet the visibility of the tower stands in contrast to the historical "invisibility" of Oris Paxton and Mantis James Van Sweringen. Leaving next to no personal papers, their careers, accomplishments, and personal lives have been traced largely through legal documents and secondary accounts. Two volumes, *The Van Sweringens of Cleveland* by Ian Haberman and *Invisible Giants: The Empires of Cleveland's Van Sweringen Brothers* by Herbert Harwood Jr. focus largely on the rise and collapse of their business empire. Largely absent in these monographs and a variety of shorter articles are the details of their personal lives and, to a substantial degree, a more focused view of their impact on Cleveland and the nation during the first two decades of the twentieth century, a time when business and industry operated in what might be considered a middle ground between the excesses of the Gilded Age and the restraints of Progressive Era regulation. That void has resulted in several myths concerning their private lives. Nor have previous works fully placed the Vans' career and accomplishments in the wider context of the history of Greater

Cleveland from the late nineteenth century to the 1930s, a period when the city experienced incredible growth in terms of both population and spatial expansion, the latter having been driven by both annexation and, particularly, suburbanization.

This volume by Lauren Pacini provides a different look at the "Vans," one that focuses strongly on their impact on the built landscape of Greater Cleveland. It also provides a more intimate story of two brothers who rose from poverty to the pinnacle of wealth and power in the roaring twenties. The narrative is supported and enhanced by numerous archival images and contemporary black-and-white photographs by the author. Importantly, the author provides a detailed history of the two Van Sweringens, drawing, in part, on early family correspondence, thus providing an image of the brothers that is more personal than that available in previous accounts. Pacini's emphasis is on their rise from poverty, and it includes accounts of the failures that occurred on their way to success. It also avoids the innuendos that have come to characterize the lives of two brothers who were brilliant but shy and closely devoted to one another.

While covering much of the story of their rise to fame and fortune, and the subsequent waning of their business empire, the focus of this work is the situating of their real estate career squarely within the broader history of the spatial expansion of the city and early suburbanization. Certainly, there is no question that their creation of Shaker Heights was of enormous importance. Indeed, it is one of the aspects of the city's history that has found its way into national overviews of suburbanization, such as Kenneth Jackson's *Crabgrass Frontier*. By using a combination of text and images, Pacini places that accomplishment into the wider context of expansion and suburbanization in the Cleveland area from the post–Civil War era to the 1930s. And it was suburban development that led to the creation of the Vans' railroad empire—one that began with the purchase of a major railroad simply to obtain a short area of trackage to complete a light-rail route from Shaker Heights to city center. This seeded their development of a national rail empire, one that almost achieved single ownership of a full, transcontinental rail route. This achievement, and its eventual collapse during the Great Depression, was what made the two men "national" figures.

In many ways the Vans were an iteration of the high and mighty that had come to characterize the early decades of the twentieth century—but they were cut from a different cloth. They were not Samuel Insull, yet they fit into the model of the time, and their legacy is perhaps still one of the most visible of that time—seen not only in Cleveland's Terminal Tower but also in the vast suburban empire they created to the east of the city. It is the evolution of that empire that anchors the narrative of this volume.

John J. Grabowski, PhD
Krieger Mueller Associate Professor of Applied History,
Case Western Reserve University
Historian/Senior Vice President for Research and Publications,
Western Reserve Historical Society
Editor, *Encyclopedia of Cleveland History*

ACKNOWLEDGMENTS

My deepest appreciation is extended to the following, without whose help this book would not be a reality:

Western Reserve Historical Society—Kelly Falcone-Hall, President and CEO; John J. Grabowski, Historian/Senior Vice President for Research and Publications; Ann Sindelar, Acting Library Director and Reference Supervisor.

City of Shaker Heights—David E. Weiss, Mayor; Cameron Roberts, former City Planner.

Shaker Historical Society—Keith Arian, President; Brianna Treleven, Executive Director.

Shaker Heights Public Library—Michael J. Bertsch, President; Amy Switzer, Director; Meghan Hayes, Local History Librarian.

Cleveland Heights Historical Society—Kenneth Goldberg, President; Korbi Roberts, Trustee

Roy Larick, PhD—Archaeologist, Bluestone Heights.

Dunham Tavern Museum & Garden—James M. Edmonson, President, Board of Trustees; Lauren Hansgen, Executive Director.

Ashtabula County—David Thomas.

Ashtabula County District Library—Martha Shippy, President; Carrie Wimer, Archive Librarian.

Holmes County Historical Society—Mark Boley, Executive Director; Candace Barnhart, Curator.

Wayne County Historical Society—Ray Leisy, President.

Jefferson Historical Society—Norma Waters, President; Dave Martin, Vice President.

Platt R. Spencer Historical Society (Geneva, Ohio)—Jamie Ortiz, President; Sue Ellen Foote, Executive Director; Barbara Pruden.

Chippewa-Rogues Hollow Historical Society—Eric Pandrea, President; Mary Mertic, Vice President; Earl Kerr, Past President.

Juniata County Historical Society (Mifflintown, Pennsylvania)—Seth Mosebey, President; Shirley Covert, Research Volunteer.

City of Cleveland—Justin M. Bibb, Mayor; Charles Mocsiran, City Archivist.

Cuyahoga County—Chris Ronanye, County Executive; Michael W. Chambers, CPA, Fiscal Officer; Portecia Montecalvo; Judith Cetina, County Archivist.

Smithville Community Historical Society—Ralph Smucker, President.

Northern Ohio Railway Museum—Steve Heister, President.

Mad River and NKP Railroad Museum (Bellevue, Ohio)—Chris Beamer, President.

Pennsylvania Trolley Museum (Washington, Pennsylvania)—Scott Becker, Executive Director.

Fort Wayne Railroad Historical Society—Kelly Lynch, Vice President.

Drone Ohio (Cleveland, Ohio)—Jeff Holbury, Senior Photographer.

Sears Holdings Archives (Hoffman Estates, Illinois)—Eddie Lampert, former Chairman and CEO.

Shaker Village of Pleasant Hill (Harrodsburg, Kentucky)—Maynard Crossland, President and Chief Executive Officer; Billy Rankin, Vice President of Public Programming & Organizational Strategy; Amy Bugg, Chief Marketing Officer.

Special appreciation is extended to all who opened their doors and agreed that my photographs of their properties would be included on the pages of this book.

EMPIRE BUILDERS

PROLOGUE

ON THE LAST PAGES OF *INVISIBLE GIANTS: THE EMPIRES OF Cleveland's Van Sweringen Brothers* (Indiana University Press, 2003), author Herbert H. Harwood Jr. said in part,

> Any Van Sweringen biographer faces a daunting job. If nothing else, this work attests to the brothers' absolute fixation on both personal and business privacy. Their associates and office staff were chosen to be close-mouthed, and their public relations people were steeped in the philosophy that the best publicity is no publicity. When public statements were necessary, reporters and writers seldom got much more than carefully crafted quotes designed to achieve a specific purpose and mention nothing else. Thus, many semi-truths and a few pure fabrications helped create the enduring and confusing Van Sweringen mythology.
>
> Furthermore, they left no journals or diaries and, beyond formal business communications, no personal letters of consequence. Without wives and children, they also left no family records or intimate memories. Indeed, few people in their home city of Cleveland could claim to know them. As just noted, their closest associates and employees were circumspect in the extreme during the brothers' lifetimes, and most remained so after their deaths—partly out of admiration for them and probably partly because of sensitivity to the many attacks which came during the last years. As a result, the Van Sweringen story has heavy doses of speculation, hearsay, and legend.

During my research for this volume, I was struck by the similarities between the Van Sweringen brothers and Levi Tucker Scofield, the architect, artist, and sculptor of the Cuyahoga County Soldiers' and Sailors' Monument. While I undertook the research for *Honoring Their Memory: Levi T. Scofield, Cleveland's Monumental Architect, and Sculptor,* there was likewise a sparsity of documentation.[1] Scofield left no letters or papers; although, unlike the Van Sweringens, he was married and had five children—four of whom participated in their father's business—who were witnesses to much of their father's life and passed stories down to their descendants. A small number of Scofield's architectural drawings are known to exist in the archives of Cleveland's Western Reserve Historical Society. They are said to have been found in a cardboard carton in the corner of a closet in the offices of Scofield's architectural firm on the fourteenth floor of the Schofield Building when the offices were being cleaned out sometime after Scofield's death.

In writing about Scofield for the 125th anniversary of the dedication of the monument, I had a firsthand account in *History of the Cuyahoga County Soldiers' and Sailors' Monument*, written by William J. Gleason—himself a veteran of America's Civil War, president of the monument's board of commissioners and chair of the executive committee—and published by the monument commissioners in 1894, the year the monument was dedicated.

The Van Sweringen brothers had no such Gleason. Other than twenty-seven letters written by the Van Sweringen brothers and their three siblings to their father during the spring and summer of 1897 while he was traveling to visit relatives throughout Pennsylvania, there is no known written record of the brothers' youth.[2]

The brothers did have Louise Clara Davidson Jenks, who, along with her husband, Benjamin Lane Jenks, was among the brothers' closest friends. Jenks was one of the brothers' longest-term employees and closest confidants. His wife, also known as Daisy, often served as a hostess when the brothers entertained business associates. At her husband's urging, Daisy wrote *O. P. and M. J.* as a gift for their son, David, on his thirtieth birthday in 1940, to share "some of the little intimate things so revealing of those two dear Van Sweringen men." In a note of explanation to David, Daisy said of the essay, "I shall try because I realize that you might remember that they seemed impatient at times and 'un-understanding' with Youth. One must not forget that they had no youth and that all of us, when worked too hard in our every day [sic] lives, are so often careless and unintentionally abrupt . . . seemingly unkind." She went on to describe the brothers as follows:

> Oris Paxton . . . with dark complexion, low blood pressure, physically slow and inactive with a quick clear mind . . . very kind and gentle until through some difficult, absorbing project, the continuity of his thoughts were [sic] disturbed. Then he would show irritation; but always afterward repentant and apologetic, willing to admit his faults and ask for forgiveness . . . An [sic] humbleness not often found in so brilliant a mind.
>
> Mantis James . . . light complexion, high blood pressure, quick and alert. Though the younger of the two brothers, he felt that O. P. was his to care for, protect and manage. From the time they went into business together they had but one common bank account; and it was for M. J. to see that his brother's bag was packed, his tickets bought and needed money given him when he departed, with all reservations made ahead in New York or where ever [sic] he was to go. Nor was O. P. the only one to be managed. Mantis wanted to take all of us under his wing and plan for us . . . never too tired to do another kindly deed for any of us, even to the people he employed in the office or on the farm.[3]

And the brothers had Raymond F. Blosser, staff writer and editor, and later bureau chief for the Associated Press in Cleveland from 1935 to 1943. His papers include his unpublished biographical manuscript, with notations and corrections by William H. Wenneman—O. P.'s private secretary, who was with the older brother at the time of his death—among others.

In this untitled biography of Oris Paxton and Mantis James Van Sweringen, Blosser described O. P. as "one of the most persuasive men the world has known."[4]

> He was the super salesman, "ne plus ultra." He showed shrewd capitalists his dreams and walked away with millions in less time than the average man needs to get into line. And he left them charmed and smiling, ready to lend more.
>
> Van Sweringen combined a prismatic personality and a swift, daring mind to hoist himself from a less-than-penniless real estate salesman to command of a railroad and real estate empire with assets of more than three billion dollars. Cleveland, Ohio, was his base, but his realm extended from the Atlantic to the Rockies.

An incurable optimist, he was incapable of doing anything on a normal scale. "I am not, thank heaven, built on a negative basis," Van Sweringen snapped to an adversary. He proved it by starting life with nothing, ending it with $80,000,000 less. Between those extremes he and brother Mantis James Van Sweringen, two years his junior, boomed their fortune to $140,000,000 or more.[5] Their power reached such heights that James W. Gerard,[6] former ambassador to Germany, included them in his famed list of sixty-four persons who were "ruling the country."[7]

Van Sweringen had the nerve of John Pierpont Morgan—and Morgan's money to work with. Millionaires found his magnetic conversation so irresistible that he pyramided to power and fortune on successive alliances with such men as William Henry Gratwick and John Joseph Albright, the Buffalo, New York, capitalists; President Alfred Holland Smith of the New York Central Railroad; the junior J. P. Morgan; and fabulously rich George Fisher Baker, Sr., of New York's First National Bank. Then, in adversity, he turned to George Alexander Ball, the fidgety Muncie, Indiana industrialist whose fruit jars lined housewives' pantries across the country.

As an obscure Cleveland land peddler, O. P. Van Sweringen fed himself by the grace of his creditors and sometimes by the perspiration of his relatives. Then he had a dazzling idea, and his infiltrative charm and earnest persistence converted empty pasture land [sic] into the pretentious dream suburb of Shaker Heights, a haven for Cleveland's wealthy."[8]

Unlike Gleason's firsthand account, Blosser's work was compiled from his interviews with those who did have firsthand knowledge to share with the writer.

NOTES

1. Lauren R. Pacini, *Honoring Their Memory: Levi T. Scofield, Cleveland's Monumental Architect and Sculptor* (Cleveland, OH: Artography Press, 2019).

2. Letters were donated to the Juniata County Historical Society by Barbara Van Sweringen, granddaughter-in-law of Herbert Van Sweringen.

3. Typescript of the second draft of "Untitled biography of the Van Sweringen brothers of Cleveland," 1946 [Container 1, Folder 1–4] MS 4543 Raymond F. Blosser Papers, Series II, Western Reserve Historical Society, Cleveland, Ohio.

4. Raymond F. Blosser (1913–1997) was staff writer/editor and, eventually, bureau chief for the Associated Press in Cleveland, Ohio, from 1935 to 1943. In his spare time beginning in 1938, Blosser conducted interviews and extensive research for a biography of Oris P. and Mantis J. Van Sweringen, developers of the exclusive suburb of Shaker Heights, Ohio, and builders of Cleveland's Union Terminal, who amassed huge holdings in railroads during the 1920s. Blosser finished his manuscript in 1946, but it remained unpublished. Blosser was public relations director for the New York Central Railroad until 1956 and vice president in charge of public relations and advertising at Union Commerce Bank in Cleveland from 1956 to 1973.

5. The personal wealth of the brothers in 1930 was more than $3 billion. The total value of their empire would exceed $56.8 billion in 2024 dollars.

6. James Watson Gerard III (1867–1951), a lawyer, diplomat, and justice in the New York Supreme Court.

7. "Gerard's List of Sixty-Four Who Rule the United States," *New York Times*, Sunday, August 24, 1930, 5.

8. Blosser, 1.

INTRODUCTION

TWO BOYS, SEVENTH-GENERATION AMERICANS, WERE BORN into abject poverty to a mother who died while they were still very young and to an alcoholic, disabled Civil War veteran father who tried but was unable to provide for his five children. At just nineteen, the eldest son became the breadwinner, and the two daughters became caregivers for the youngest siblings, who would go on to reshape the concept of suburban life in Cleveland, Ohio. As young men, the brothers envisioned a garden community built on the "Heights" above what was then the sixth-largest city in the nation. As Frederick Lewis Allen said in *The Lords of Creation: The History of America's 1 Percent*,[1] "These two young men were the Van Sweringen brothers of Cleveland, upon whom had been bestowed the singular names of Oris Paxton and Mantis James. They were not twins by birth, for O. P. Van Sweringen was two years older than M. J.; but they were twins by choice. They lived together, worked together, planned together; bachelors both, they were almost inseparable; they even slept in twin beds. Each knew everything the other did. They were almost like two halves of a single personality. And they had a joint and very remarkable career." Given the obstacles they faced in their youth, they were well equipped to overcome the challenges they faced in creating a business empire, unequaled in the 1920s.

This book places the life and career of the Van Sweringen brothers into the larger context of the history of Cleveland. It begins with the founding, growth, and changes of the city during its first century and some of the events that set the stage for the young Van Sweringen brothers' creation of a beautiful and affluent suburban community on the border of Cleveland, all while assembling the third-largest railroad empire in the nation. Using photographs that illustrate the changing built environment of Cleveland, the book links the early history of the city and the first developments in what became known as the Heights to the Van Sweringens' careers. That history of architecture and suburbanization served as their classroom. The successes and failures of others served to inform their own development of Shaker Heights. Against all odds, the brothers' boundless vision became a reality. That meteoric rise and the brothers' unending drive for success ultimately set them up for catastrophic failure despite their incredible ambition and their dependence on and commitment to each other. Nearly a century after their deaths and the collapse of their empire, what they created remains central to the identity of the cities of Cleveland and Shaker Heights to this day.

Unlike the work of previously published biographies of the brothers, this volume is intended not for the bookshelf but for the coffee table. As an architectural photographer, I prefer to tell the story through contemporary photographs wherever possible. Words alone do not do justice to the splendor of the architecture of the Vans' real estate developments. Images, therefore, are central to the story. Previous biographies contain little more than a passing glance at the brothers' early years. I believe that understanding the environment in which the brothers were born, grew, and developed their drive is essential to fully appreciate who they became and what they accomplished.

Likewise, I do not believe that the story of the Van Sweringens ended with the end of their lives. To believe so would be to diminish the importance of those lives. The epilogue, therefore, contains a discussion of the events that have transpired in the nearly nine decades since their deaths and poses what I hope will prove to be thought-provoking questions for the reader to ponder and answer in the context of their own life experiences.

Beyond the book: throughout this book, you will see Quick Response (QR) codes like the one to the right, which will allow you to view additional content on your mobile device. Go to the App Store or Google Play to download a QR code reader and scan this code and the others.

NOTE

1. Frederick Lewis Allen, *The Lords of Creation: The History of America's 1 Percent* (New York: Open Road Media, 2017).

ONE

BUILDING A CITY

CLEVELAND . . . THE EARLY DAYS

Cleveland was founded in 1796 when General Moses Cleaveland, a veteran of the American Revolution and one of thirty-six founding investors in the Connecticut Land Company, led a surveying party from Canterbury, Connecticut, to the Western Reserve, a part of Connecticut's old colonial claim.[1] The land was divided into five-mile square townships, including Cleveland Township, East Cleveland Township, Euclid Township, Newburg Township, Bedford Township, and Warrensville Township. Cleveland Township was laid out around a ten-acre town commons and smaller lots, where homes would be built. The remaining townships were divided into one-hundred-acre lots suitable for farming. The surveyors also recorded the natural resources, including details about the terrain, trees, plants, animals, and water, before returning to Connecticut for the winter.

Although Moses Cleaveland remained in Connecticut, the rest of the surveyors returned the following year. With them were Lorenzo Carter and Nathaniel Doan. Carter became Cleveland's first permanent settler, building a small log cabin, and later a larger one on the east bank of the Cuyahoga River that would serve as a hotel and tavern, a town hall, a jail, and an informal religious meeting house. In 1802, having bought more than twenty-three acres of land, Carter began to build the first frame house in the village, but it was destroyed by fire before the construction was completed.

Doan, a blacksmith, who oversaw the livestock during the journey to the Western Reserve, would return to Connecticut with the surveying party for the winter, returning with his wife and six children in 1798. The following year, he purchased a one-hundred-acre lot near the intersection of a trail and a brook, five miles to the east of the public commons that we know as Public Square—where he first set up a blacksmith's shop, followed by a hotel and tavern, a store, and a saleratus (sodium bicarbonate) factory. The trail, a part of the historic Native American Lake Shore Trail, would become known as the Buffalo Road that extended from Buffalo, New York, to Detroit, Michigan. In 1825 it was renamed Euclid Street, and in 1870, Euclid Avenue. The brook would be named Doan Brook, as it remains known to this day. In 1906, when the Cleveland City Council adopted an ordinance changing north–south street names to numbers, and houses were renumbered accordingly, Doan Street became East 105th Street. Contemporary street names will be used once the historic names have been introduced.

Map of the Western Reserve including the Fire Lands, 1826. Courtesy of Cleveland Public Library Map Collection.

The early growth of the hamlet was slow due to the inhospitable conditions and prevalence of ague (malaria) in the lowlands along the Cuyahoga River. Most of those who first settled in Cleveland Township moved on to Newburg or Doan's Corners to escape the intolerable conditions. As the new century dawned, the population of Cleveland stood at seven (see app. A).

Lorenzo Carter Replica Log Cabin, 1976–2021. This replica of the original Lorenzo Carter cabin was commissioned by members of the Women's City Club of Cleveland in celebration of the city's bicentennial in 1976; it stood at the intersection of Merwin and West Avenues (less than a quarter of a mile from the site of the original log cabin) until it was demolished in 2021.

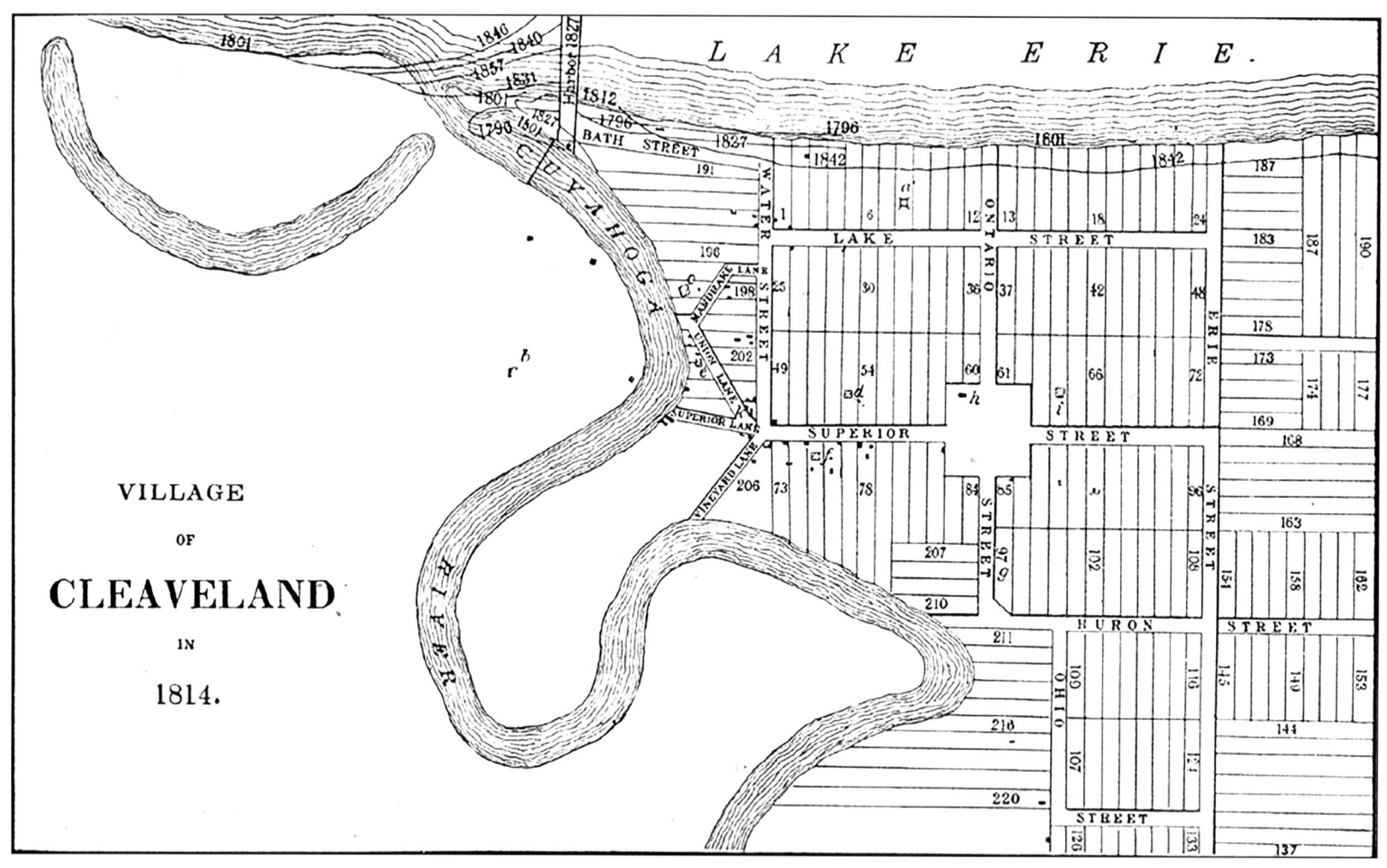

The Village of Cleaveland, Amos Spafford, 1801. Corrected by Alfred Kelley, 1814. Reproduced in *A History of the City of Cleveland*, James Harrison Kennedy, 1896. Courtesy of Cuyahoga County Archives.

The main gate of Erie Street Cemetery, 2254 East 9th Street, 1826.

Settlement in the Western Reserve was not for the faint of heart. On June 3, 1797, David Eldridge died while attempting to cross the Grand River with his horse on his way to Cleveland. He was the first known European to die in the Western Reserve and to be buried in what became known as the Ontario Street Cemetery, south of Public Square. He was joined that year by William Andrews in July and Peleg Washburn in August, both succumbing to dysentery. Eldridge's remains were relocated to the Erie Street Cemetery in 1835. Located on the east side of East 9th Street, between Erie Court and Sumner Avenue, and extending to Brownell Street (East 14th Street), Cleveland's second cemetery had been established in 1826, replacing the original community burial ground.

Following the opening of the new cemetery, the remains of unknown pioneers were relocated from the Ontario Street Cemetery to a common grave on East 9th Street, later marked by a bronze plaque placed by the Early Settlers Association of the Western Reserve in 1946. Other early pioneers buried in the Erie Street Cemetery included Lorenzo and Rebecca Carter and John W. Willey, Cleveland's first mayor. Willey's remains have since been relocated to Lake View Cemetery in East Cleveland, although the original headstone remains in the Erie Street Cemetery.

The first recorded deed in the records of Cuyahoga County documents that on April 14, 1808, Timothy and Mary Burr of Hartford, Connecticut, conveyed 260 acres of land in Tract 8 in Cleveland Township to Timothy and Maria Beardslee Burr for $260. The deed was recorded in book 1, on page 1, on July 14, 1810. Page 2 of the same book shows that the State of Connecticut, Andrew Kingsbury, Treasurer, conveyed 5,320 acres in "Township No. 6"—Rockport Township—to Ephraim Root of Hartford, Connecticut, on April 7, 1810, as recorded on July 20 by John Walworth.

By 1814 there were more than a dozen log cabins along a four-block section of Euclid Avenue beginning at Public Square. Some of the cabins doubled as businesses, including a brewery, stone yard, carpenter's shop, and doctor's office. In 1819 Rufus and Jane Pratt Dunham arrived in the Western Reserve from Mansfield, Massachusetts. On May 14, 1824, they purchased 23.63 acres on Euclid Avenue for $147.68. By 1827 they had increased their holdings to nearly eighty-two acres. They began to build the north portion of the structure at what is now 6709 Euclid Avenue, and known as the Dunham Tavern Museum and Garden, likely completing it in 1832. That was followed by the main block of the home immediately to its south. By 1838, with the addition of the west wing, the house looked very much as it does to this day. The frame house served as their home and a tavern for weary travelers on the Buffalo Road.

Cuyahoga County records show that the Dunhams initially moved to sell their home and its immediate surrounding acreage to the Wilbur family, relatives of their son-in-law James S. Welch. Title transfer complications ensued, resulting in the sale of the property instead to Cleveland banker George Williams and his wife Mary for use as a private residence in October 1857. The nearly two-hundred-year-old home has had remarkably few owners. It remained in the Williams family until 1889 when George Williams died; Dr. James A. and Oriana L. Stephens then acquired the property, making it their home until Dr. Stephens's death in April 1930.

In 1932 landscape architect A. Donald Gray rented the tavern from the doctor's widow, restoring much of the building and replanting the orchard. For a time, the tavern served as a studio for artists and printmakers sponsored by the Works Progress Administration. On December 24, 1936, Mrs. Stephens sold the property to Dunham Tavern, Inc., funded in part by a gift from Mrs. Benjamin P. Bole, who had grown up on the "most beautiful street in America," in a mansion designed by Levi T. Scofield and built in 1875 at 7809 Euclid Avenue. Today the Dunham homestead is the oldest structure on its original foundation in Cleveland, thought to be the first structure east of Willson Street, now known as East 55th Street.

Dunham Tavern Museum & Garden, 6709 Euclid Avenue, 1824.

Lock 38 with Lockkeepers House and Tavern on the Ohio and Erie Canal,
7104 Canal Road, 1825–1827.

Tinkers Creek Aqueduct, 7300 Canal Road, 1825–1827.
Restored between 2011 and 2021.

CLEVELAND'S CHANGING ECONOMY

Initially an agricultural community, Cleveland became a mercantile center with the War of 1812. In 1825 the decision was made to build a 308-mile-long canal from the mouth of the Cuyahoga River in Cleveland, south through Columbus, and then to the Ohio River near Portsmouth, 110 miles east of Cincinnati. The thirty-eight-mile section between Cleveland and Akron consisted of forty-four locks and three aqueducts. When the canal was completed in 1832, there were 146 locks, built to a standard of ninety feet long by fifteen feet wide, to raise and lower the canalboats. Six aqueducts were constructed to bridge the canal above creeks. Lock 38, at the twelve-mile mark, includes what was likely the lockkeeper's house and an inn or tavern. Six-tenths of a mile upstream, the reconstructed Tinkers Creek Aqueduct carries the canal and beside it the towpath, north and south above the creek, which wends its way west to join the Cuyahoga River.

Cleveland began to experience rapid growth with the influx of Irish immigrants drawn to work on the canal as unskilled and semiskilled laborers. With the canal's completion and the discovery of iron ore in Michigan's Lake Superior range in 1844, the city was on a course to become one of the leading industrial cities in the nation and consequently one of the wealthiest. In 1857 Henry Chisholm invested in one of the first rolling mills in Cleveland, and in 1873 Charles Otis founded America's first open-hearth steel mill. By the dawning of the twentieth century, Cleveland ranked fifth in the nation in steel production.

The pace quickened as John D. Rockefeller invested in an oil refinery in 1863, leading to the creation of Standard Oil just seven years later. In 1870 Henry Sherwin, formerly a paint distributor, and Edward Williams formed Sherwin Williams & Company to manufacture paste paints, oil colors, and putty. In 1876 Jacob Cox moved a small machine tool company from Dunkirk, New York, and established the Cleveland Twist Drill Company. In 1881 Worcester Warner and Ambrose Swasey moved their fledgling machine tool company from Chicago to Cleveland, establishing the Warner & Swasey Company east of Willson Avenue on East Prospect Street at the Cleveland & Pittsburgh Railroad overpass, now known as East 55th Street and Carnegie Avenue.

At their heights, Standard Oil Company was the world's leading producer of petroleum products, Cleveland Twist Drill was the world's largest producer of high-speed drills and reamers, and Warner & Swasey was the world's leading manufacturer of turret lathes and a leading manufacturer of telescopes and observatories. Only Sherwin-Williams, the world's largest producer of paints and pigments, remains.[2]

THE MOST BEAUTIFUL STREET IN AMERICA

European immigrants flocked to the city, drawn by the abundance of jobs in iron and steel, oil and chemicals, and heavy manufacturing industries that would make Cleveland the nation's fifth-leading city by 1920, both in population and in industrial output. As the city's factories, mills, plants, and refineries prospered, so did their owners, many of whom built some of the forty sprawling mansions on Euclid Avenue, east to East 40th Street—Millionaires' Row—known as "The most beautiful street in America." At its peak, some 250 luxurious homes extended four miles along Euclid Avenue. Included among them were the homes of John D. Rockefeller, Henry Chisholm, Charles Otis, Jacob Cox, Henry Sherwin, Worcester Warner, and Ambrose Swasey.

Nathan Perry, a merchant and fur trader who had bought and sold numerous parcels of land in the Western Reserve beginning in 1813, bought one hundred acres of land on the north side of the Buffalo Road, extending to Lake Erie. He cleared the land for farming and, in about 1830, had a frame-and-brick home built by master builder Jonathan Goldsmith, three hundred feet from the street. As Jan Cigliano described in her book *Showplace of America: Cleveland's Euclid Avenue, 1850–1919*, "The first houses on Euclid Street were fairly modest frame dwellings. They were rooted stylistically in the plain vernacular of the villages in upstate New York and New England."[3] Perry's new home, although larger than the earlier houses closer to Public Square, was no exception, but the deep setback that would be copied in the houses that followed set the

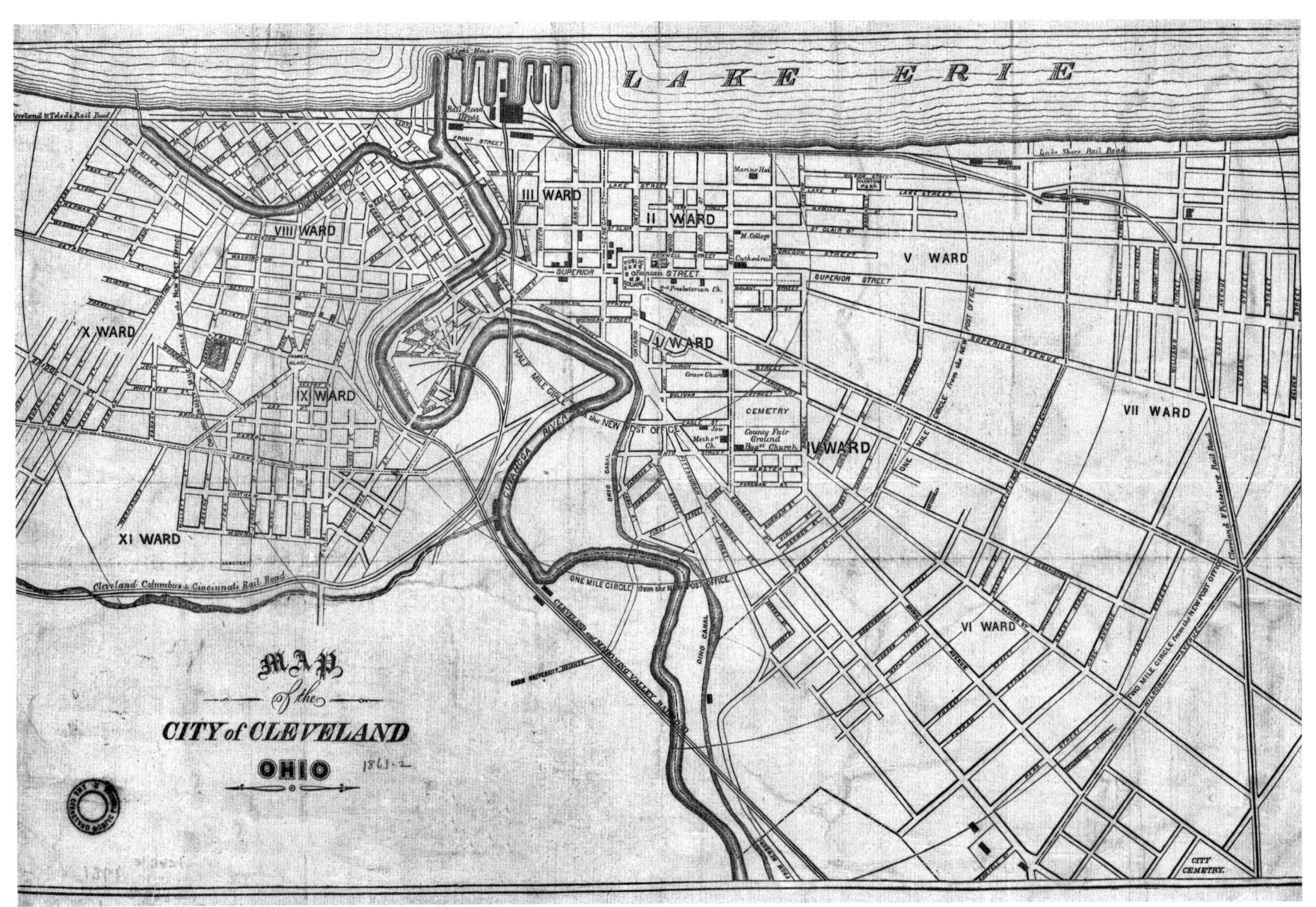

Map of the City of Cleveland, 1862. Courtesy of Cleveland Public Library Map Collection.

Stager-Beckwith Mansion, 3823 Euclid Avenue, 1866.

character of future development along Euclid Avenue. In 1832 merchant Peter M. Weddell, followed by carpenter Samuel Dodge in 1838 and then Dodge's sons Henry and George, built along the north side of the street.

The Stager-Beckwith House is today the longest-standing mansion on Euclid Avenue, built in 1866 for Anson Stager, general superintendent of Jeptha Wade's Western Union Telegraph Company. In 1868 Stager sold the mansion to T. Sterling Beckwith, a principal in Beckwith, Sterling and Company, which specialized in carpeting and interior decorating. After Beckwith's death, his family remained in the house until 1909. Originally designed by Joseph Ireland, the mansion was redesigned in 1912 by J. Milton Dyer and Henry H. Walsh. In 1913 the mansion became the University Club, originally an invitational young men's social club and temporary residence with apartments on the upper floors for graduates of any of forty select colleges and universities. In 1980 the University Club became a meeting and social place for business and professional women and men. Today, the mansion is home to the Children's Museum of Cleveland.

The glory days of Euclid Avenue spanned much of the era of Victorian architecture, including early Gothic Revival, Folk Victorian, Greek Revival, Italianate, Second Empire, Stick, Romanesque Revival, Shingle, Colonial Revival, and Queen Anne styles.[4] Originally, homes were built only on the north side of Euclid Avenue from Public Square to East 40th Street, on parcels that extended to what today is Payne Avenue. When development extended beyond East 40th Street, parcel depth was constrained by Mason Street (today, Commerce Avenue) and Hough Avenue as development extended almost to Doan Avenue (today, East 105th Street) with the home of Mrs. F. L. Ford at 10302 Euclid Avenue.[5] Parcels on the south side of Euclid were much shallower, constrained by Prospect Avenue.

By the mid-1880s Millionaires' Row had begun to change. The first commercial building, the Stillman Hotel, was erected at the intersection of Euclid Avenue and East 12th Street in 1884. The elegant eight-story hotel and apartment building was the subject of an article in the *New York Times* on April 12, 1885, when the structure, believed to have been fireproof, proved not to be. The headline of the article read "A Cleveland Hotel Ruined." Ruined but not destroyed, the Stillman was restored and served Cleveland until it was razed in 1902. On September 29, 1916, the Stillman Theater opened on the site of the former hotel. The first true movie palace in Cleveland, the eighteen-hundred-seat Stillman Theater was one of the Midwest's largest and most luxurious theaters ever built. With moviegoers preferring suburban theaters, the Stillman closed in 1963 and was demolished in 1965. A parking garage for the Statler Hotel (now the Statler Arms Apartments) was built on the site.

Euclid Avenue was often compared to the Champs-Élysées in Paris, Unter den Linden in Berlin, and Prospekt Nevsky in Saint Petersburg. What differentiated Euclid Avenue from the others was what ultimately led to its demise. The grandeur of Euclid Avenue—its variety of exquisite architecture, vast lawns, iron fences and gates, and tree-lined streets—was not dictated by city ordinances but was self-imposed by those who lived there. The residents wanted to improve Euclid Avenue by creating a boulevard and took their request to City Hall, but the mayor had other priorities.

Cleveland's mayor, Tom Johnson, mounted an effort to create a new "downtown." Johnson established the Group Plan Commission to address the need for larger, modern public buildings to house municipal, county, and federal offices. The city engaged architects Daniel H. Burnham—the mastermind behind Chicago's 1893 Columbian Exposition—Arnold W. Brunner, and John M. Carrère to develop a master plan in keeping with the City Beautiful movement. Many of those who served on the Group Plan Commission were residents of Euclid Avenue. The concept of a park boulevard on Euclid Avenue failed to gain traction, but the development of Cleveland's Mall surrounded by neoclassical buildings succeeded as it was seen to serve the greater good.

Other forces were at work that would ultimately spell the end of America's most beautiful street. Property values began to skyrocket, and with them, the burden of property taxes. For example, the two-and-a-half-acre estate of Sylvester Everett, with its Romanesque Revival mansion, valued at $39,000 in 1890, was valued at $604,000 in 1920, and property taxes rose from $1,100 to $14,000 during the same period. In addition to the increase in property taxes, residents were faced with steep increases in the cost of operating and maintaining their aging properties and their staffs of as many as one hundred servants. In 1911 the last new residence, that of Anthony Carlin, was built at 3233 Euclid Avenue. With the ratification of the Sixteenth Amendment in 1913, federal income tax, abolished in 1872, was restored. In 1914 the Corlett Building was built as the home of the Cadillac Motor Car Company, an automobile dealership at the northwest corner of Euclid Avenue and East 20th Street, the former site of the Victorian-era mansion of Dr. William T. Corlett, built circa 1882–1885 and attributed to Cleveland architect Levi T. Scofield.

HOW EVOLVING TRANSPORTATION CHANGED CLEVELAND

Urban transportation began in Cleveland with the founding of the horse-drawn, trackless Cleveland & Newburgh Railroad in 1834. Service went from Public Square, east on Euclid Avenue, then muddy and rutted, to East 101st Street just short of Doan's Corner, and then on to a quarry at the top of Cedar Glen. In 1859 Cleveland City Council awarded franchises to two companies to lay rails in the streets. The East Cleveland Railway Company began laying iron-strapped wood rails from Euclid Avenue at what is now East 55th Street to what is now West 6th Street. The Woodland Avenue Street Railroad Company laid rails as well. As the popularity of the street railroads grew, so did the lines, extending service to other streets.

Three suburban steam lines were established to extend service into the countryside. First, organized in 1867, the Rocky River Railroad ran from West 58th Street and Bridge Avenue through Lakewood to Sloane Avenue in the vicinity of the Rocky River. Second, the Cleveland & Newburgh Railroad was organized in 1868, running from East 55th Street and Woodland Avenue to Broadway and Miles Avenue. It was called a "dummy" railroad because the steam engines were disguised as passenger cars to avoid spooking horses. Ironically, the railroad was forced into receivership in 1877, after numerous accidents. The third steam line was the Lakeview & Collamer Railroad, extending from the intersection of Becker Avenue (now East 71st Street) and Superior Avenue, where it connected with the Superior Street Railway and continued along Superior Avenue and then Euclid Avenue to Euclid Village.

Steam failed to provide the answer for powering street railroads. In 1884, the first attempt to use electricity failed, but four years later, the first successful use of electrical power prompted all but two street railroads to switch from steam. That year the Cleveland Railway Company built a power-generating substation with steam-powered generators on Ashland Avenue near Cedar Road. A second building was constructed in 1890 and was expanded in 1892 to keep up with the demand for electric power.

By 1901 street railroads were unanimous in their use of electricity. In 1909 Cleveland City Council adopted a resolution, and in 1910 the voters approved the consolidation of all the many street railroads into a single franchise—the Cleveland Railway Company. Unable to keep up with the demand, the generation of electricity was outsourced to the Cleveland Electric Illuminating Company in 1917. The Van Sweringens purchased the railway in 1930, owning it until 1937, and in 1942 the City of Cleveland purchased the company's shares, and the municipally owned Cleveland Transit System assumed control of the city's transit operations.

As Cleveland prepared for its centennial year, a new era was being ushered into the Western Reserve. Manufacturers of bicycles and carriages were beginning to retool their shops to enter the era of the automobile. Akron, set to become the nation's rubber center, due largely to the automobile, was home to the Western Reserve's first self-propelled vehicle. In 1892 Akron resident Achille Philion patented a steam-driven vehicle that he exhibited at the 1893 Chicago World's Fair.

Just five years later, Robert Allison, a mechanical engineer from Port Carbon, Pennsylvania, arrived by train in search of the Winton Motor Carriage factory. Later that day, with Alexander Winton's promise that the automobile would be delivered within a week, Allison signed an order and paid the $1,000 price in advance. With the sale of the first

Cleveland Railroad Power Station, 2162 Ashland Road, 1888.

1899 Winton Phaeton. Western Reserve Historical Society Crawford Auto Collection.

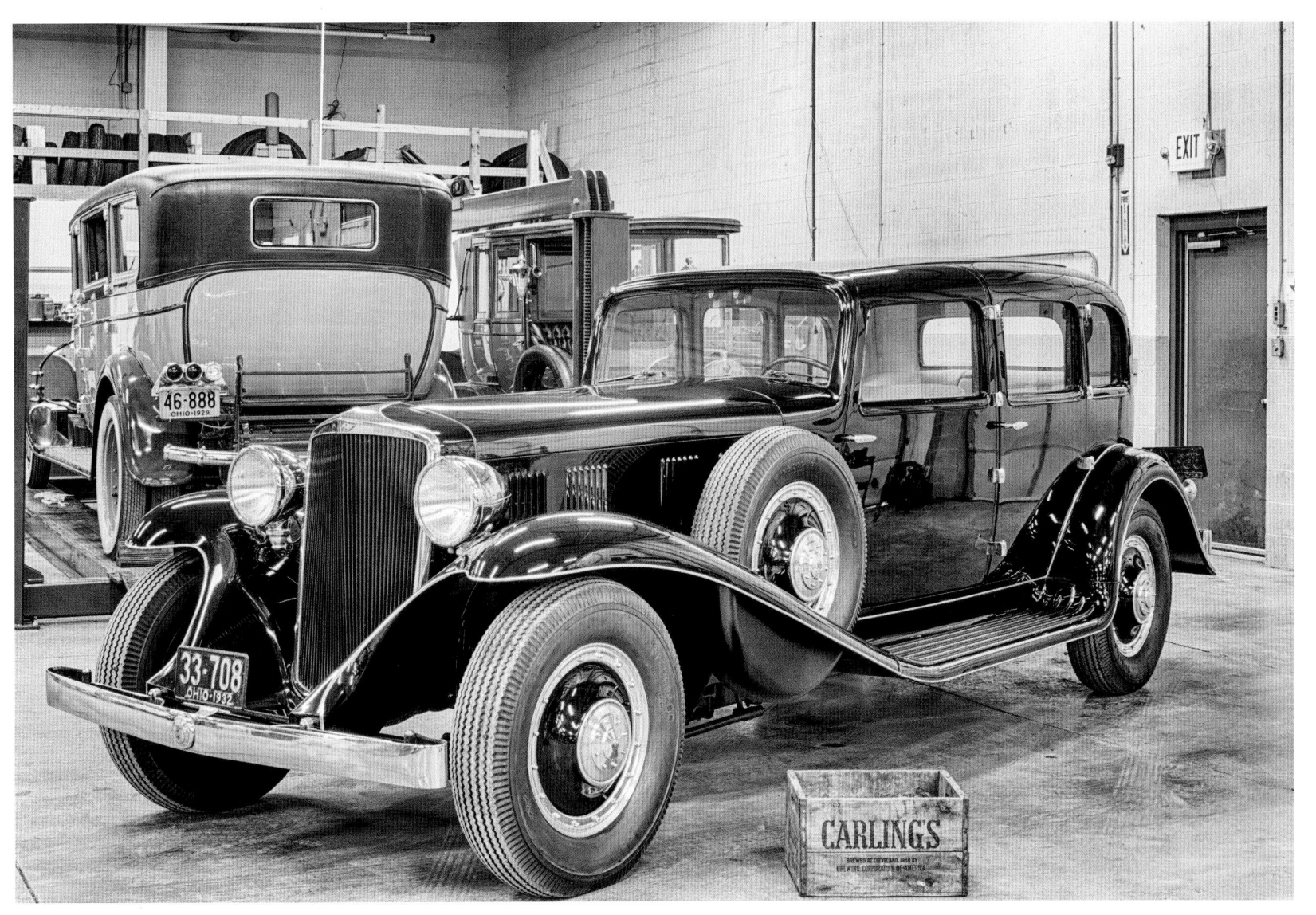

1932 V-16 Peerless Prototype. Western Reserve Historical Society Crawford Auto Collection.

American-made, standard-model gasoline-powered vehicle, Cleveland and America entered the automobile era. Cleveland's remarkable history as an automobile city would span nearly thirty-five years. During that time more than eighty manufacturers of luxurious, high-quality, high-priced vehicles operated in Cleveland. With mass production, automobiles were soon within the reach of all Americans, and the title of America's automobile center shifted from Cleveland to Detroit. Peerless, the last of the Cleveland luxury automobile manufacturers suspended operations in November 1931.

The advent of the automobile and streetcar changed life in Cleveland. They made it convenient to live greater distances from work, and the pollution and noise of the industrial city made doing so highly desirable as well. Cleveland's wealthy residents began to move from Millionaires' Row to Glenville and East Cleveland, while others were drawn to "the Heights."

THE CHANGING ARCHITECTURAL LANDSCAPE

The World's Columbian Exposition of 1893 marked a turning point for the architectural landscape in Cleveland and America and set the tone for the development of the Heights. Although short-lived in the United States (1893–1929), the Beaux Arts style had an enduring influence on the landscape of major American cities—most notably, Cleveland, New York, and Washington, DC.[6] Architects of government, cultural, and academic buildings embraced the French neoclassical style that was the centerpiece of Daniel H. Burnham's "White City" at the Columbian Exposition. This was the style of the City Beautiful movement, an attempt to establish a sense of order and dignity, generally absent in American urban planning at the time.

By 1900, Cleveland was the seventh-largest city in the nation, having grown twenty-three-fold in the prior fifty years, and by 1920, it would be the fifth largest. The federal and city governments wanted new, larger, and more modern facilities, as did the Public Library. There was pressure from the city leaders for a new train station as a hub for all transportation.

Burnham, Brunner, and Carrère introduced the Group Plan to Cleveland in 1903. The original plan called for construction directly north of Public Square, in an area that was a part of the city's commercial district at the time. The decision was made to locate the project on a parcel of land northeast of Public Square to eradicate one of the city's most disreputable sections. At the same time, Millionaires' Row was beginning to lose its luster. Between Public Square and East 9th Street, the early mansions had been replaced by shopping arcades and office buildings. Built in 1890, the five-story Arcade financed by John D. Rockefeller, Steven V. Harkness, Louis Severance, Charles Brush, and Marcus Hanna was designed by John Eisenmann and John H. Smith and inspired by the Vittorio Emanuele in Milan, Italy. Nicknamed Cleveland's Crystal Palace, the Arcade holds the distinction of being the first indoor shopping center in the nation. Although a departure from the stately mansions of Millionaires' Row, the Arcade was consistent with the avenue's architectural splendor.

The concept behind Cleveland's Group Plan was the development of a mall, a long public park surrounded by the city's major civic and governmental buildings of uniform height in the neoclassical style. In late 1901 and early 1902, even before the Group Plan Commission submitted its plan, preparation was well underway. The post office vacated its building on Middle Street, later designated East Second Street, facing Public Square, and relocated to the Wilshire Block. The Case Block, only recently renovated by Levi Scofield, was likewise vacated. City Hall moved to temporary space across Wood Street (now East Third Street), on the land now occupied by the Cleveland Public Library. The former post office and Case Block were demolished, and the site was prepared for the New Federal Building, now known as the Howard M. Metzenbaum US Courthouse. The cornerstone was set on May 20, 1905, and the first building to be built as part of Cleveland's Group Plan was dedicated on March 20, 1911.

In answer to the dramatically increasing cost of heating Euclid Avenue mansions in winter, Cleveland oilman, investor, and real estate speculator George Canfield, the founder and president of the Canfield Oil

The Arcade, 401 Euclid Avenue, 1890.

Howard M. Metzenbaum US Courthouse, 201 Superior Avenue, 1911.

Stockbridge Hotel, 3328 Euclid Avenue, 1911.

Company, announced an agreement with Samuel Mather for a ninety-nine-year lease on a parcel of land on the south side of Euclid Avenue, just east of East 32nd Street. Plans were developed for a five-story luxury apartment building that opened in 1911. In the heart of Millionaires' Row, the design of the luxurious Stockbridge Hotel consisted of four apartments on the first floor and two four-thousand-square-foot apartments on each of the next three floors, each with sixteen rooms and two bathrooms, offering an affordable alternative that allowed residents to close their mansions for the winter. The amenities included a restaurant on the lower floor (the suites did not include kitchens) and a ballroom on the top floor. Although the suites were spacious enough for several servants, housekeeping services were also available.

Euclid Avenue was undergoing a substantial change. One by one, the spectacular largely Victorian-style homes of the rich and famous that lined the most beautiful street in America were demolished and replaced with commercial buildings. Today, in addition to the Stager-Beckwith mansion, six of Cleveland's Millionaires' Row mansions—and a carriage house—stand as a testament to the grandeur of Cleveland's heyday. Three other structures have been incorporated into more recent buildings.

The Stockbridge remains as well, having served as temporary homes for traveling entertainers the likes of Bob Hope, Jack Benny, Dean Martin, and Lucille Ball, in town to perform at the Hippodrome, or headliners with the Metropolitan Opera in town for their annual performances. An addition to the rear of the Stockbridge provided space for lesser performers and others traveling with the stars. Today the spacious suites have been transformed into forty much smaller but comfortable apartment units.

THE VAN SWERINGEN FAMILY

Sixty miles south of Cleveland's Public Square is Wooster, the seat of Wayne County, Ohio. Oris Paxton (1879–1936) and Mantis James (1881–1935) Swearingen, the youngest of five children of James Tower and Jennie Curtis Swearingen, were born in Chippewa Township, outside Wooster. Their fifth-great-grandfather, Garrett van Sweringen, a son of nobility, was born in Rijnsaterwoude, South Holland, in 1636, and emigrated from Beemsterdam (now part of Amsterdam), Holland. Departing on December 21, 1656, at the age of twenty, aboard the *Prins Mauri* bound for colonial America, the ship went aground off the shore of Long Island's southern coast. The journey continued aboard the *Beaver*, arriving in New Amstel—now known as New Castle—on the bank of the Delaware River on April 25, 1657.

Garrett married Barbarah de Barrette, with whom he had nine children. The third was a son, Thomas, who Americanized the family name, dropping the "van"—which he later gave to his second son as his first name—and changing the spelling of the family to "Swearingen." The first evidence of the revision of the spelling back to "Sweringen" appears on O. P.'s birth certificate, but it was not until 1900 when the elder of the young brothers was twenty-one that "Van Sweringen" reappeared. It was around the same time that the brothers formally adopted their initials in place of their first and middle names.

At the age of twenty-eight, their father James Tower Swearingen—third great-grandson of Thomas—left his home in Bealetown (now Honey Grove) in Juniata County, Pennsylvania, drawn to the fertile, rolling land in Wayne County, Ohio. He had every intention of becoming a farmer, but a crowded public meeting at the Wayne County Courthouse in Wooster inspired him to respond to President Lincoln's call for volunteers. On June 4, 1861, he and more than one hundred other volunteers boarded the train from Wooster to Camp Dennison, a military recruiting and training post near Cincinnati. On June 6 James mustered into Company E, 4th Ohio Infantry, and quickly saw the horrors of war in Virginia, at Winchester and other battlefields in the Shenandoah Valley. After moving to the eastern front, he fought at Fredericksburg and Chancellorsville.

On May 7, 1864, Swearingen was seriously wounded at the Battle of the Wilderness (May 5–7, 1864), a turning point, both in the Civil War and for young James Swearingen. It was the first battle of Lieutenant

General Ulysses S. Grant and General George G. Meade's 1864 Virginia Overland Campaign against General Robert E. Lee and the Confederate Army of Northern Virginia. Both armies suffered heavy casualties, with approximately five thousand soldiers killed in the three-day battle. Swearingen mustered out on June 21, 1864, and when he was able, returned to Bealetown.[7] The physical and emotional scars of war would remain with Swearingen for the rest of his life.

Following his mother's death in 1866—his father having died in 1855—James Swearingen decided to try his luck in the oil fields of northwestern Pennsylvania. Although Swearingen had done well initially, he soon lost everything as oil that had once brought twenty dollars a barrel dropped to ten cents. He married Jennie Curtis, twelve years his junior, and they settled down in Franklin, Pennsylvania. The couple's first four children were born in northwestern Pennsylvania, where their father seems to have bounced from odd job to odd job, unable to pursue jobs for which he was qualified as an oilfield engineer because of the wounds he sustained in battle. Herbert Curtiss was born in 1868; Maude Alene in 1870, dying in infancy; Carrie Blanche in 1872; and Edith Elizabeth in 1874. In 1878 the couple and their three surviving children moved to Wayne County, Ohio, where James hoped that he would be better able to provide for his young family.

The Swearingen family moved to a farm (Dwelling Number 473) in Chippewa, northeast of Wooster.[8] The family struggled to make ends meet. Jennie helped where she could by taking in sewing. Oris Paxton was born on April 24, 1879. The story is told that his father heard a mother calling her son, probably "Horace," but he heard it as "Oris." The infant's middle name—Paxton—was in honor of their friend and neighbor, S. Paxton Downing, who looked out for the family, providing food when they were hungry and coal or wood when they were cold. It is apparent that James Swearingen was in a downward spiral, and Jennie was growing even more frail.

The family moved to Rogues Hollow, south of Doylestown, Ohio. It was there that Mantis James was born on July 8, 1881, and where the three oldest children attended the local one-room school no. 5. The schoolhouse was built in 1861 and served the children of the area until 1938. Today the former schoolhouse at 12017 Rogues Hollow Road is a private residence (see app. B).

When Oris was three and Mantis was one, the family moved again—this time to Geneva, Ohio, in Ashtabula County, where one of Swearingen's friends had settled earlier. They first lived at 15 Park Street (now 95 Park Street), believed to have been built before the Civil War, and then at 34 Eastwood Street (now 269 Eastwood Street), built in 1880.[9] On September 25, 1882, James filed for a disability pension and worked as a fireman. For the first time, life was good. Then, on January 18, 1886, when the eldest child was eighteen, and the youngest was just four, Jennie succumbed to tuberculosis that had plagued her for years. Her death left her husband to see to the needs of their five children. James, perhaps devastated by the loss of his beloved Jennie, who though frail for years had been the strength of the family, lost his job as a fireman, leaving only his pension and kindly neighbors and church members to provide for the family. Taking matters into his own hands, nineteen-year-old Herbert walked the sixty miles to Cleveland in search of work. He landed a job at the Cleveland Storage Company, and, once again, the family moved.

Following the move to Cleveland in 1887, the family lived first at 733 Ansel Avenue near the intersection of Euclid Avenue and Doan Street—where the boys undoubtedly played along Doan Brook in what would a decade later become Rockefeller Park—and later at 920 Doan Street (south of Cedar Avenue on East 105th Street).[10] They first attended the Bolton School at East 90th Street and Carnegie Avenue, and then the Fairmount School at East 107th Street and Euclid Avenue. Whether James's growing alcoholism was a consequence of the pain from the memories and wounds of war or the loss of his wife, he no longer made any effort to work. While Herbert worked at Cleveland Storage, the two sisters cared for the younger brothers.

In 1894 when the young brothers were fourteen and twelve, respectively, Oris and Mantis had a *News and Herald* newspaper route, consisting of fifty farmhouses on the escarpment, many of them scattered around the site of the old Shaker colony. In summer, they spent a great

Sweringen Residence, 269 Eastwood Street, Geneva, Ohio, ca. 1860.

Sweringen Residence, 95 Park Street, Geneva, Ohio, 1880.

deal of time exploring the abandoned Shaker buildings and the Reader Quarry.

Each brother's formal education ended after the eighth grade. The boys went to work at the Bradley Chemical Company, where their elder brother was then working, each of them starting as office boys before being promoted to clerks. They rode their bicycles the five miles to and from work. Oris named his bicycle "The Vaness." It was soon clear that for Oris, if not also Mantis, office work did not portend a fulfilling career. Oris was becoming the visionary and planner, Mantis the implementer and manager that would make them the inseparable business partners and empire builders they became.

On December 8, 1897, Herbert married Mabel Adams. Moving into a house of their own meant that the family was losing its best wage earner. Despite occasional baskets of food left on the front porch, there never seemed to be enough money left at the end of the month to clear the tab for the family's food. It was ten years later that Oris cleared up the family debt with the kindly neighborhood grocer.

In 1900 the Bradley Fertilizer Company closed. Oris was twenty-one and Mantis was nineteen when the boys, still living at home, sought to fulfill their childhood dream of entering the world of real estate. It was then that the brothers assumed their initials in lieu of their first and middle names. The first-known recorded transaction involving O. P. Sweringen was his purchase on April 27, 1900, of a lot on South Logan Avenue (now East 96th Street) from Mrs. Minerva Fuller for $1,900. Lot 409, Sublot 7 measured 30 feet of frontage and 128 feet, 9 inches of depth and was located on the west side of the street.[11]

Selling houses part-time in Cleveland's western suburb of Lakewood taught the brothers some hard lessons and resulted in judgments against them. They placed an advertisement in the *Plain Dealer* on May 3, 1900: "Fine corner lot on heights: 138 feet adjacent boulevard: $1,500: easy payments. Or will build. Phone 2752; Doan 730 J. O. P. Sweringen."

The brothers appear to have tried their hands at acquiring undeveloped parcels on Doan Street, bidding at auction on properties with tax delinquencies, but there is no indication that they had any luck. Try though they might, the brothers sank deeper into debt. And try, they did. They tried selling stone from an abandoned quarry near the former Shaker settlement, calling the business "The Pioneer Stone Company." They established the "Prospect Storage and Cartage Company" and made a little money with weekly sales of unclaimed goods. They took to selling butter and eggs from a wagon with "O. P. & M. J. Van Sweringen"—the first reappearance of "Van"—painted on the side.

O. P. met a Cleveland lawyer by the name of Frederick L. Taft, a partner in the law firm of Smith, Taft, and Arter. Taft was well-connected among a syndicate of Cleveland businessmen with an interest in utility ventures. Impressed by Van Sweringen, Taft assigned him a variety of projects that necessitated that O. P. travel to other cities. It was through those projects that Van Sweringen came to understand the intricacies of high finance. Combined with the lessons they had learned from the failures of their earlier business ventures, the stage was set for the rest of the brothers' lives, first as real estate developers and then as railroad magnates as well.

NOTES

1. The spelling of the city's name was changed from Cleaveland in 1831 by *The Cleveland Advertiser*, an early city newspaper. For the name to fit on the newspaper's masthead, the first "a" was dropped, reducing the city's name to *Cleveland*. Contemporary spelling will appear throughout this book.

2. In 1885, Rockefeller relocated Standard Oil from Cleveland to New York. In 1911 the US Supreme Court ordered dissolution of the company having been found in violation of the Sherman Antitrust Act. Cleveland Twist Drill and National Acme merged to form Acme-Cleveland in 1968, and in 1994 Cleveland Twist Drill was sold to Greenfield Industries. In 1980, Warner & Swasey was acquired by Bendix Corporartion and in 1992 the Solon plant was closed.

3. Jan Cigliano, *Showplace of America: Cleveland's Euclid Avenue, 1850–1919* (Kent, OH: Kent State University Press, 1991). Published in cooperation with the Western Reserve Historical Society.

4. Victorian architecture exteriors include steeply pitched roofs, plain or colorfully painted brick, ornate gables, painted iron railings, churchlike rooftops, finials, sliding sash and canted bay windows, octagonal or round towers, and turrets to draw the eye upward. They feature two to three stories, generous wraparound porches, small gardens, and asymmetry. Interiors include grand staircases; complicated layouts with multiple rooms, including formal dining rooms, libraries, and parlors; high ceilings; ornately carved wood paneling; geometric tile hallways; decorative fireplaces; stained glass windows; dark wood furniture; heavy drapes; decorative wallpaper; and hardwood floors covered with rugs. See The Spruce, https://www.thespruce.com/victorian-architecture-4769162.

5. Cigliano, *Showplace of America*, 171.

6. Named for the École des Beaux-Arts in Paris, the legendary school where the principles of this popular late nineteenth- and early twentieth-century architectural style were taught, Beaux Arts architecture is characterized by grandiose, ornate, and theatrical design based on the symmetry and proportions of Roman and Greek classicism, combined with more flamboyant French and Italian Renaissance and Baroque influences. Beaux Arts became a favorite architectural style for government and institutional buildings such as art museums, train stations, libraries, university campuses, and courthouses in Europe and the United States.

7. Frequent reference is made to James Tower Sweringen's wounds having been sustained during the Battle of Gettysburg. The *Family Register of Gerret van Sweringen and Descendants* specifies the Battle of Spotsylvania, but military records specify the wounds were sustained during the Battle of the Wilderness, immediately preceding Spotsylvania.

8. 1880 United States Census.

9. Now 239 Eastwood Street and 303 Park Street, Geneva, Ohio.

10. 1900 US Census. In 1906, the Cleveland City Council passed an ordinance providing for "the renaming of streets and the renumbering of houses to conform to one general system." Contemporary street names and house numbers will appear throughout this book.

11. Book 754, page 292, AFN 190005050052, Recorded May 5, 1900. Mrs. Fuller purchased the property and the adjoining lot (Lot 9) from Emily A. Thorp on April 17, 1890. On May 21, 1892, Fuller sold Lot 9 to Robert Quigley.

TWO

THE EMERGENCE OF EASTERN SUBURBS

The city's first eastern suburbs grew up in East Cleveland Township. In 1785, to create a way whereby the lands of the Northwest Territory would be sold to states and in turn to individual landowners, the Confederation Congress defined how the land was to be divided. Six-mile-square townships were to be further divided into thirty-six 640-acre sections. The Land Ordinance of 1785 remained in effect until the passage of the Homestead Act of 1862. Moses Cleaveland's surveyors had modified the dimensions but not the concept. As Cleveland grew, it became necessary to annex land from East Cleveland Township. In June 1847 the Cuyahoga County Commissioners approved new boundaries for the township. Instead of due east to Mayfield Township, the approved configuration extended from Lake Erie southeast onto the Portage Escarpment and continued to the border with Warrensville Township, including what would become Cleveland Heights.

In 1850, with 17,034 residents in Cleveland and an additional 2,313 dotting the landscape of East Cleveland Township, the first village in the township—Collamer—was established. The township attracted Cleveland's wealthy, who built summer homes and a golf course. A twelve-acre cemetery was established in August 1859, across Euclid Avenue from where Lake View Cemetery would be founded ten years later. Collamer was followed in 1870 by Glenville and in 1883 by Collinwood. The City of East Cleveland that we know today was incorporated as a village in 1895. Collamer was included as a part of the new Village of East Cleveland when the latter was established. In 1911 East Cleveland received its charter as a city. Glenville, Collinwood, and East Cleveland became Cleveland's first eastside suburbs. Growth soon began to spread onto the escarpment.

THE ROLE OF THE BROOK

Doan Brook dates back to the end of the Ice Age some fifteen thousand years ago. As the ice receded, a series of waterways emerged to carry the melt from the Portage Escarpment, the western edge of the Appalachian Highlands, to Lake Erie. In addition to Doan Brook, there were Walworth Run, Burke Brook, Giddings Brook, Dugway Brook, Nine-Mile Creek, and more. Only the nearly eight-and-one-half-mile Doan Brook remains, albeit redirected and culverted in several places to meet human needs. Fed by groundwater, the three headwaters that form Doan Brook bubble up from aquafers east of Warrensville Center Road. The northern two, between Fairmount and Shaker Boulevards, merge east of Lee

Outline Map of **CUYAHOGA Co.** OHIO.

Scale 2 Miles to an Inch.

EXPLANATION FOR TOWNSHIP MAPS

Farm Line	Private Road
Section or Lot Line	Public Road
Range Line	Rail Road
Township Line	Residence Res.
Stream	Building

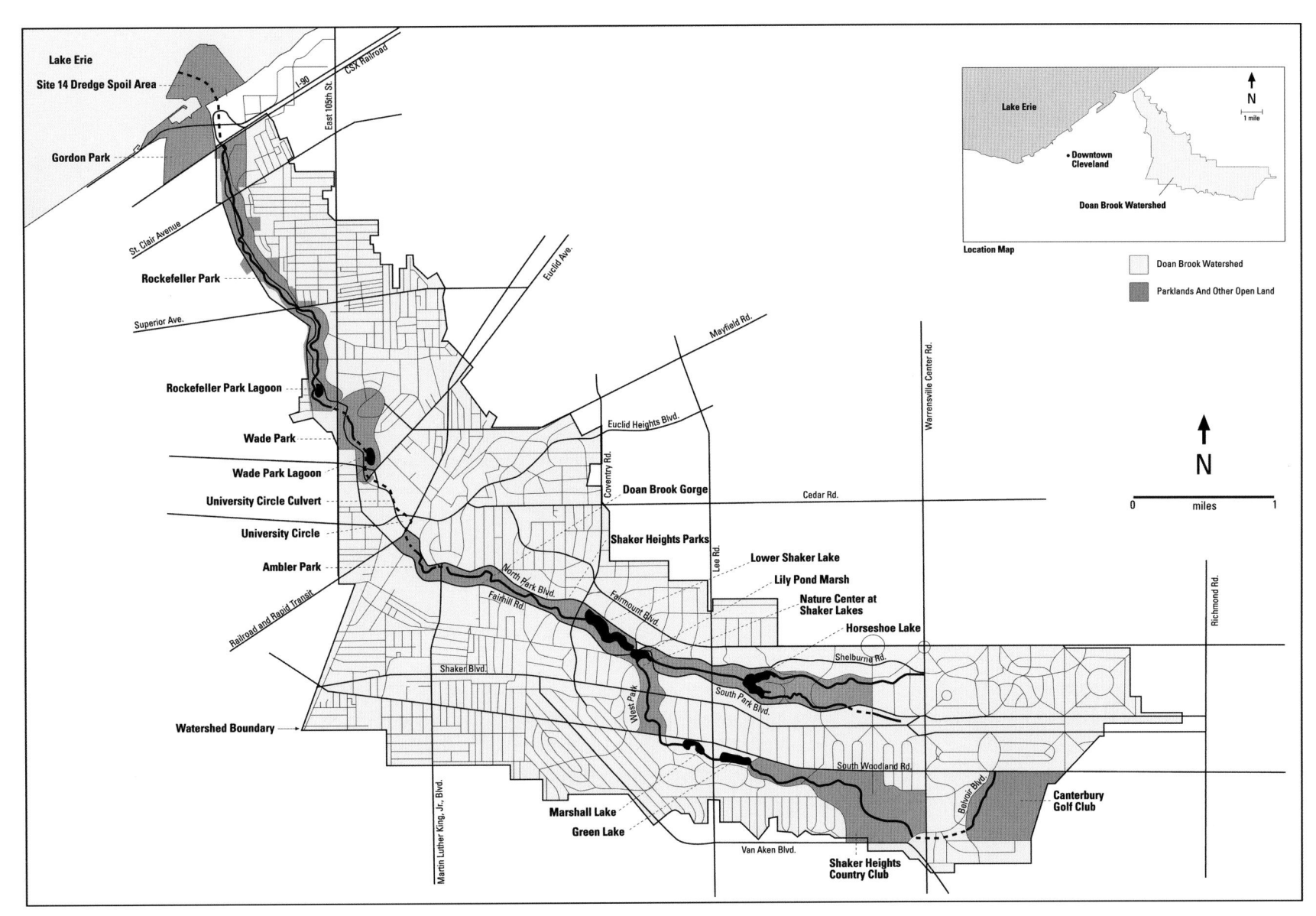

Facing, Map of Cuyahoga County, 1874. Courtesy of Cleveland Public Library Map Collection.

Map of Doan Brook, *The Doan Brook Handbook,* 2001. Courtesy of Laura Gooch.

Road between North Park and South Park Boulevards, forming the upper branch of the brook. The southern headwater, or lower branch, bubbles up in the vicinity of South Woodland Road, east of South Belvoir Boulevard. From there it was redirected to follow the western boundary of Canterbury Country Club during the construction of the golf course. Today it is culverted from South Belvoir just north of Chagrin Boulevard under the commercial area—known for many years as the Van Aken Shopping Center, and today as the Van Aken District—before emerging on the grounds of Shaker Heights Country Club. The two branches merge in the marsh west of the Nature Center at Shaker Lakes and east of North Woodland Road, continuing north to the edge of the escarpment as a single body of water where it is culverted and remains so under University Circle. Doan Brook resurfaces near the Cleveland Museum of Art, where it winds its way through Cleveland's Cultural Gardens in Rockefeller Park. Just before the railroad bridge at the north edge of the Gardens, the brook is once again culverted before entering Lake Erie.

Access to fresh running water for drinking, cooking, and washing has always been an important factor in the development of settlements. Nathaniel Doan would likely not have settled where he did along an Indian trail had it not been for its intersection with the brook. Likewise, the Shakers must have considered the brook when they began to develop the North Union Community. Cleveland archaeologist Roy Larick, PhD, says that "saw milling along the length of Doan may go back to the 1800s, certainly to the 1810s. At both the Lower and Upper dam sites, the Shakers purchased land that had saw milling operations dating to the 1810s. The Shakers in some sense improved dams already in place, but we don't know what those early dams looked like or how the Shakers continued to use them. One could say, in any event, the Shaker Lakes predate the Shakers."[1]

SETTLING "THE HEIGHTS"

Five miles east of Public Square, the Great Plains touch the foothills of the Appalachian Highlands, the first rise into the Alleghany Mountains.

In 1808, twelve years after the founding of Cleveland, Moses Warren, a veteran of the Revolutionary War, accompanied his son Daniel; Daniel's wife Margaret Prentiss Warren; and their toddler son William from Acworth in Sullivan County, New Hampshire, to Painesville in Lake County, Ohio. Moses returned to Acworth, walking all the way. Daniel, an accomplished brickmaker, made the bricks for the Ashtabula County Courthouse, the first brick courthouse in the Western Reserve, before moving on to settle in Cuyahoga County.

On October 3, 1810, Daniel Warren purchased a 161-acre parcel of land from Gideon and Mindwell Granger in "Township number seven in the Eleventh Range of Townships in said Cuyahoga County being lot number thirty-two" for $280, where he built a log cabin.[2]

Moses Warren's three daughters died in the spotted fever epidemic that ravaged New England in the springs of 1812 and 1813. He and his wife Priscilla Nourse Warren and Daniel's father-in-law James Prentiss decided to move from New Hampshire to join Daniel and his family in the Western Reserve in 1815. They first lived with Daniel, and on December 2, 1815, Moses purchased seventy-four acres of land on the west half of Lot 54 in Township Seven for $259 from James Prentice Jr.; here he too built a log cabin. On May 21, 1816, Moses purchased an additional 154 acres of land in Lot 53 from Gavis and Philura Pease for $456, bringing his total land ownership to 228 acres. On November 21, 1816, Daniel Warren purchased 164 acres for $1,446, bringing the combined ownership of father and son to 456 acres.[3]

The township was organized in that same year, and Daniel's wife Margaret Prentiss Warren, the first woman to settle in the township, had the privilege of naming the township. She named it Warrensville. The following year, Moses erected the first frame house in the township, at 3535 Ingleside Road. The two-story house measured twenty-six feet by thirty-two feet, with a substantial setback from the road. The foundation was built of sandstone quarried nearby, and the frame and siding were fashioned from trees from the surrounding forest. The 1817 home has undergone several remodelings, including expansion and reconfiguration as a two-family house in 1947.

Map of Warrensville Township, 1874. Courtesy of Cleveland Public Library Map Collection.

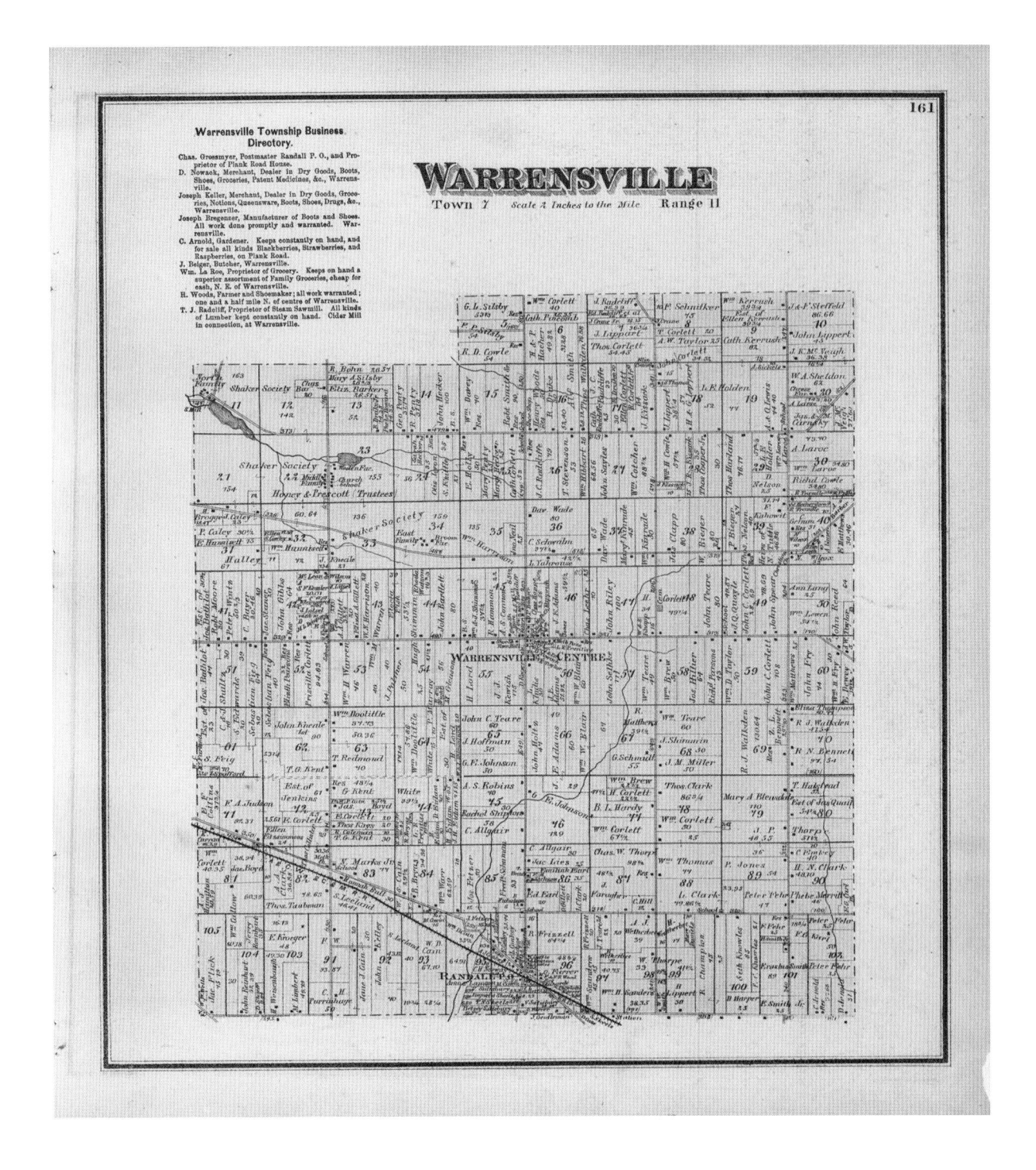

Moses Warren House, 3535 Ingleside Road, 1817.

Among other early settlers in the township was Asa Upson, whose home, built in 1836 and expanded in 1941, stands at 19027 Chagrin Boulevard. Asa and Chloe Upson came to the Western Reserve from Connecticut and settled in Twinsburg Township in Portage County sometime before 1834, when they assembled 277 acres of land in Warrensville Township for $1,265. On September 30, 1834, the Upsons leased an eight-acre square parcel to William Truesdell for the construction and operation of a sawmill. Asa served the township as its treasurer and as a trustee, and Chloe was a founding member of the Warrensville Methodist Episcopal Church, which stood on the parcel on what we know as Warrensville Center Road, north of Chagrin Boulevard, where Christ Episcopal Church, built in 1945, stands today.

Another early settler was Jacob Strong, whose home at 18829 Fairmount Boulevard was built between 1839 and 1847. Strong came to the Western Reserve from Burlein in Trumble County, Ohio, in 1830. In 1835 he purchased 140 acres of land for $1,120, farming 100 acres and selling the remaining 40 acres, purchasing additional acres in 1850. In 1853 the Strongs sold 100 acres to Richard and Clarissa Hecker for $4,000, and two months later, they sold the rest of their land before moving to Indiana. Three generations of Heckers lived on the farm until John A. Hecker, the grandson, sold the property to the Van Sweringen Company. Hecker worked in purchasing for the Van Sweringens, served Shaker Heights as a member of its city council for thirty-three years, and was a founding member of the Shaker Historical Society.

Among the other early settlers in Warrensville Township, several hundred emigrated from the Isle of Man in the Irish Sea. B. Robert and Elizabeth Corlett built their home at 21710 Fairmount Boulevard in 1844, and William and Jane Kewish built their home on sixty-seven acres of land at 19620 Chagrin Boulevard in the same year. William Kewish died in 1849 and was buried in the Warrensville West Cemetery, as were Elizabeth Corlett, who died in 1856; Robert Corlett, who died in 1861; and Jane Kewish, who died in 1872.

Asa Upson House, 18629 Chagrin Boulevard, 1836.

Jacob Strong House, 18829 Fairmount Boulevard, c. 1839–1847.

The Emergence of Eastern Suburbs

Robert Corlett House, 21710 Fairmount Boulevard, 1844.

William Kewish House, 19620 Chagrin Boulevard, c. 1844–1847.

Thought to have been built about 1825, the Curtis-Preyer House is the oldest-standing structure in Cleveland Heights, then a part of East Cleveland Township. Located at 14299 Superior Road, the stone house may have been built from material quarried in the nearby Dugway Creek ravine by Richard Curtis, who had purchased seventy acres of land for $225 in 1819; Curtis is thought to have farmed the land until 1835. During the next three decades several early real estate speculators purchased the land, along with other families, including Duranson and Helen Dart. The Darts attempted to convert the former farm, by then turned meadow, into a dairy farm, with no success.

In 1863 Benjamin and Mary Phillips bought the land and house as an investment, selling them on July 12, 1864, to John Peter Preyer. Preyer, who had emigrated from Prussia with his wife, Charlotte, and their six children, created the Lake View Wine Farm, increasing the land from 54 to 131 acres and building a wood-frame addition on the rear of the house. The family built two additional houses and a carriage house—the Emil Preyer House (son) stands next door to the Curtis-Preyer House, and the Hellwig House (son-in-law) stood just down the street.

In 1853, East Cleveland's board of education purchased more than three-quarters of an acre on which to build the East Cleveland District 9 School. The original school was demolished in 1882, and the first story of the current structure was constructed of sandstone. In 1901, when Cleveland Heights was designated a hamlet, the new board of education took over the structure as the new community's first school, and in 1915 the frame second story was added. When classes moved to new buildings in 1924, the schoolhouse became home to the Cleveland Heights Board of Education. Today it is home to the Cleveland Heights Historical Society.

The Asa Cady House that now stands at 3921–3923 Bluestone Road was built in 1841, at what is today the intersection of Monticello and Noble Roads, where Cady operated a steam-powered sawmill. The Cadys were involved in the antislavery movement, he serving as vice president of the Cuyahoga Anti-Slavery Society, and the house may have been a station on the Underground Railroad. In 1851 Asa and Teresa Cady were

Curtis-Preyer House, 14299 Superior Road, c. 1825.

Cady House, 3921–3923 Bluestone Road, 1841.

Quilliams House, 884 Quilliams Road, 1867.

Superior School House, 14391 Superior Road, 1859.

Cleveland Heights Methodist Episcopal Church, 14280 Superior Road, 1904.

among fourteen members of the First Presbyterian Church of Collamer who broke away from that church because it "maintained fellowship with slaveholders." The Cady's house is believed to have been moved to its present location around the turn of the twentieth century.

In 1867 Hugh Quilliams built a farmhouse for his son and daughter-in-law, William T. and Nancy Quilliams, at 884 Quilliams Road. A carpenter and Union Army veteran, William went on to become a civic leader, serving as a trustee for East Cleveland Township and later for the hamlet of Cleveland Heights.

In 1904 shortly after the founding of Cleveland Heights Village, the Cleveland Heights Methodist Episcopal Church was dedicated on Superior Road, just feet north of the Preyer House. The oldest-standing house of worship on "the Heights" stemmed from Fairmount Methodist Episcopal Church, which was built near the Superior Schoolhouse in 1878.

EARLY DEVELOPMENT OF "THE HEIGHTS"

Located on the Portage Escarpment, the area of East Cleveland Township that today is Cleveland Heights was largely home to farms and quarries in the latter quarter of the nineteenth century. As Cleveland approached its centennial year, five miles from downtown Cleveland, developers set out to attract Millionaires' Row residents who had begun migrating eastward, away from the city's pollution, noise, taxation, and the encroachment of commercial businesses. Development benefited from the advent of electrified streetcars, which were able to climb the steep grades leading up to the Heights. The first interurban line onto the Heights was completed along Mayfield Road in 1899.

The development of Cleveland Heights can be most easily understood by viewing it through the lens of the area's neighborhoods, many of which have been designated historic districts. Euclid Heights, Cedar Heights, M. M. Brown's Mayfield Heights, Ambler Heights, Grant Deming's Forest Hill, Euclid Golf, and Inglewood each had a different developer, and each had its own characteristics, appealing to different demographics. The development of Shaker Heights was in many ways much easier because it was the undertaking of a single developer—the Van Sweringen brothers—appealing primarily to a single demographic.

EUCLID HEIGHTS ALLOTMENT, 1892–1930

Patrick Calhoun, a lawyer with the Atlanta and New York Railroad and the grandson of John C. Calhoun—twice vice president of the United States, first under James Monroe and then under John Quincy Adams—traveled to Cleveland on business in 1890. While he was in Cleveland, Calhoun rode to Lake View Cemetery to visit the recently dedicated memorial to slain President James A. Garfield. As he rode, he noticed the building boom going on in the East End (Hough area) and wondered what the future held in store.

Calhoun had been involved with the Richmond Terminal Railroad project in Virginia and was familiar with the groundbreaking work that Frank J. Sprague, the "Father of Electric Traction," had done there in using electric railroads to promote urban development.[4] Knowing that the East Cleveland Railway Company had recently done some innovative work electrifying streetcars, Calhoun saw an opportunity to develop an important streetcar suburb at the top of Cedar Glen. With J. G. W. Cowles—who had managed real estate for John D. Rockefeller—attorney William Lowe Rice, and merchant John Hartness Brown, Calhoun had development plans drawn up by 1892.

In 1893 Cleveland architect Alfred H. Granger designed and built for himself the first home in the new Euclid Heights Allotment, an imposing three-story Jacobean Tudor with half-timbering, decorative stonework, and a Gothic castellated turret. The Panic of 1893 put further plans for the development of Euclid Heights on hold. By 1896 an amended site plan was recorded, with Euclid Heights Boulevard bisecting the site from the southwest corner at the crest of Cedar Hill. The northeast corner of the development was designated as a commercial district—what we now know as Coventry Village.

Alfred Hoyt Granger Residence, 2141 Overlook Road, 1893.

Patrick Calhoun Residence, Meade and Granger, 2460 Edgehill Road, 1896.

In 1896 Frank B. Meade and Alfred Hoyt Granger designed Patrick Calhoun's first home in Euclid Heights, a Tudor, in the Queen Anne style that was popular during the last two decades of the nineteenth century and the first decade of the twentieth century. That same year, the partners designed the residence of John Hartness Brown, a Richardsonian Romanesque mansion with Tudor and Gothic details. Brown is said to have introduced Calhoun to the land on which he would develop Euclid Heights. A commercial real estate developer himself, in 1900, Brown had acquired land on the north side of Euclid Avenue, between what is now the 925 Euclid Building and just west of East 12th Street. Although his project ended in bankruptcy, Brown is credited with having inspired the redevelopment of Euclid Avenue between East 9th and East 14th Streets as a retail shopping district.

The Briggs Estate, on five and a half acres of land, bounded by Mornington Lane, East Overlook, Coventry, and Edge Hill Roads was designed by Charles Schweinfurth and completed in 1909. The thirty-room mansion had thirty-inch outer walls, fifteen fireplaces, mahogany paneling, and handblown leaded glass windows. The stone Tudor castle–like mansion stood in contrast to the outbuildings, including the Tudor Revival carriage house that was as large as all but the largest Cleveland Heights homes, containing a sixty-foot-long ballroom.

In 1911, Frank B. Meade and James M. Hamilton joined forces, and in 1915, they designed the home of John T. Gill. Gill was the son of John Gill, an immigrant from the Isle of Man who became one of the leading masonry contractors in Cleveland. The son learned the trade as a stonemason's apprentice and joined his father as a partner. Together, they built the Northern Ohio Lunatic Asylum, the post office building in Washington, DC, the Baltimore Courthouse, and the Missouri State Capitol, among others. At some point, John's brother Kermode joined the firm as a partner. Following their father's death, the firm built the Hanna Building and Theater, the Bulkley Building, and the Allen Theater in what we know as Playhouse Square, the Federal Reserve Bank, and the Van Sweringens' Cleveland Union Terminal.

John Hartness Brown House, Meade and Granger, 2380 Overlook Road, 1896.

Briggs Estate Carriage House, Charles F. Schweinfurth, 1965 Mornington Lane, 1904.

John Gill House, Meade and Hamilton, 2465 Euclid Heights Boulevard, 1915.

Wilson B. Hickox House, Meade and Hamilton, 2647 Berkshire Road, 1916.

In 1916 Meade and Hamilton designed a Georgian home at 2647 Euclid Heights Boulevard for Martha and Wilson Begges Hickox. Martha was Patrick Calhoun's daughter, and Wilson was the president of the Lemur Company, a manufacturer of permanent waving equipment and cosmetics. His mother was a first cousin of President Woodrow Wilson.

Two significant events occurred that would attract upper-class families to Euclid Heights. The first was the incorporation of the Euclid Golf and Country Club on August 30, 1900. Plans included an eighteen-hole golf course and a clubhouse with several sleeping rooms for its members. Real estate developer Patrick Calhoun furnished the land and funded the project. The Euclid Club opened with a gala on August 15, 1901, with more than 350 members and guests in attendance. The entrance to the club was where the Alcazar Hotel now stands, and a winding road led to the Tudor clubhouse on the south side of Derbyshire Road east of Norfolk Road.

Among the early members of the club were leading citizens, the likes of Andrew Squire, Dr. Dudley P. Allen, Myron T. Herrick, Horace E. Andrews, Wilson B. Chisolm, and Henry S. Blossom. In addition to bowling alleys, a billiard parlor, and tennis courts, the club facilities included a nine-hole course that was laid out between Euclid Heights Boulevard and Cedar Road. An additional nine holes were completed on adjacent property south of Cedar Road, donated for the purpose by John D. Rockefeller—a strict Baptist—with the stipulation that it would not be used for golf on Sundays.

The second event was the award in 1904 of a franchise to the Cleveland Railway Company to extend its streetcar line up Cedar Glen and east on Euclid Heights Boulevard to Coventry Road. This franchise would have a positive benefit, not only to the development of the Euclid Heights Allotment but to the development of Cedar Heights and Ambler Heights as well. A second franchise, in 1906, extended the streetcar line up Fairmount Boulevard to what would be the Van Sweringens' Shaker Farm Allotment and would later benefit the development of Barton Deming's Euclid Golf Allotment.

The Emergence of Eastern Suburbs

The club thrived until 1908, when some members withdrew to organize the Mayfield Country Club in Euclid Township. In September 1910 an article in the *Plain Dealer* announced that because "the property had become too valuable to be longer retained for club purposes," the Euclid Club would close on October 1. It appears that that article was premature, as the Euclid Club continued for several more years. In 1913, however, additional members withdrew and founded the Shaker Heights Country Club. It would be just a matter of time before the Euclid Club closed its doors.

CEDAR HEIGHTS, C. 1892–1925

While Calhoun began the development of Euclid Heights, the Walton brothers, William and Edmund Jr., who had developed a portion of what is now known as Cleveland's Little Italy, laid out two streets running from Cedar Road south to North Park Boulevard, calling the development Cedar Heights and naming the streets Bellfield and Grandview Avenues. In contrast to the elegant architecture of Euclid Heights and later Ambler Heights, Cedar Heights was laid out with small lots on which simple single- and two-family homes were built largely in the plain American Foursquare style, and apartment buildings were included as well, to appeal to the working class. Among the earliest homes in the development were those located at 2200 Grandview and 2190 Bellfield, built circa 1893. By 1898 nine homes stood on Grandview, with eight more on Bellfield.

In 1903 O. P. Van Sweringen acquired two lots at the south end of Grandview, one at the northwest corner of the intersection with North Park and the other immediately adjacent to the first to the north. As compared to the 40- by 138-foot lots laid out by the Waltons, the combined frontage of the lots purchased by Van Sweringen was 177 feet on Grandview and 175 feet on North Park. Across the street, contracting builder J. Wentworth Smith was constructing a mansion—in stark contrast to the

2200 Grandview Avenue, c. 1893.

2190 Bellfield Avenue, c. 1893.

2435 Grandview Avenue, Charles F. Schweinfurth, c. 1920.

North Park Manor, 2425 North Park Boulevard, 1925.

homes being built elsewhere in Cedar Heights—at 2435 Grandview. The mansion was designed by noted Cleveland architect Charles Schweinfurth, with whom Smith often worked. In 1925 the eight-suite North Park Manor would be built on the lots that O. P. had acquired years earlier.

M. M. BROWN'S MAYFIELD HEIGHTS, 1898–1937

On October 12, 1895, Marcus M. Brown, a real estate attorney in Chicago, purchased thirty-five acres of land from Peter R. and Lucy Hewitt Everett for $20,000. The next year, Brown and his family moved to Cleveland, settling in East Cleveland Township. Over the next five years, the allotment increased with the purchase of thirty-five additional acres from members of John Peter Preyer's family. Bounded by Mayfield Road, Superior Road, Euclid Heights Boulevard, and Coventry Road, the land was designated Mayfield Heights—not to be confused with today's suburban Mayfield Heights, five miles further to the east.

Brown built a fifteen-room Queen Anne Victorian mansion for himself and his family at 2893 Euclid Heights Boulevard, with bricks in varying shades of yellow on the ground floor—a style popular in Chicago at the time—with clapboard and cedar shingles on the upper levels and mahogany, cherry, and quartered oak throughout the interior. Also on the grounds is a carriage house with additional living space. The pool house has been converted to a home facing Wilton Road, and the barn is no longer standing. Brown laid out his plans for the new community, with brick-paved streets. In contrast to Euclid Heights, designed to attract the wealthy, and Cedar Heights, designed to attract the working class, Mayfield Heights was largely built for professionals and the middle class.

Following the Crash of 1907, Cleveland Trust Company took ownership of the allotment and marketed it as builder-designed homes in the American Foursquare, Arts and Crafts, Craftsman, Bungalow, colonial, and Queen Anne styles for working-class families.

The Emergence of Eastern Suburbs

Marcus M. Brown House, 2893 Euclid Heights Boulevard, 1899.

Sillman House, 1786 Cadwell Avenue, 1909.

Doty House, 2945 Euclid Heights Boulevard, 1909.

Phillips House, 2983 Euclid Heights Boulevard, 1910.

AMBLER HEIGHTS ALLOTMENT, 1903–1927

Situated on the bluff just beyond Cleveland's southeast border, Ambler Heights is bounded by Cedar Glen Parkway on the north, North Park Boulevard on the south, South Overlook Road on the east, and Ambleside Road and Martin Luther King Jr. Boulevard on the west. Dr. Nathan Hardy Ambler was a dentist who made his fortune during the California Gold Rush, where he was paid for his services with gold dust. Upon his return to Cleveland, Ambler turned to land speculation, buying property on Cleveland's city limits and selling it for development as the city grew outward.

After his death, Dr. Ambler's widow donated twenty-five acres to Cleveland for the formation of Ambler Park, overlooking University Circle. Ambler's adopted son Daniel O. Caswell, who had worked with his father in land development, and his nephew, William Eglin Ambler, joined forces to develop 350 acres of two- and three-story homes, ranging

The Emergence of Eastern Suburbs

Kermode F. Gill House, 2178 Harcourt Drive, Meade and Hamilton, 1910.

George Canfield House, 2232 Elandon Drive, Bohnard & Parsson Architects, 1913–1914.

G. Buckwell House, 2005 Chestnut Hills Drive, Walker and Weeks, 1916.

Joseph O. Eaton House, 2207 Devonshire Drive, Meade and Hamilton, 1917.

in size from three thousand to more than eighty-seven hundred square feet, built to the specifications of wealthy Clevelanders and designed by leading architects. The duo named the development Ambler Heights.

Kermode F. Gill, the younger son of John Gill and brother of John T. Gill, built a mansion in 1910. Designed by Frank B. Meade of Meade and Hamilton in the Jacobean style, it is located at 2178 Harcourt Drive. Standing on the bluff, the beautifully restored mansion, now known as Harcourt Manor, overlooks Cedar Glen Parkway.

George R. Canfield, the investor and real estate speculator who built the Stockbridge Hotel, built a house at 2232 Elandon Drive. Designed by Bohnard & Parsson Architects, the house is one of Ohio's finest examples of the Prairie School design and was built in 1913–1914.

Edward G. Buckwell, secretary and general sales manager and a member of the board of directors of the Cleveland Twist Drill Company, built a home in 1916 at 2005 Chestnut Hills Drive. Designed by Walker and Weeks, the English Georgian house is unusual in that its narrow end faces the street and the front door faces the next-door neighbor.

The Emergence of Eastern Suburbs

Grant Deming House, 3154 Redwood Road, 1909.

In 1917, Joseph Oriel Eaton, the founder of the Eaton Axle Company—now Eaton Corporation—built a house at 2207 Devonshire Drive. The house was designed by Meade and Hamilton in the English cottage style.

GRANT DEMING'S FOREST HILL ALLOTMENT, 1909–1928

Not to be confused with John D. Rockefeller's Forest Hill subdivision, Grant Deming's Forest Hill Allotment was opened in June 1909 on land previously owned by John D. Rockefeller and James Haycox. The 194-acre allotment was generally bounded by Coventry Road on the east, Euclid Heights Boulevard on the north, Lee Road on the east, and Derbyshire and East Derbyshire Roads on the south.[5] Grant W. Deming was a prominent developer responsible for several allotments in the Glenville section of Cleveland's east side, near Rockefeller Park.

Nathan Weisenberg House, 1999 Coventry Road, 1917.

2976 Lincoln Boulevard, 1910.

2956 East Overlook Road, George H. Burrows, 1917.

The Emergence of Eastern Suburbs

Barton R. Deming House, 2485 Fairmount Boulevard, 1914.

Grant Deming's house, the first house built in the allotment, is located at 3154 Redwood Road, just west of Lee Road. Built in 1909, the Victorian Queen Anne is in the shingle style with a matching carriage house with a gambrel roof.

The structure at 2976 Lincoln Boulevard, built in 1910, is believed to be the second oldest in Grant Deming's Forest Hill. It stands at one of the two original designated entrances to the allotment and takes advantage of its curved corner lot to maximize its visual impact.

Built in 1917 at 2956 East Overlook Road, a Swiss chalet–influenced Craftsman house is one of two known designed by architect George H. Burrows in Deming's Forest Hill. Burrows was a prolific architect, designing nearly one thousand homes in the Heights in the early twentieth century.

In 1917 Nathan Weisenberg, the president of Consolidated Oil Company, built a home at 1999 Coventry Road. The Italian Renaissance stucco house has a recessed arcaded front porch flanked by casement windows and a flat roof with a combination parapet and balustrade. It also has flat-roofed, one-story wings on both ends.

Francis J. Osborne House, 2603 Fairmount Boulevard, 1924.

J. Wentworth Smith House, 2504 Fairmount Boulevard, Charles F. Schweinfurth, 1919.

Model Home, 2645 Fairmount Boulevard, Philip E. Robinson, 1914.

The Emergence of Eastern Suburbs

3064 Corydon Road, The Sears Ashmore, ca. 1920.

EUCLID GOLF ALLOTMENT, 1913

The developer and builder Barton Roy Deming, brother of Grant Deming, purchased land originally owned by John D. Rockefeller that had been leased to the Euclid Club. The allotment was bounded by Nottinghill Lane and Clarkson Road on the north, Coventry Road to the east, Scarborough Road and West Saint James Parkway to the south, and Ardleigh Drive to the west. The allotment includes Fairmount Boulevard from Cedar to Coventry, part of the Fairmount Boulevard Historic District. Deming engaged the architectural firm of Howell & Thomas to design model homes built by the B. R. Deming Company and to approve the work of other architects designing for the allotment.

Barton R. Deming built 2485 Fairmount Boulevard on a sliver of land at the intersection of Fairmount Boulevard and Cedar Road. The four-story French Renaissance mansion served as the gateway to Deming's Euclid Golf Allotment. Philip E. Robinson designed the first model home within the allotment, located at 2645 Fairmount Boulevard.

3347 Ormond Road, The Sears Crescent, ca. 1921.

3402 Ormond Road, The Sears Ardara, ca. 1920.

3407 Clarendon Road, The Sears Columbine, ca. 1924.

The Emergence of Eastern Suburbs

CRAFTSMAN AND KIT HOMES

Cleveland Heights includes a wide range of architecture, including sprawling Victorian and Tudor mansions with gatehouses and carriage houses, the work of many of Cleveland's most highly acclaimed architects. At the other end of the spectrum are the Craftsman homes of the Arts and Crafts era and kit homes. Two of America's leading mail-order retailers, Sears, Roebuck & Company (Sears Modern Homes, 1908–1940) and Montgomery Ward & Company (Wardway Homes, 1910–1931), included kit homes, fixtures, and appliances in their catalogs. Sears is said to have sold an estimated seventy-five thousand kit homes in nearly 450 models, and Montgomery Ward sold more than thirty-two thousand kits. Today, there are dozens of Sears homes throughout the Greater Cleveland area that were fabricated in and shipped from mills in New Jersey, Ohio, and Illinois. The wooden pieces were numbered at each end to aid in the assembly. In June 1919 James and Stella Humpal purchased a 50-by-160-foot lot at 3064 Corydon Road, where they built a six-room, three-bedroom Sears Ashmore kit home the next year. Also in 1920, George Beyerley bought a similar lot a couple of blocks away, at 3402 Ormond Road, where they built a Sears Ardara, a one-floor bungalow with five rooms, including two bedrooms and one full bath. Just down the street, Frank Marten and Susie Carlson bought a lot at 3347 Ormond Road, in July 1919. In 1921, a five-room Sears Crescent, including two bedrooms, was completed. Two blocks away, at 3407 Clarendon Road, William and Grace Sunderman purchased a lot in February 1923, and the following year, construction of a six-room, three-bedroom Sears Columbine was completed.

The Van Sweringen brothers paid close attention to what was going on in Cleveland Heights, learning from the successes and failures of the various developers. Whereas what we now know as Cleveland Heights was developed by numerous independent developers, and except for Calhoun's Euclid Heights Allotment, largely unconstrained by standards and restrictions, the Van Sweringens took a very different approach as they developed Shaker Heights.

Perhaps the greatest lesson that O. P. learned from his own failures was not to disclose too much, too soon, saying,

> People will size you up as a dreamer and the reputation alone will defeat you.... I have been unwise often enough to know this from experience. The average man has to be sold with results. You have to convince him of what you will do by what you have done.... Of course, there is a time when you have not done anything when you have to make a start. If you have to sell your vision before you can start, reduce it to statistics. They are a lot easier to market than vision in terms of vision. All of which is just saying that the world knows enough to favor men with a well-balanced combination of idealism and practicality. You sometimes find men of vision who do not think ordinary business methods are worth troubling over. You find other men, a much larger class, who make a God of their matter-of-fact ways and care nothing for vision. The progress of either type is usually hard and meager.[6]

NOTES

1. Email from Roy Larick to Lauren Pacini, January 16, 2023.
2. Deed, Gideon Granger & Wife (Grantors) to Daniel Warren (Grantee), signed October 3 and recorded October 20, 1810, book 1, pp. 21 and 22, John Walworth, Recorder.
3. Deed, Gavis & Philura Pease (Grantors) to Moses Warren (Grantee), signed May 21, 1816, recorded June 4, 1816, book 2, p. 210.
4. The National Inventors Hall of Fame (https://www.invent.org/).
5. Boundaries are for general reference and are not the legal description.
6. Blosser, 27.

THREE

BUILDING SHAKER HEIGHTS

I looked over the land and considered its possibilities. Then and there I had a vision of how the whole region could be developed, but I did not say much about it. My experience is that it is best not to reveal all of your vision at first. Make good on part of it, and then you will be in a better position to take the next step.[1]

O. P. Van Sweringen

THE COMING OF THE SHAKERS

In 1813 another Revolutionary War veteran, Jacob Russell, purchased 475 acres of land in the upper Doan Brook valley from Lemuel Storrs, a land agent for the Connecticut Land Company. Born in 1746 in Windsor, Connecticut, Russell moved with his wife, Esther, to what would become Warrensville Township. On August 8, 1822, a year after Jacob's death, the land he had acquired was distributed to his heirs. His son Ralph received 32.1 acres. Ralph had visited the United Society of Believers in Christ's Second Appearing in Union Village near Lebanon, Ohio, where he became a "believer."

Founded in England in 1747 by James and Jane Wardley, the "Believers" stemmed from the English Quakers. They were known for their simple lifestyle, practice of celibacy and communal living, pacifism, charismatic worship, and equality of the sexes. They were also known for their technological innovation, architecture, and furniture design. Led by Mother Ann Lee (1736–1784), who taught them to "do all your work as though you had a thousand years to live, and as you would if you knew you must die tomorrow," the "Believers"—who would come to be known as the "Shakers"—came to colonial America in 1774.[2] They established a number of colonies, including Union Village in southwestern Ohio, which Ralph Russell visited and where he was converted.

An elder from Union Village had persuaded Ralph to establish a colony on the Russell property. On September 12, 1826, the first recorded transfer of land to the North Union Shakers was signed by Ralph's brother Return and his wife Jerusha when they deeded Lot 22 to the United Society of Believers at North Union Village. It was on that land, at the site where Jacob Russell's log cabin once stood, that the first family dwelling house of the North Union Settlement was built in 1826. The two-story dwelling house measured thirty by forty feet. The next acquisition by the

Shakers was fifty-nine acres in Lot 34, deeded by Ralph Russell and his wife Laura on September 20, 1828.

In 1840 a two-story addition measuring twenty by sixty feet was added to the rear of the dwelling house. The first floor was the kitchen and a dining room containing two long tables, each seating twenty-five. The sisters sat at one table and the brethren at the other. On the second floor above the dining room was a chapel, where services were held three evenings a week and on Sunday. Above the kitchen that consisted of the cookroom and bake room were two living rooms and two shops for the sisters. On the roof was a 326-pound bell.

By 1840 there were one hundred men, women, and children in the North Union Settlement. As the population of the village grew, so did its land. These were the first two of nearly twenty-five parcels of land acquired by the Society between 1826 and 1880. As land was acquired for the growing colony, it was placed in trust for the United Society at North Union Village, first overseen by Deacons Nathan Sharp and Daniel Boyd. The colony quickly grew from one to three families, and by 1850 it had three hundred members.

The Center Family, living in the dwelling house on the west side of Lee Road, between Shaker and North Park Boulevards, was the first of three families to be formed. At its peak, the family inhabited four dwelling houses, one for the elders and eldresses, one for adults, another for boys, and yet another for girls. There was also a meetinghouse for religious services, a blacksmith shop, a carpentry shop, and a tannery.

The North Family, also known as the Mill Family, was the next to be formed. Located at Coventry Road and North Park Boulevard, the family consisted of fifty members at its peak. Driven by the need for board lumber for the construction of their dwellings, a sawmill was constructed on the west side of Coventry, on the north side of the brook. In 1829, the sawmill was joined by a gristmill about a quarter mile farther downstream. A small dam powered the mills near where the Lower Lake dam stands today. As the need for water increased, the dam was rebuilt, until finally, in 1837, a twenty-acre reservoir provided more than enough water to power the mills. In 1843 the original gristmill was replaced by a massive five-story one built of stone.

The East (or Gathering) Family was established on what is today Fontenay Road, between Shaker Boulevard and South Woodland Road. In 1852 the dam that had been built in the early years of the nineteenth century further upstream, forming what we know as Horseshoe Lake, was expanded and a woolen mill and broom shop were built and powered by water that was carried by a series of wooden troughs. In 1854, that dam was rebuilt, including a stone spillway and reinforcement to the upstream face. Although threatened by plans to demolish the Horseshoe Lake Dam and return the space to nature, the dam stands today as a tribute to the ingenuity and commitment of the hardworking Shakers.

The practice of celibacy meant that the colony was dependent on recruitment to sustain its population. It is also likely that the families took in orphans as well. Following the Civil War, the membership that had peaked at around three hundred began to dwindle. The East Family was the first to disband. By 1889, only twenty-seven members remained in the North Union Settlement. The colony disbanded, with the members moving to other settlements, likely in southwest Ohio. On April 23, 1890, the last North Union Shaker departed the community, but not before witnessing the Mill Family dwelling house in flames. As the *Plain Dealer* reported the next day, the twelve-room dwelling house, once home to sixty Shakers, and the adjoining buildings, including a two-story cheese house, a carpenter shop, and a laundry, all built in 1845, were reduced to charred ruins. It remains unclear who set them ablaze. Much of what we know about what the Shaker's North Union Settlement looked like comes from the photographs and hand-drawn maps of lifelong Clevelander Louis Baus (1875–1949), *Plain Dealer* staff photographer from 1911 until the time of his death.

On June 10, 1891, Lawrence Lamb, an attorney from Memphis, Tennessee, purchased 1,393.4 acres of land that had been held in trust for and was home to the North Union Shakers for nearly seventy years. Lamb

Map of North Union Settlement, 1874. Composite created by the author.

Center Family Dwelling, built in 1826. Louis Baus, 1898. Courtesy of Shaker Historical Society.

The Dam at Upper Lake.

The Dam at Lower Lake.

Jacob Russell Grave, South Park Cemetery.

Shaker Common Grave, Warrensville West Cemetery, 3451 Lee Road.

69

paid the United Society of Believers $316,000 in an agreement with Joseph R. Slingerland and Oliver C. Hampton, Trustees. It is not clear why the deed was not recorded by the Cuyahoga County Recorder until April 14, 1892. Recorded on that same day was a deed signed on April 1, 1892, by which Lamb transferred the land to the Continental Development Company, a Virginia corporation with offices on the eighth floor of the Society for Savings Building on Public Square, for $400,000. The *Plain Dealer* reported that the officers of Continental Development Company included William Hamlin of Detroit, Michigan, president; Lawrence Lamb, vice president; and Thomas A. Lamb, secretary and treasurer. Directors included Henry Avery of Avery Stamping, Luther Allen of Globe Iron Works, and William L. Rice, attorney-at-law with the firm of Russell and Rice. On June 16, 1893, Continental Development transferred the former Shaker land to Joseph A. Oaks, a resident of Buffalo, New York, for $1.00, and Oaks assumed the second mortgage that had secured the $316,000 paid to the trustees of the United Society in June 1891, on which there was a balance of $313,000 remaining.

On June 30, 1893, Joseph Oaks and his wife, Phillippina, transferred the nearly fourteen hundred acres of land on the "Heights," five miles from downtown Cleveland and once a thriving Shaker community, to William Henry Gratwick Sr.'s Shaker Heights Land Company of Buffalo, New York, for $1.00.

Selected photographs of North Union Settlement by Louis Baus. Louis Baus Collection, 1843–1898. Digitized by Brianna Treleven, Shaker Historical Society.

THE VANS' REAL ESTATE DEVELOPMENT

The abandoned Shaker land was now in the hands of the Shaker Heights Land Company, a Buffalo syndicate headed by William Henry Gratwick Sr., a lumber merchant and Great Lakes freighter operator. The syndicate hired civil engineer Fred Alwood Pease, formerly the deputy engineer for Cuyahoga County, to lay out streets and lots. Owen C. Ringle was their sales agent and Clifford W. Fuller was their attorney. However, there was no demand for land, as the nation, indeed, the world, was in the grip of the Panic of 1893, an economic depression that would last until 1897. This prompted the Shaker Heights Land Company to donate more than 278 acres of the upper Doan Brook Valley, including the Shaker Lakes, that had been designated as parkland to the City of Cleveland on April 10, 1896. With the elder Gratwick's death in 1899, control of the land company passed to his eldest son, William Henry Gratwick Jr., W. H. Sandrock, Charles Gurney, and Otto Lautz.

Following the 1896 donation to the City of Cleveland, the Shaker Heights Land Company's next two transactions did not take place until May 23, 1903. In the first, Cleveland brewer, entrepreneur, and real estate investor George F. Gund purchased two parcels of land measuring a little more than four and one-quarter acres along Coventry Road (in the section now known as Shaker Boulevard), south of Main Park Drive (now North Park Boulevard). The property was still undeveloped at the time of Gund's death in March 1916 when it was transferred to his widow. On December 19, 1918, Anna Gund sold the parcels to the Van Sweringen Company.

In the second transaction on that same day in 1903, banker, railroad man, and John D. Rockefeller associate John Vickers Painter purchased eight and one-half acres of land at the southeast corner of the intersection of Fairmount Boulevard and Center Road (now Lee Road). Unlike George Gund, Painter hired an architect, John Skeel, to design a sixty-five-room Jacobean-style summerhouse. However, Painter did not live to see the completion of the mansion. Following his death in 1903, the deed was transferred to his widow, Lydia Ethel Farmer Painter.

Under Lydia Painter and her son, Kenyon Vickers Painter, the estate grew to fifty acres. Following Lydia's death in 1909, Kenyon, who later became president of the Union Trust Bank—one of the Van Sweringens' primary banking relationships—continued the project, transforming

Painter Mansion, 3240 Fairmount Boulevard, John Skeel, 1905.

71

Painter Gatehouse, 17412 Shelburne Road, 1909.

the architecture to Tudor with Gothic details. The estate became a year-round residence in 1915.

The Shaker Heights Land Company sold two more lots in December, bringing the total for 1903 to four. Three more lots were sold in 1904. O. P. and M. J. Van Sweringen met with the syndicate's land manager, O. C. Ringle, and obtained and promptly sold several lots. Their strategy was to have payment from their buyer before their own payment was due to the Shaker Heights Land Company, thus working, whenever possible, with other people's money. The brothers then met with members of the Buffalo syndicate, including William Henry Gratwick Jr. and Herbert P. Bissell, and negotiated a two-year agreement. Effective May 1905, the terms of the agreement included a 5 percent commission—with a minimum selling price of $2,500 per acre—and "a good touring car for transportation of prospective purchasers." The "good touring car" was a big, heavy, impressive Cleveland-built Royal.[3]

O. P. opened an office on the ninth floor of the Williamson Building on the southeast corner of Cleveland's Public Square—where the F. A. Pease Engineering Company had its offices and where 200 Public Square, the former BP Tower, now stands. M. J. joined him, and they formed a fifty-fifty partnership. They opened a joint bank account in which they deposited $1,800, including money from M. J. and their sister Edith. Soon the brothers were operating under the name of the Sedgewick Land Company.

SHAKER FARM, 1904–1915

The brothers' first development was a 266-acre tract on both sides of Fairmount Boulevard, one of the original Shaker roadways, and the north/south side streets between Fairmount and Scarborough Road. The development extended east from Coventry Road to the intersection with Wellington Road; today, it is known as the Shaker Farm Historic District.

Among the homes that were built in the district were the French Normandy–style mansion at 2787 Fairmount Boulevard with seven bedrooms–each with its own bathroom–designed by Frank B. Meade and James M. Hamilton and built in 1923 for J. Prescott Burton Jr.; the nine-thousand-square-foot Tudor at 2900 Fairmount Boulevard designed by Philip L. Small in 1923 for Studer Thompson; the Meade and Hamilton Georgian Revival located at 2905 Fairmount Boulevard that became home to William Fowler Nash and his wife Anna, a niece of John D. Rockefeller; and the stunning mansion, combining Second Renaissance Revival and Beaux Arts styles, at 3001 Fairmount Boulevard designed by Frederic W. Striebinger for Henry A. Tremaine, who sold it to Michael Gallagher just three years later.

O. P. met with Horace E. Andrews, president of the Cleveland Railway Company, and proposed that if Cleveland Railway would provide trolly service, he would pay for laying track up Fairmount Boulevard and subsidize Cleveland Railway's operating loss up to $1,000 per month. Andrews agreed to extend service from Coventry to Lee Road. Although the trip from Public Square to Fairmount and Lee would take forty-five minutes, the Van Sweringens saw that as an acceptable temporary solution, convinced that the payment to cover the railway's loss would be more than made up through lot sales.

It was during this time that the brothers met bankers Joseph R. Nutt, president and board chair of Union Trust Company, and Charles L. Bradley, vice president of Union Trust, who became close friends, confidants, and associates. And they renewed their boyhood friendship with Benjamin Lane Jenks, who became their attorney; he and his wife, Louise, known as "Daisy," would likewise become among the brothers' closest friends. Although he was ten years older than O. P., Jenks knew the brothers from their days as newsboys when he was secretary of his father's lumber company. Daisy was one year younger than M. J. The Jenkses and the brothers became nearly inseparable—so much so as to be the basis of unfounded rumors. Daisy would tell the story in *O. P. and M. J.* many years later, as follows:

Building Shaker Heights

J. Prescott Burton Jr. House, 2787 Fairmount Boulevard, Meade and Hamilton, 1923.

Studer Thompson House, 2900 Fairmount Boulevard, Philip L. Small, 1923.

J. B. Crouse Residence, 2905 Fairmount Boulevard, Meade and Hamilton, 1915.

Tremaine-Gallagher House, 3001 Fairmount Boulevard, Frederic W. Striebinger, 1914.

When we first lived on Shaker Heights, corner of Lee and Shaker Boulevard, M. J. went away for a few days. In his absence O. P. got very lonely. He was a young man who did much pondering and was very shy with people. Real estate at that time was his great absorbing interest and he spent much time going over his newly acquired land.

One evening he dropped in on us. As it grew late, we invited him to spend the night. He did, and the next night mustered up courage enough to invite himself. Then again, the next night! He found we had much in common. We were all teetotalers, we had been brought up by strict parents to observe the Sabbath (the brothers had not been allowed even to whistle on Sunday), and we agreed on ideas of Christian behavior.

Then M. J. returned, and on finding O. P. had done the unusual and stayed away from home, he was very jealous and came directly to me. Shaking his little blond head, he told me I had been too nice to his brother and would thank me not to pay him more attention. I asked him what he would have done under like circumstances and advised him when his brother wanted to stay another night to remain and sleep in the bed next to him. This he did, and we almost never saw one brother without the other.[4]

O. P. Van Sweringen would do whatever it took to close a deal. In the book for her son, Daisy told this story to make that point:

How O. P. chuckled at the mention of cod fish! When he heard the Jenkses were in the market for a home, O. P. used his influence in the direction of his holdings on the Heights. Upon returning from the first trip, I invited him to have dinner with us, explaining that I had no maid and had simple food. My allowance for all household expenses being ten dollars a week at that time. We had cod fish and baked potatoes, and O. P. ate it with relish. It was almost a year after he dined with us in our new home, and we again had cod fish and he emphatically refused it and asked for a fried egg. I reminded him of his having had two helpings the first night I ever knew him, and he said with a merry twinkle, "Yea, but I sold that lot and I don't have to do it again."[5]

SHAKER VILLAGE, 1905–1931

O. P. had grown tired of the politics necessary to get the needed infrastructure improvements made by East Cleveland Township. His solution was to form his own village—an exclusive, white, Anglo-Saxon, Protestant community. An article in the *Plain Dealer* on July 6, 1911, announced the approval by the county commissioners of the secession and formation of Shaker Heights as a village, with John L. Cannon, O. P. Van Sweringen, and William J. Van Aken as trustees. The village was incorporated in 1912 and as a city in 1931.

Shaker Village was bounded by Fairmount Boulevard on the north, Lomond Boulevard on the south, Warrensville Center Road on the east, and Coventry Road on the west. The village was later expanded to include the area roughly bounded by Lomond Boulevard, Lytle Road, Scottsdale Boulevard, and Lindholm Road. The Van Sweringen brothers named the community Shaker Heights. It soon became clear that streetcar service would be essential to the success of the project, and negotiations began to build two lines—one on Shaker Boulevard and the other on Moreland Boulevard, known today as Van Aken Boulevard. Cleveland Railway Company finally agreed to build the line on Shaker Boulevard but not the second line on Moreland.

When they encountered an objection, the Vans quickly found a way to overcome it. By way of example, an article in the *Plain Dealer* on September 20, 1909, described the length to which the brothers would go.

Every school day in the year the school kids who live out on one portion of Shaker Heights get staked to a snug little joy ride.

The Van Sweringen boys, when they began to offer lots for sale out that way, were met by the objection from parents: "It's too far for the children to go to school."

"We'll haul 'em to school," declared the Van Sweringens, and the objection was swept aside.

They didn't promise to take the youngsters to school in a big auto. But that's what they're doing. They have a man who gives practically his entire time to gather up the bunch of kids in the morning, taking them home at noon, back to school, and home again in the evening.

"Pretty soft for those kids, pretty soft," remarked one parent of that vicinity who used to walk three miles to school all winter long.

The brothers owed much to their siblings. Their brother, Herbert, eleven years older than O. P., and thirteen years older than M. J., to whom they were never particularly close, had become the breadwinner when their father was either unwilling or unable to fill that role. Their sisters, Carrie and Edith, with whom they remained close for the rest of their lives, had cared for the brothers following the death of their mother. It is said that the brothers built a home for the sisters on Lee Road that they never occupied, thought to have been the house at the southwest corner of Lee Road and Shaker Boulevard—the same house that Benjamin and Daisy Jenks lived in after they first moved to Shaker Heights. Instead, the sisters lived in the brothers' town home on South Park Boulevard, even after the brothers had moved to their country estate, Roundwood Manor, in Hunting Valley in 1924.

Frustrated by the slow pace of development in Shaker and believing that activity bred activity, O. P. was determined to do whatever it took to create more building activity. He entered into a contract with George W. Hale, a builder, to work in collaboration with architect H. T. Jeffrey. Hale hired large numbers of tradesmen and often had between fifteen and twenty houses under construction at a time.

Meanwhile, track was laid on the section of Coventry (that would become Shaker Boulevard), east to Fontenay Road, just under one and three-quarter miles. On December 17, 1913, the Shaker Lakes Trolley began operating from Fontenay Road, west to Coventry Road and then north to Fairmount Boulevard, where the line joined the existing tracks of Cleveland Railway, continuing west along Fairmount to Cedar, and then down through Cedar Glen to University Circle and Euclid Avenue, continuing west on Euclid to downtown—a ten-mile commute taking forty-five minutes.

O. P. and M. J. had begun to think about rapid transit to eliminate the reliance on Cleveland Railway and reduce the forty-five-minute commute between residences in Shaker Heights and offices in downtown Cleveland to fifteen minutes. On July 18, 1911, the brothers incorporated the Cleveland & Youngstown Railroad, with a broad railroad charter rather than a narrow street railway franchise. The older brother had spent many hours poring over area maps, studying all the possible routes. His plan was for an eight-and-one-half-mile route that would run from Warrensville Center Road, west on the grass median of Shaker Boulevard. From there they needed the most direct route to Public Square, and they found it along Kingsbury Run in the shadow of Rockefeller Refinery No. 1 and Grasselli Chemical Company.

The best location for a transit terminal, they found, was not at the north end of the mall as the Group Plan Commission had recommended in 1903, and of which Cleveland's former mayor Tom Johnson was a strong proponent, but on Public Square. This meant diverting from Kingsbury Run at East 34th Street, leaving the brothers with a two-mile stretch that was heavily urbanized. They considered tunneling as suggested by civil engineer William Pease but turned their attention first to acquiring the land needed for their terminal before settling on the final two-mile right-of-way.

Just to the southwest of Public Square was the four-acre Haymarket District. Originally a marketplace surrounded by fine homes, the district had evolved into a combined residential and commercial space before degenerating into the city's first slum. Given the blighted condition of the area, the cost of land would be low, and O. P. reasoned that he could leverage a terminal by opening it up to traction lines and smaller steam railroads. Everyone would win. The city would be rid of the slum; he would deliver on his promise of a fifteen-minute commute from Shaker Heights homes to downtown offices; and steam and traction lines would have access to the fine new terminal. Best of all, it would be paid for by fees for the use of the terminal and increased land sales in his growing new suburb, maximizing the brothers' philosophy of using other people's money.

The Van Sweringen brothers began to acquire property in the former Haymarket District, and in the summer of 1911 they organized two new companies: the Terminal Building Company and the Terminal Realty & Securities Company. On May 6, 1912, the Cleveland City Council awarded the Van Sweringens the necessary franchise for the Cleveland & Youngstown Railroad, with hardly any discussion and even less opposition. The following year, O. P. incorporated the Cleveland Interurban Railroad Company to manage and operate the rapid transit system, and that same year he formed the Van Sweringen Company, taking the place of the Sedgewick Land Company that had been formed in 1907 to conduct the business activities in Shaker Heights. He also incorporated the Long Lake Company to hold the farmlands that were continuing to be acquired east of their Shaker development. With the creation of new companies, new jobs were created as well. With the offices in the Williamson Building outgrown, the brothers negotiated for the top floor of the planned twelve-story Marshall Drug Building on the northwest corner of Public Square where the Sherwin Williams Company's new corporate headquarters is today under construction.

The Van Sweringen brothers—especially O. P.—were opportunistic, and likely the older brother never saw an opportunity he did not want to undertake. In December 1911, the brothers took advantage of its availability and purchased twenty-five acres of land in Hunting Valley from the heirs of Jesse H. Luce for $125 per acre. The deed was recorded in the name of Benjamin L. Jenks, a practice that would frequently be repeated in the coming years. This was the first purchase of what would ultimately assemble 660 acres of land at S. O. M. Center Road between Shaker Boulevard and Old Kinsman Road for the development of luxury country estates that the visionary O. P. had in mind.

The Luce property consisted of a farmhouse and several barns. It was hilly, with woods and ravines, and soon it became the picturesque weekend getaway of the brothers and the Jenkses. The brothers considered naming it Orman Farms—a contraction of their first names—but they decided on Daisy Hill instead. Whether it was named for the omnipresent Daisy Jenks or for the flowers that were found in abundance on the slopes remains unclear. Daisy Hill became a place to entertain business associates and prospective buyers or to get away to think and reflect—something the always-thinking O. P. did often.

Land acquisition was a delicate balancing act that offered a narrow window of opportunity. The brothers were well recognized, and the per-acre price of farmland suddenly jumped one hundred dollars on the suspicion that the Van Sweringens might be buying the land. The brothers hired land agents to acquire acreage, stressing a smaller down payment and longer terms, counting on being able to sell the land before too many payments had been made. As farmers worked every minute of the daylight hours, the land agents worked at night, often in teams, simultaneously meeting with adjacent landowners, knowing that prices would soar once neighbor told neighbor that there was land acquisition going on Although the brothers had seemingly limitless credit, the same could not be said about their cash.

In a fortuitous meeting with Alfred Holland Smith in 1913, scheduled to discuss the purchase of an adjacent twenty-five-acre parcel belonging to Smith's sister Caroline Chapman, the recent widow of railroader Harry Chapman, the discussion soon turned to the subject of the brothers' rapid transit. "Mr. Smith," as O. P. would always call him, had a similar youth as that of "Van," as he would call O. P. He shared with O. P. that he had once stayed in bed while his mother repaired the seat in his only pair of pants, something with which O. P. could most certainly have related. Smith was now the senior vice president and soon to become the president of the New York Central Railroad. The two quickly reached an agreement on the Chapman land and went on to the discussion that was on Smith's mind.

The New York Central's freight station was located on the lakeshore near Cleveland's downtown. It was old and overcrowded. If a new union terminal was constructed at the north end of the mall to replace the existing decrepit station built in 1866, it would be seventy-five feet above the level of the lake, and the existing trackage would have to be rerouted. Because of the 7 percent grade from the track to the top of the bluff, cartage companies charged a surcharge that had cost the New York Central half of its cargo tonnage. Moreover, Smith was planning the extension of the New York Central into the Midwest. That would necessitate a new freight facility and tracks through the busy Cleveland downtown, preferably following a route to the south of the business district, which would coincide nicely with the brothers' plans for their rapid transit. Smith felt that a local company would be looked on more favorably in terms of the necessary city council approval.

"Van" and "Mr. Smith" reached an agreement whereby the brothers would build tracks and a freight station stretching between East 91st Street and East 34th Street. The agreement would give the New York Central the two tracks and freight station it needed, and the Van Sweringens would get the two tracks they needed for their rapid transit. The brothers would pay for it all out of advances from the New York Central. All that was required now was the approval of Cleveland voters. Approval of the Cleveland City Council was necessary to put the issue on the ballot, and that came, but not easily. Smith had been correct that the council would look more favorably on a local company, and it did, but not without long and heated discussion. The council knew, as did Smith, that the New York Central's financial support of the new union terminal on the mall was in the balance. In the end, Mayor Baker and officials of both the New York Central and Pennsylvania Railroads met and came to an informal agreement on the terms of a new terminal on the mall. A second issue—the voter's approval of the freight terminal—was added to the November 1915 ballot. Both were approved.

The Van Sweringens assembled a syndicate of investors to acquire the land for the promised New York Central freight station. Members of the syndicate included Joseph Nutt, Warren Hayden, Otto Miller, Charles Bradley, and Parmely Herrick, but not the brothers. In the process of acquiring the necessary land, it was discovered that the Baltimore & Ohio Railroad (B&O) owned a small but critical piece. During a meeting in Baltimore, B&O officials expressed interest in the brothers' project of a union terminal on Public Square, suggesting that the B&O, Wheeling & Lake Erie, and Erie Railroad could potentially be interested in the site if it was upgraded from a traction terminal to a steam-railroad terminal.

The tracks of the New York, Chicago & St. Louis Railroad, known as the Nickel Plate Road—owned by the New York Central—were perfectly located for the rapid transit's access to the brothers' proposed transit terminal. O. P. attempted to negotiate for the use of the Nickel Plate's right-of-way, but the New York Central denied access. However, Mr. Smith had other ideas. With the passage of the Clayton Antitrust Act in 1914, Attorney General Thomas W. Gregory had notified Smith, by then president of the New York Central, that its ownership of both the Nickel Plate and the Lake Shore & Michigan Central constituted an antitrust violation.[6] Freight service between Buffalo and Chicago was dominated by the Lake Shore & Michigan Southern, the Lake Shore & Michigan Central, and the New York, Chicago & St. Louis Railroad.

The Lake Shore & Michigan Southern had been fully merged into the New York Central, and the other two lines were direct competitors between Buffalo and Chicago, so the New York Central had to divest itself of one of the lines. O. P. still needed access to the terminal, and Mr. Smith did not want a competitor to purchase the line, especially the New York Central's archrival, the Pennsylvania Railroad. Nor did he want anyone to purchase the railroad who could not be trusted not to sell it to the Pennsylvania Railroad, regardless of the offer. On July 6, 1916, the

Van Sweringens acquired the 513-mile Nickel Plate Road for $8.5 million, and with it, one of the New York Central's up-and-coming executives, John J. Bernet, thought by some to have been Mr. Smith's handpicked successor. On July 15, 1916, John J. Bernet was elected president of the Van Sweringens' Nickel Plate Road. Then O. P. added as a vice president a top-notch legal executive, H. D. Howe, a partner in a Chicago law firm that had done a great deal of work for the New York Central.

With the land for Shaker Heights acquired and the matter of the right-of-way for the rapid transit resolved, the brothers hired F. A. Pease Engineering Company to implement their plans for a Garden City suburb in keeping with the City Beautiful movement. Company founder Frederick A. Pease and his chief engineer, Harry C. Gallimore, were primarily responsible for the design of Shaker's roads, transit, lakes, and parks, and for determining individual neighborhood lot sizes. All these items were successfully integrated into a larger community master plan that created an ideal setting in which architects could design a variety of residences, community buildings, schools, shops, and churches.

The New York Central's Orange Avenue freight complex had been given a wartime priority and opened in January 1918. The Shaker Rapid Transit, however, was at a standstill. The grading of the roadbed to the west of Shaker Heights had been completed by the end of 1916, but track and overhead wires had been held up by the war effort, and the Van Sweringens had released the stockpile of rail for the Moreland Boulevard line to meet wartime needs overseas. An operating contract was finally signed in September 1919, and the official rapid transit service began in April 1920, with four cars built in 1914 by Cleveland's G. C. Kuhlman Car Company and leased from the Cleveland Railway Company.

Three permanent stations were constructed—one at the end of the Moreland Boulevard line at Lynnfield Road; another at the end of the Shaker Boulevard line at Courtland; and the third on Shaker Boulevard at Coventry Road. As they do today, the Shaker and Van Aken (Moreland) Boulevard lines merged just east of Shaker Square, and the combined line continued on its dedicated track to East 34th Street. From there the cars followed the existing streetcar track along Pittsburgh and Broadway Avenues to East 9th Street, north to Superior Avenue, and west to Public Square. The new two-mile route cut ten minutes off the commute.

When completed, the Shaker Rapid boasted railroad-standard construction over the six-mile route from Union Terminal to Shaker Square, unimpeded by automobile traffic. The transit crossed over three railroad rights-of-way and several streets while navigating the long stone-cut ascent to the Heights. Beyond Shaker Square, the lines continued over the wide grass medians of Shaker and Van Aken Boulevards—the new name of Moreland Boulevard, renamed to honor Shaker Heights's first mayor, William J. Van Aken—with stops approximately every one-third of a mile, where several streets came together to be served by a single transit stop.

The investment in rapid transit not only served as an incentive to prospective homeowners to purchase and develop lots in Shaker Village but was financially profitable for the Van Sweringens. Unlike other commuter transit systems that experienced one-way rush hours as commuters packed the cars when they went from home to work in the morning and from work to home in the evening, the Shaker Rapid experienced two-way rush hours, as servants packed the otherwise empty cars to their jobs in the growing suburb in the morning and returned to their downtown homes in the evening.

The dramatic increase in the population of the City of Cleveland—from a little more than 560,000 in 1910 to nearly 800,000 in 1920—prompted the Greater Cleveland Transportation Committee to release a report projecting a countywide population of three million by 1960. In fact, the population of Cuyahoga County in 1960 was only slightly more than one-half of the projection, but the report had encouraged the Van Sweringens to initiate a comprehensive rapid transit plan. The resulting plan called for a transit line from Rocky River on the west side through Union Terminal to Chardon Road on the east. Two additional lines were planned for the west side. One was to follow the New York Central right-of-way to West 98th Street and then west to the interurban tracks to Elyria. The other was to follow the New York Central right-of-way to

Berea. Two more lines were planned on the east side from the terminal to East 55th Street along the existing Shaker Rapid tracks. There, one would follow the Erie Railroad right-of-way through Kingsbury Run to North Randall. The other would follow the Wheeling & Lake Erie right-of-way to East 93rd Street and Broadway Avenue, connecting with the Northern Ohio Interurban tracks to Akron.

The plan for the existing Shaker Boulevard line included an extension to Brainard Circle, where the line would split. One set of tracks would follow Gates Mills Boulevard northeast to Mayfield Road where it would follow the former Eastern Ohio Interurban to the Village of Gates Mills. The other set of tracks would go southeast to connect with the Eastern Ohio Interurban tracks to Chagrin Falls.

Some of the brothers' plans for regional rapid transit were abandoned or modified early on, while work was started on others. On the Shaker Boulevard line, grading was completed to Brainard Circle and on Gates Mills Boulevard nearly to Mayfield Road. Plans for the lines on the New York Central, Erie Railroad, and Wheeling & Lake Erie rights-of-way were abandoned. The plan for the Rocky River/Chardon Road line was shortened to East 110th Street (between Detroit and Clifton) on the west and Ivanhoe Road on the east, and construction was begun on the east side in 1928. The roadbed was prepared from East 55th Street to East Cleveland, and bridges were widened to allow for the additional tracks. Stairwells were constructed at Cedar Glen and Mayfield in Cleveland, and Lakeview, Lockwood, Hower, and Superior Roads in East Cleveland, to permit access to the elevated tracks. Construction was stopped in 1930 as the country slipped into the Great Depression. That same year, the Van Sweringens acquired the Cleveland Railway Company, holder of the transit franchise for the City of Cleveland. Although some work was begun, only one line, that from Windermere to the east to Cleveland Hopkins Airport to the west, has ever been completed.

The Shaker Village's original nearly 1,400-acre tract had grown to 4,000 acres, extending east to Warrensville Road and south to Scottsdale Road. A Van Sweringen Company sales and engineering office was built

Car 1218—G. C. Kuhlman Car Company, 1914. Property of the Illinois Railway Museum, Union, Illinois.

Pullman Standard Company, 1948. Pennsylvania Trolley Museum, Washington, Pennsylvania. Courtesy Scott Becker.

Coventry-Shaker Rapid Station, 14040 Shaker Boulevard, 1923.

Lynnfield-Shaker Rapid Station, 18800 Van Aken Boulevard, 1922.

End of the line, Shaker Rapid, Shaker Boulevard east of Green Road Station.

Gates Mills Boulevard extension cleared and graded.

at the northeast corner of Shaker Boulevard and Lee Road, formerly the site of the Shaker meeting house. The building also served as the first village hall and schoolroom, and it housed the municipal offices, police, fire, and service departments until 1931, when it is presumed to have been demolished. At some time before 1921, a neoclassical building was built at the northwest corner of the intersection of Shaker Boulevard and Coventry Road. It too was used as a sales office by the Van Sweringen Company. When the company opened a new subdivision east of Warrensville Center Road in 1927, the building was moved to the southeast corner of the Warrensville Center Road/Shaker Boulevard intersection, and an addition was built on the rear.

As had been the case in Patrick Calhoun's Euclid Heights, the Van Sweringens developed strict standards in 1925, which were modified in 1928. The standards specified allowable building materials, construction details, color schemes, and acceptable architectural styles. Homes were to be architect-designed, in English, French, and colonial styles, and no two could be the same.[7]

As African Americans sought to purchase property in Shaker Village, the Van Sweringen Company, in collaboration with a committee of the Shaker Heights Protective Association, devised and implemented deed restrictions that, although containing no overtly discriminatory language, largely succeeded in achieving the company's discriminatory objective of maintaining Shaker Heights as an exclusive community. In 1925, the African American physician Dr. E. A. Bailey purchased a center-hall brick colonial home on Huntington Road. The family was subjected to hostility at the hands of their white neighbors, who threw bricks and stones at the house. A fire was set in the family's garage, and police, assigned to protect the family, harassed the Baileys, searching them and their friends as they entered and left the home, leading the family to sell and move out of Shaker Heights. It wasn't until after January 1956, when a firebombing destroyed the garage and damaged the house under construction for prominent Cleveland attorney John Pegg and his wife Dorothy, on Corby Road in the Ludlow neighborhood, that things began to change in Shaker Heights. The following year, the Ludlow Community Association was formed.

Discrimination was not limited to race but included religion as well, prohibiting the sale of homes to Jews or Catholics. The prohibition of Jews, although largely enforced, appears to have been arbitrarily applied. For example, in August 1927, a building permit was issued to Jewish community leader Salmon Halle, a descendant of Jewish immigrants and the co-owner of the Halle Brothers department store. His fifteen-thousand-square-foot French Renaissance/neoclassical home at 2701 Park Drive is just a short walk from the Van Sweringens' Shaker Heights mansion. Prospective home buyers who felt they had been unfairly discriminated against were welcomed to petition their prospective neighbors and obtain the signatures of a minimum of eleven of the closest twenty-one, although it is unclear just how effective petitioning was in practice.

It was not until October 1945 that Shaker's first and only Catholic parish was established; parishioners worshipped in the basement of Lomond School until the dedication of the Church of St. Dominic in August 1948. There remains no temple, synagogue, or mosque in Shaker Heights to this day.

The Van Sweringen Company and, later, the City of Shaker Heights continued to enforce these restrictions, requiring personal and character references into the 1960s, well beyond the 1948 US Supreme Court ruling that rendered religious and racial covenants unenforceable.[8] (See apps. C and D.)

Not only did the Van Sweringens develop strict standards and deed restrictions but they enforced them as well. In June 1926, the K. V. Painter Building was under construction at the northeast corner of the intersection of Warrensville Center and South Woodland Roads, a location restricted to residential development. Described as "being designed with a special view to making an attractive and well-adapted retail structure," the building was being built to hold eighteen commercial tenants. When the building was completed, the Van Sweringens purchased it from Painter and the structure was demolished.

VAN SWERINGEN RESIDENCES

On August 29, 1909, O. P. Van Sweringen purchased approximately 5.4 acres of land from the Shaker Heights Land Company for $3,488. Fronting South Boulevard—now South Park Boulevard—the parcel measured approximately 533 feet wide and extended 440 feet in depth. The parcel was a part of a twenty-five-acre lot, half of which had been bought by Cleveland capitalist and philanthropist Frank A. Arter in November 1907. The brothers engaged architect H. T. Jeffrey to design and build their mansion.

Built at a cost of more than $75,000, it was an absolute showplace—the best of the best. O. P. wanted nothing less for himself, his guests, and his customers. He explained that his best ideas came to him when he set his own interests aside and viewed a project through the eyes of the customer. A gatehouse served as servants' quarters over a six-car garage, and owing to O. P.'s paranoia, it housed the furnaces and boilers that provided heat and hot water, which was piped to the mansion through an underground tunnel. An article in the *Plain Dealer* on July 3, 1910, described the residence "as large, apparently—sizing it up at a glance—as the royal stables of the czar, and as elegant as a genii palace in the Arabian Nights, and yet as homelike and refined in general appearance as a seven-room cottage in a Max Parrish drawing."[9]

After a dozen or so years, the town home was looking shabbily dated. O. P. consulted with architect Philip L. Small, whom he had engaged to design and build demonstration homes on South Woodland, telling Small, "We didn't know any better when we built it, but we want a house that we won't be ashamed of and that won't be inferior to the others around it," and admitting, "Except for the addition of a sunroom as a surprise for their sisters, nothing had been done to the home since it was completed in 1910."

Small renovated and enlarged the mansion, including a new facade that softened the medieval fortress appearance. The inside was gutted to its eighteen-inch stone walls and redesigned with fourteen generous rooms, including four large bedrooms. The walls of the spacious living room were finished in rough plaster with carved oak paneling and wainscoting. The dining room was paneled in carved walnut. The floors were finished with irregular planks of pegged oak. A servant's wing was added to the east end of the house, balanced by an enclosed porch on the west end.

In 1913, the brothers had purchased an additional seven acres of land, extending their property to Shaker Boulevard (formerly Coventry Road). A driveway entered the property from Shaker Boulevard and wound its way past the gatehouse to a stone wall separating it from the mansion. Entrance to the mansion was through the first of two magnificent gates created by Rose Iron Works, the other gate serving as the exit. Today the three-story Shaker Heights mansion includes nine rooms on the ground level and eight bedrooms on the second floor.

Photographs of Van Sweringen Mansion in Shaker.

Photographs of Van Sweringen Gatehouse in Shaker.

Daisy Hill was originally planned as a golf course and clubhouse for entertaining Van Sweringen clients and business associates, but that

Van Sweringen Mansion, 17740 South Park, as designed by H. T. Jeffrey, 1909. Courtesy of the Shaker Historical Society, Shaker Heights, Ohio.

Van Sweringen Mansion as redesigned by Philip L. Small, 1923.

Van Sweringen Gatehouse—17715 Shaker Boulevard, 1910.

gave way to the broader idea of a 4,000-acre luxury community extending from the eastern boundary of Shaker Heights at Warrensville Center Road on the west to the Chagrin River on the east, and from Fairmount Boulevard on the north to Chagrin Boulevard on the south. To be developed as Shaker Country Estates, the development was meant to appeal to the wealthiest buyers.

The brothers had assembled approximately 660 acres of land in Hunting Valley. Six and a half miles east of the center of Shaker Heights, Daisy Hill was developed between 1920 and 1927. Early in the development was the construction of a concrete barn to house O. P.'s prize-winning Holsteins. The brothers were so pleased with the result of their $250,000 investment in the upgrading of the Shaker Heights estate that O. P., who had grown tired of raising the Holsteins, decided to convert Daisy Hill to a country estate.

The visual center of the Van Sweringens' 660-acre country estate was the fifty-four-room, ninety-thousand-square-foot red-brick Roundwood Manor, designed in the colonial style by Philip L. Small and Charles Bacon Rowley. Across the way, the Jenkses' house, originally two farmhouse joined with a facade and portico, was remodeled in the colonial style as well, the Jenkses having lived there since before O. P. decided to make Daisy Hill his new home.

Construction of Roundwood Manor began in 1923. The concrete-walled cow barn was transformed into the one-and-one-half-story main lounge known as the Ship Room, and its silo was converted into an observatory, accessed by a circular stairway. Overall, the front elevation extended 250 feet, west to east, with the center wing, including the swimming pool and staff and guest bedrooms, extending 150 feet to the rear. The kitchen, including the basement preparation and storage areas, was large enough to prepare dinner for two hundred guests. M. J. oversaw the construction, and Daisy Jenks was responsible for the interior decor, tastefully blending antique and modern. O. P. once said, when asked why they wanted such a large home, that it was so that he could entertain the directors of both the Pennsylvania and New York Central Railroads at the same time without their encountering each other.

A farmhouse, too close to and in clear sight of the manor, clearly offended O. P.'s sense of beauty and solitude. Repeated attempts to buy the property had failed, so he had a group of five spacious garages built—three feet from the property line. The owner sold the structure to the Van Sweringens, who promptly had the farmhouse demolished. Although the construction of Roundwood Manor was not completed until well into 1925, the brothers moved in December 1924, leaving the Shaker Heights townhome in the hands of Edith and Carrie, who lived there until after O. P.'s death, when they moved to Moreland Courts.

Photographs of Roundwood Manor and Garages.

As early as 1908, Herbert, the eldest Van Sweringen brother, had purchased a lot from his brothers from time to time for resale, even as he was employed at Cleveland-Cliffs Iron Company. In addition, financed by several friends, Herbert acquired lots from the brothers, on which he built houses that he sold at a modest profit. In 1912, Herbert resigned from his job as an auditor at Cleveland-Cliffs to work with his brothers. O. P. gave him an office in the Williamson Building and a position in the real estate development company. The brothers sold six streets around Lee Road, on which they were to build a specified number of houses, and Herbert was put in charge of supervising the construction. In 1913, only thirteen houses were built in Shaker Village. One of them, designed by Cleveland architect Reynold Hinsdale, was on Sedgewick Road, one block west of Lee Road between Shaker Boulevard and South Woodland, and became the home of Herbert and Mabel Van Sweringen and their son, Raymond. Not satisfied with the role to which he had been relegated, Herbert and his friends also acquired lots in Florida, which quickly sold. Realizing that there was no real future for either himself or

Roundwood Manor—3450 Roundwood Road, Philip L. Small, 1923–1927.
Courtesy of the Shaker Historical Society.

Roundwood Manor as redesigned by Small, Smith & Reeb, for Gordon and
Mary Stouffer, 1946.

Roundwood Garages, 3425 Roundwood Road, 1929.

Daisy Hill Gatehouse, 36040 Shaker Boulevard/3025 Roundwood Road, 1927.

Daisy Hill Farm Group, 33919 Hackney Road, ca. 1930.

H. C. Van Sweringen Residence, 2931 Sedgewick Road, Reynold Hinsdale,
Georgian Revival, 1913.

Van Sweringen Demonstration House, 19300 Shaker Boulevard, Howell and Thomas, 1922.

Van Sweringen Demonstration House, 2834 Courtland Boulevard, Howell and Thomas, 1922.

Van Sweringen Demonstration House, 2833 Courtland Boulevard, Howell and Thomas, 1922.

Van Sweringen Demonstration House, 19600 Shaker Boulevard, Howell and Thomas, 1922.

his son working for his brothers, Herbert sold the house on Sedgewick to O. P. and moved to Miami in 1924 to pursue real estate development under the name of Sun City Holding Company, of which he was president. He and his associates developed a large part of Sun City, between Tampa and Bradenton, including the Sun City Motion Picture Studio, before the real estate bubble there burst in 1926.

VAN SWERINGEN DEMONSTRATION HOMES

To encourage the development of Shaker Village, the Van Sweringens contracted renowned local architects to design and supervise the construction of demonstration homes in the styles and quality of homes appropriate in Shaker Heights. The homes were clustered together to make it easy for prospective buyers to park their cars, to walk from one house to another, and to be inspired by a variety of architectural interpretations. In all, twenty-five such homes were built, designed by acclaimed architects Philip L. Small, Bloodgood Tuttle, and Howell & Thomas.

On September 11, 1922, building permits were issued to Howell & Thomas for the first four demonstration homes, designed in the Tudor Revival style and built by W. W. Jepson. The site was on the south side of Shaker Boulevard at the end of the Shaker Boulevard Rapid Transit line, where Courtland Boulevard and Manchester and Montgomery Roads converge. Of the four, two of the houses face Shaker, with the other two facing Courtland. Two of the four had short lives as demonstration homes. On July 2, 1923, John J. Bernet, the president of the Nickel Plate Railroad, and his wife Helen, purchased the home at 19300 Shaker Boulevard for $28,000. Less than five months later, Colonel William A. Colston, the Nickel Plate's vice president and general counsel, formerly the finance director of the Interstate Commerce Commission, and his wife Virginia purchased the adjacent house, at 2834 Courtland. The other two demonstration homes in the original cluster stand at 2833 Courtland Boulevard and 19600 Shaker Boulevard.

In 1924, four more clusters of demonstration homes were built. Philip L. Small designed a cluster of five homes on South Woodland Road, between Kingsley and Morley Roads, that were built by Ed Foley, four in the English style and one in the French style. Bloodgood Tuttle designed two clusters in the English, French, and Dutch colonial styles on Van Aken Boulevard, one just east of Southington Road, built by W. W. Jepson, and the other midway between Ingleside and Norwood Road, designed in the French style and built by J. L. Brasee. Finally, Howell & Thomas designed a second cluster, in English and French styles, also built by W. W. Jepson, this time, seven homes on the south side of Parkland Drive, from Ingleside Road to just past Maynard Road. Of the twenty-five demonstration homes built, twenty-two have since been designated Shaker Heights landmarks.

Photographs of Van Sweringen Demonstration Homes.

Photographs of the Bernet House, 19300 Shaker Boulevard.

MASTER MODEL HOMES

Immediately following World War I, the Better Homes movement debuted to encourage people to own, build, remodel, and improve their homes. The program was launched in *The Delineator*, a women's magazine focusing on fashion, culture, and fine arts, published by Butterick Publishing Company in 1922.

Building Shaker Heights

Master Model Home, 18305 Scottsdale Boulevard, Fox, Duthie & Foose, 1928.

Herbert Hoover, the US secretary of commerce and president of Better Homes in America, wrote in the foreword of the *Guidebook of Better Homes*, "The encouragement of sound and durable construction of houses and better-considered buying of household articles enables families throughout America to obtain more for the funds they have available. The construction of better-built houses is a civic and economic asset to the community as well as to the families that own them."[10]

On May 29, 1928, in a first-page article, the Cleveland *Plain Dealer* announced that Cleveland was one of thirty-eight cities selected for the program under the headline, "Ten Master Model Homes to Be Built in Shaker Heights." Between July 18 and May 13 of the following year, building permits were issued to the Robert V. Clapp Company to build a series of eight Master Model Homes. Designed by the firm of Fox, Duthie & Foose in English, French, and colonial styles, the homes were built on Scottsdale Boulevard in the Sykes and Thompson Lomond section of Shaker Village. Seven of the eight Master Model Homes have been designated Shaker Heights Landmarks (see app. E).

Photographs of Master Model Homes.

WINSLOW ROAD

The only street in Shaker Heights that consists exclusively of two-family homes is Winslow Road, running parallel to Chagrin Boulevard and Van Aken Boulevard, beginning at Avalon Road, just east of Lee Road, and ending at Farnsleigh Boulevard, just west of Warrensville Center Road. The first two of what is now more than 170 houses on 45-feet-wide by 130-feet-deep lots were built in 1924. Construction of the first, designed by J. A. Reese, was completed on January 9, by L. D. Stouffer for E. H. Taylor. The second was completed on September 29 by R. F. Gaiser for F. J. Erthal and designed by the firm of Brooke and Burrows.

By 1929 nearly three-quarters of all the houses that would be built on the street were completed, including forty-three designed by George R. Burrows and fourteen more by Fox, Duthie & Foose, the architects of the Master Model Homes just blocks away. The Winslow Road houses were built to the same standards and restrictions as the rest of Shaker Heights, and the single entrance conceals the fact that the structures are two-family dwellings. The last structure was completed at 20005 Winslow Road on February 4, 1957, by Widlus Builders, designed by George H. Burrows, who by the end of his career had designed nearly one thousand homes throughout Cleveland Heights, Shaker Heights, and other eastern suburbs.

INVESTMENT IN SUCCESS
Shaker Heights Country Club, 1915

Along with adequate transportation, the Van Sweringen brothers had seen how the Euclid Club had attracted the well-to-do to Euclid Heights, and they understood the role those social opportunities would play in developing Shaker Village. Growing dissension among members of the Euclid Club had caused some of that club's members to resign their membership and found the Mayfield Country Club in 1909. Others left to found the Shaker Heights Country Club in 1913. On August 3, 1914, the Van Sweringens deeded four parcels of land for the Shaker Heights Country Club. In addition, Frederick C. Green, E. W. Sloan, and O. P. Van Sweringen, trustees, deeded additional land that had been placed in trust on April 1, 1911, to be used as public parkland. The total donation to establish the club was 110 acres. The deed stipulated that the Shaker Heights Country Club complete the construction of a clubhouse, at a value of not less than $40,000, within twenty-four months.

The brown brick clubhouse was designed by Frank B. Meade in the sixteenth-century English style. Doan Brook was filled in and redirected to follow the design of the eighteen-hole golf course.

Shaker Heights Country Club, 3300 Courtland Boulevard, Frank B. Meade, 1915.

Larchmont Avenue was vacated, and additional property was purchased to provide adequate parking. The clubhouse was officially opened on May 29, 1915, with five hundred members and guests in attendance for a dinner dance. The first nine-hole rounds of golf were played two days later, and the first eighteen-hole rounds were played on July 4. Not surprisingly, O. P. and M. J. Van Sweringen were founding members and were members of the original House Committee, but it is unlikely that they were in attendance for the May 29 celebration.

Photographs of Shaker Heights Country Club.

Plymouth Church, 1919

On April 21, 1915, the Van Sweringens donated two parcels of land in the vicinity of Coventry Road and Shaker Boulevard to the Congregational Union of Cleveland, and on November 26, 1919, building permits were issued for the construction of Plymouth Church. Sixty-five years earlier, thirty members of Old Stone Church had broken from the church because of the pastor's moderate antislavery stand. The group of abolitionist parishioners formed a new church at the corner of Euclid and East Ninth Street, naming it Plymouth Church in 1852 at the suggestion of Henry Ward Beecher, a nationally known abolitionist. The church closed its doors in 1913, due to a loss of membership and a lack of money. While the first church in Shaker Village was under construction, the members held their services in the auditorium of the newly constructed high school. Among the founding members were Carrie and Edith Van Sweringen, and the brothers' grandnephew, James Paxton Van Sweringen, who remained an active member of the church until his death in 2020.

In addition to the winding streets of the garden community, with rapid transit and a spectacular country club with a beautiful golf course, the Van Sweringens recognized the value that their customers placed on education. To attract more buyers to Shaker Heights, they induced three private schools, one for boys and two for girls, to move to Shaker Heights with the offer of the donation of land.

Hathaway Brown School was originally founded in 1876 as the Brooks School for Ladies. Anne Hathaway Brown purchased the school in 1886, changing the name to Miss Anne H. Hathaway Brown's School for Girls. The architectural firm of Hubbell & Benes was hired to design a new building at East 87th Street and Euclid Avenue, into which the school moved in 1905. On July 17, 1925, Kenyon V. and Maud Wyeth Painter quitclaimed the land at 19600 North Park Boulevard to the East End School Association, a nonprofit organization doing business as Hathaway Brown School, as a part of a three-way transaction whereby the Van Sweringens were the donors.

In February 1925, a contract was signed, and on August 28, 1926, a building permit was issued to Hunkin & Conkey to build a brick-and-stone building designed by Walker and Weeks. The school moved into its new campus in 1927, and on September 19, 1929, the East End School Association executed a deed transferring the land at 1945 East 97th Street to Harshaw Chemical Company. In 1984, the Cleveland Clinic acquired the former Hathaway Brown School, demolishing it in January 2010.

University School was incorporated on May 21, 1890, as a college preparatory school for boys. Its purpose was to provide the technical training its founders believed necessary to prepare young men to be industry leaders. Originally located on the former ten-acre Thomas Bolton Estate on Gidding Avenue (now East 71st Street), between Hough and Lexington Avenues, the school erected a building measuring fifty feet by eighty feet by fifty-one feet. In February 1925, the school awarded a contract to Hunkin-Conkey Construction for a new campus in Shaker Heights near the intersection of Shaker Boulevard and Warrensville Center Road. On December 30, 1925, all the equipment and materials were relocated from Hough to Shaker Heights, and on January 5, 1926, students and faculty

Plymouth Church of Shaker Heights, 2860 Coventry Boulevard, Charles S. Schneider, 1915.

Hathaway Brown School, 19600 North Park Boulevard, Walker and Weeks, 1926.

University School, 20701 Brantley Road, Walker and Weeks, 1925.

Laurel School, 1 Lyman Circle, John Graham, 1927.

filled the classrooms on the new thirty-five-acre campus. In June of that year, the school deeded the former Bolton estate to the Cleveland Board of Education.

Laurel School was founded in 1896 as Miss (Jennie Warren) Prentiss's Wade Park Home School, located in a house at 116 Streator Avenue (now East 100th Street). The following year, the school added a second house at 95 Streator to accommodate its growth. A new name, Laurel Institute, was adopted in 1899, and by the next year, the rapidly growing school had moved to 2165 (now 10001) Euclid Avenue, opposite Streator Avenue. With the new school year in 1904, Sarah E. (Mrs. Arthur E.) Lyman was introduced as the school's new principal. On May 13, 1927, the Van Sweringen brothers deeded eleven acres of land to the school, and a building permit was issued to Crowell & Little Construction Company to build a cluster of buildings that had been designed by architect John Graham. Reminiscent of a sixteenth-century English manor house, the design included a main building flanked by kindergarten classrooms on the right and a residence hall on the left. Later that year, the school again changed its location, moving to 1 Lyman Circle in Shaker Heights, and changed its name to Laurel School.

In addition to Hathaway Brown, Laurel, and University School, John Carroll University, a private Jesuit university, was under construction in what is today neighboring University Heights. With the concentration of schools being developed in the vicinity of the intersection of Fairmount Boulevard and Warrensville Center Road, the Cleveland Transit System agreed to extend bus service from Fairmount and Eaton to the newly completed Fairmount Circle.

DEVELOPING "LITTLE SHAKER HEIGHTS," 1920–1930

Just as the Van Sweringens did not limit their business interests to real estate development, they did not limit their development to Shaker Village. In 1920, the Van Sweringen brothers' Shaker Heights Improvement

Longwood Fountain.

Longwood Stables.

Empire Builders

Ben Brae Wall.

Glen Allen Wall and Columns.

Company bought forty-one acres of land in Cleveland Heights from the third-generation timberman Charles Lathrop Pack.

The intersection of Mayfield and Taylor Roads in Cleveland Heights was once the site of three Severance family country estates, built as an escape from the pollution and congestion on Millionaires' Row. On the southeast corner stood Longwood, the first and by far the largest and most opulent estate. Built in 1911 by John Long Severance on land he had inherited from his father, Louis Henry Severance, the fifty-room Longwood was designed by J. Milton Dyer with construction beginning in 1898, and in 1914, Longwood was redesigned by Charles Frederick Schweinfurth.

The northeast corner of the intersection had previously been farmland owned by John Severance's sister Elisabeth Severance Allen Prentiss and their cousin Julia Wadsworth Severance Millikin. It was there that the understated home of Benjamin and Julia Millikin, known as Ben Brae, was built in 1913, and next to it, the imposing forty-plus-acre Glen Allen estate of Elisabeth Severance Prentiss was built in 1915.

Today, the only remaining signs of the sprawling Longwood estate are the Carrara marble fountain from the inner courtyard, now on the grounds of the Cleveland Heights City Hall on the northwest corner of the former estate, and the stable, located east of where the mansion once stood, now owned by the Cleveland Heights Board of Education. The rest of the 161-acre estate was redeveloped in 1963 as Severance Town Center, a mixed-use retail and commercial center. Only the stone wall remains to mark where Ben Brae once stood, replaced by a Cleveland Heights fire station. Walls and columns and a farmhouse serve as a reminder of days gone by, while a high school occupies the spot on the forty-plus acres where the Glen Allen mansion once stood.

Along the Cleveland & Eastern Mayfield Road interurban line, once again the Van Swerigens' vision for Inglewood was an architect-designed garden community with winding streets and homes in English Tudor, French, or colonial styles. Among the architects who designed homes in Inglewood were Howell & Thomas, Walker and Weeks, Charles

Building Shaker Heights

1334 Inglewood, the first house completed in 1922. The architect and original owner are unknown.

Lucretia J. Prentiss House, 1255 Oakridge Drive, Charles S. Schneider, 1925.

William Tonks House, 1259 Oakridge Drive, Harold Ott Fullerton, 1926.

H. F. Bash House, 1365 Yellowstone Road, the last house completed in Inglewood in 1975.

115

Schneider, Bloodgood Tuttle, and Abram Garfield. The same restrictions the brothers imposed in Shaker Village existed in Inglewood, including the stipulation that no two homes were to be exactly alike. On September 26, 1920, the *Plain Dealer* included the first advertisement for Inglewood, describing the development as "A Natural Park of Great Beauty," and "A Select Neighborhood for Fine Homes." In 1922 the first house in the new Inglewood development was completed at 1334 Inglewood. Nothing is known about either the architect or the original owner of the Georgian Revival home. Today there are eighty homes in Inglewood; all but eight were built before the end of the 1950s. The most recent was built at 1365 Yellowstone Road in 1975.

Built in 1925 in the Georgian Colonial Revival style, the structure at 1255 Oakridge Drive, a short walk from Glen Allen, is the home built for Lucretia J. Prentiss. She was the unmarried second cousin of the late Francis Fleury Prentiss, whose widow was Elisabeth Severance Prentiss. Miss Prentiss was an invalid for much of her life, and Charles S. Schneider's design for her home included an elevator between the first and second floors and an oversized bathroom off the master bedroom. Today the elevator is gone; in its place is a circular staircase between the first floor and the basement.

Next door to the Prentiss residence, at 1259 Oakridge Drive, stands a six-bedroom home designed by Harold Ott Fullerton in the Tudor Revival style. It was built in 1926 for William Tonks, vice president of the Union Trust Company, who named his new home "Twin Oaks" for the Siamese twin—half-red and half-white oak tree—that stood in front of the house. The wildflower garden, designed by Phillip W. Koellisch, enjoyed a national reputation. Behind the houses on the north side of Oakridge Drive between Yellowstone and Quilliams Roads is the ruggedly picturesque Inglewood Berea sandstone bluff marking the area that was quarried by Alanson Tainter as early as 1846. Stone columns on the bluff above the quarry are the remains of the Rotunda, a gathering place for family and friends, undoubtedly built of stone from that quarry.

In May 1939 Twin Oaks was purchased by Dr. R. Richard Renner, one of the founders and chief of staff at Doctors' Hospital, which was located at the convergence of Euclid Heights Boulevard and Cedar Road. Renner went on to become one of the founders and the first chief of staff at Hillcrest Hospital, now a part of the Cleveland Clinic, on Mayfield Road, east of S. O. M. Center Road in Mayfield Heights, in 1968. Inglewood had become known as "Pill Hill" due to the many physicians at University Hospitals, the Cleveland Clinic, and Doctors' Hospital who chose to live there. Five initial owners of homes in Inglewood were doctors, and many followed, including Dr. Benjamin Spock, author of *Baby and Child Care*, first published in 1946 and one of the best-selling books of the twentieth century. The Spock family lived at 1285 Inglewood during a part of his time as a visiting professor at the Western Reserve University Medical School. The last home to be built in the Inglewood District was completed in 1975 for H. F. Bash, in the modern style by an unknown architect.

Photographs of Lucretia Prentiss House.

Photographs of Twin Oaks—William Tonks House.

MORELAND COURTS AND SHAKER SQUARE, 1923–1929

A major apartment complex was conceived by Josiah Kirby in 1922 when he acquired a fifteen-hundred-foot stretch of land from the Van Sweringens on the north side of Shaker Boulevard, west of Coventry. To describe Kirby as controversial may be understating the facts. Having failed in a business in Cincinnati, he came to Cleveland in 1911 and formed the Cleveland Discount Company, which had grown to be the largest mortgage company in the nation by 1922. Kirby hired Alfred W. Harris to design a luxury apartment complex to be built on his land. Harris's vision was every bit as grandiose as Kirby's. It consisted of a panorama of English architecture, including Elizabethan, late Gothic, Tudor, Jacobean, and Georgian. In early August 1922 Kirby named Ralph P. Stoddard, secretary and manager of the Common Brick Manufacturers' Association, as vice president of the Moreland Courts Company.

In 1923, with only six of the fifteen planned buildings completed—from the Point Building at Coventry Road, to the West Tower, Kirby's Cleveland Discount Company went into receivership, and all his assets, including Moreland Courts, were liquidated. The Van Sweringens reacquired the land and hired Philip Small to complete the project. The first apartments in the original buildings were available for occupancy in November 1924. Six more buildings were designed by Small. The styles were graduated to complement the styles of the existing buildings to the east and the Georgian style of Shaker Square to the west.

By 1929, with the addition of fifty-six apartments, Moreland Courts consisted of 147 apartments ranging in size from six to twelve rooms—fifteen hundred to four thousand square feet—in twelve buildings. A central corridor extends the full length of Small's buildings and is accessible from Kirby's West Tower as well. The corridor includes two gathering areas, including a space for relaxing to live musical presentations and an art gallery. Small's design included four women's shops, exclusively for residents. The Van Sweringens' plan was for a second set of like buildings on the south side of Shaker Boulevard, but that was not to be. In 1978 Moreland Courts transitioned from landlord-owned apartments to a resident-owned condominium association.

Photographs of Moreland Courts.

SHAKER SQUARE, 1927–1929

In 1926, the Van Sweringens hired Philip Small to design a tranquil village green setting consisting of an open space enclosed by buildings in an octagonal form, with the Shaker Rapid tracks and Shaker Boulevard cutting through from west to east. Roadways entered the traffic circle on the north and south sides. Shaker Square was one of the earliest planned suburban shopping centers in the nation, and it serves as the junction point of the two eastern divisions of the Shaker Rapid Transit.

Each of the four quadrants contains a two-story center building flanked by one-story wings and square corner pavilions. In 1946, one of the two-story central buildings became home to Shaker Square's crown jewel, first known as Stouffer's Shaker Tavern, a two-hundred-seat restaurant with four intimate dining rooms. The restaurant was directly accessible to residents of Moreland Courts through a private entrance in the common wall, and the manager of the restaurant soon began freezing menu items for residents to take back to their apartments. The second floor contained eight guest rooms for guests of residents of Moreland Court. Stouffers remained at the location of their first suburban restaurant until 1981.

The other two-story buildings housed a bank, a movie theater, and a variety of specialty retail establishments, with the second-floor housing

The Pointe Building, 13901 Shaker Boulevard to Shaker Square.

The Tudors, 13805 Shaker Boulevard, Alfred W. Harris, 1925.

East Tower, 13705 Shaker Boulevard, Alfred W. Harris, 1925.

The Gallery Buildings, 13415 Shaker Boulevard, Philip L. Small, 1929.

The Gallery Buildings, 13301 Shaker Boulevard, Philip L. Small, 1929.

Shaker Square aerial view. Courtesy of Drone Ohio.

Shaker Square Northeast Quadrant.

Shaker Square Northwest Quadrant.

Shaker Square Southwest Quadrant.

Shaker Square Southeast Quadrant.

office space. Cleveland Trust was one of the first merchants at Shaker Square when it opened a branch bank in the northwest quadrant in 1929. The Colony Theater, designed by noted theater architect John Eberson, opened in the southwest quadrant in 1937 and was renamed Shaker Square Cinemas in 2000. Today, it is known as Atlas Cinemas. Although the Georgian Revival motifs vary, making the overall architecture more interesting, the similarity of style and materials such as red brick, white trim, and slate roofs contribute to the harmony of Shaker Square. The square is central to a sixty-four-acre mixed-use neighborhood combining single-family dwellings and apartment and commercial buildings, built mainly between 1920 and 1930, although some are midcentury.

SHAKER COUNTRY ESTATES

O. P. Van Sweringen's vision for Shaker Heights, like his vision for virtually everything else, knew no bounds. Beginning with the original nearly fourteen hundred acres once inhabited by the North Union Shakers, Shaker Heights grew to four thousand acres with the expansion of the eastern boundary to Warrensville Center Road and the southern border to Scottsdale Boulevard. The Van Sweringens had begun acquiring additional land as it became available as early as 1911. O. P.'s vision was for further expansion from Warrensville Center Road east to the Chagrin River, following Gates Mills Boulevard on the north and Kinsman Road on the south, on which estates not unlike those on Daisy Hill—where he had built Roundwood Manor beginning in 1923—would be built. Central to Shaker Country Estates was The Country Club on Lander Road, just north of Shaker Boulevard.

The Country Club was founded in 1889 on the shore of Lake Erie between Doan Brook and Eddy Road in the section of Glenville that is now Bratenahl. On fifteen acres, with a spectacular view of Lake Erie, The Country Club was an outgrowth of the Bit & Bridle Club, whose members rode their horses to the club from their mansions along Millionaires' Row for picnics and other social activities. In 1895 the first golf course west of the Appalachian Mountains was founded as a subsidiary of the Country Club. In 1929, enticed by the Van Sweringens' offer of two hundred acres of land, the Country Club relocated to the proposed Country Estates, opening on August 10, 1930, adjacent to Pepper Pike Country Club, which had opened in 1925.

Today Shaker Country Estates is a cluster of midcentury colonial-style homes in an area between Richmond Road and Interstate 271, between Fairmount and Shaker Boulevards.

NOTES

1. Herbert H. Harwood Jr., *Invisible Giant* (Bloomington: Indiana University Press, 2003), 9.

2. The words of Mother Ann Lee, the founding leader of the United Society of Believers in Christ's Second Appearing, inscribed on the plaque placed at the site of the grave of Ralph Russell in South Park Cemetery by the Shaker Historical Society on September 2, 1949.

3. Blosser, 31.

4. Louise Davidson Jenks, *O. P. and M. J.* (Cleveland, OH: Brooks Company [privately printed], 1942). Written for the birthday of David Jenks, May 7, 1940. Western Reserve Historical Society.

5. Jenks, *O. P. and M. J.*, 14.

6. The Clayton Antitrust Act was enacted in 1914 by the US Congress to clarify and strengthen the Sherman Antitrust Act. Whereas the Sherman Act only declared monopoly illegal, the Clayton Act defined as illegal certain business practices that are conductive to the formation of monopolies or that result from them.

7. Beaux Arts, which is sometimes called Academic Classicism, American Renaissance, or Beaux Arts Classicism, became a favorite architectural style for government and institutional buildings such as art museums, train stations, libraries, university campuses, and

courthouses in Europe and the United States. Representing the height of European style and flair, Beaux Arts also became a signature style for the opulent private mansions of the privileged few in wealthy enclaves such as Newport, Rhode Island. Many of the world's most celebrated and admired buildings are examples of Beaux Arts architecture.

8. As late as August 1971, the restrictive covenants remained in the sales agreement; however, this buyer was instructed to sign, indicating understanding that the language was null and void.

9. Maxfield Parrish (July 25, 1870–March 30, 1966) was an American painter and illustrator active in the first half of the twentieth century, known for his distinctive saturated hues and idealized neoclassical imagery.

10. The Better Homes movement was launched in 1922 by the Better Homes Advisory Council with Better Homes Week. The *Plain Dealer* cosponsored the construction of master model homes and reported their progress.

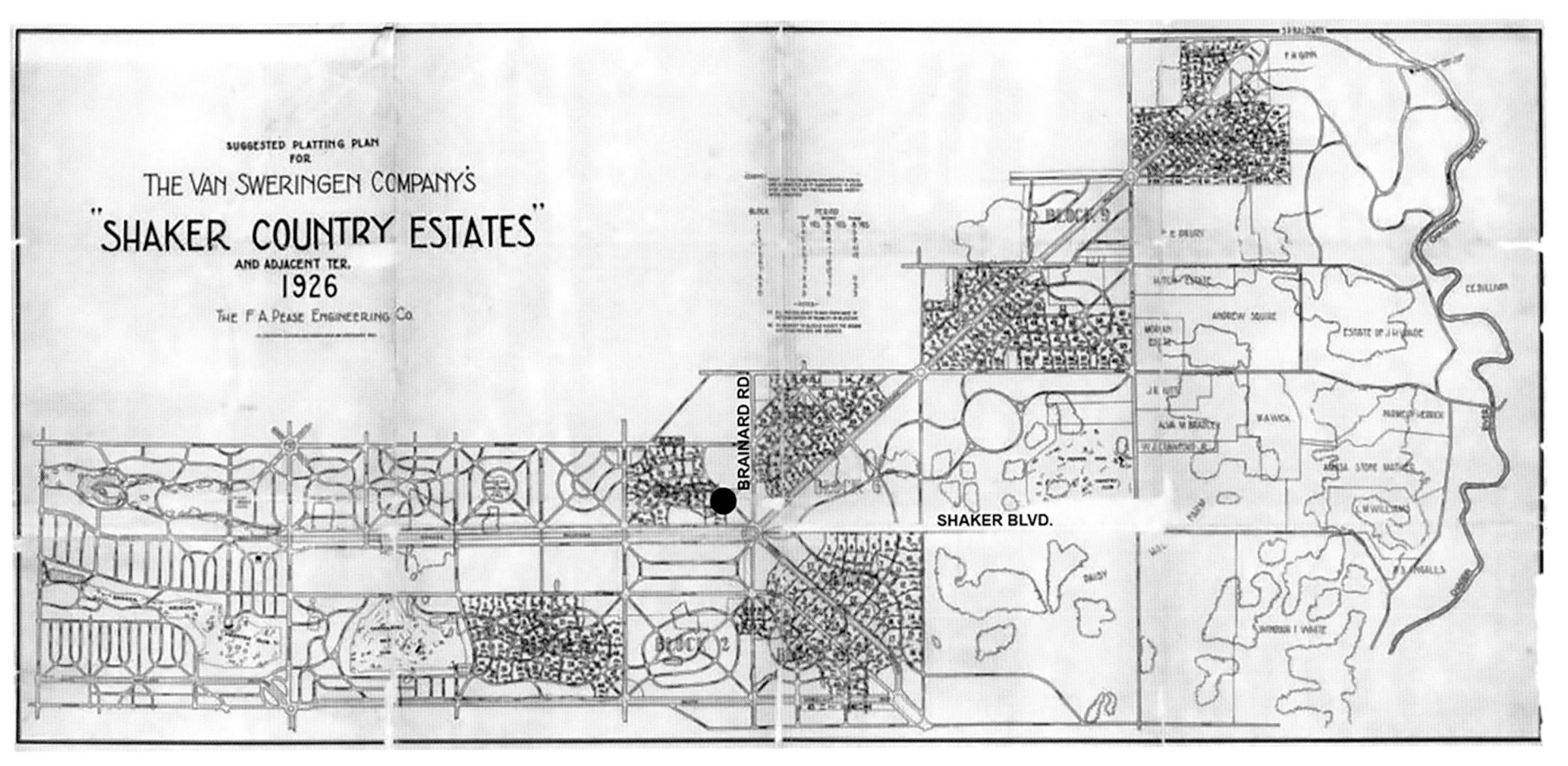

Map of Shaker Country Estates, F. A. Pease Engineering Company, 1926.

FOUR

CREATING AN EMPIRE

THE HOTEL CLEVELAND, 1916–1918

On September 12, 1916, the *Plain Dealer* reported that "an unnamed man" was negotiating a long-term lease for the site of the former Forest City Hotel in downtown Cleveland. An earlier article by W. R. Rose recounted that, although there was no record of the transaction until 1815, sometime in 1812 Samuel Huntington sold lot 82, on the west side of Public Square with sixty-five feet of frontage on Superior Street to Phinney Mowrey for $100. Mowrey "built an extremely modest structure on the land and this he used as a place of entertainment for man and beast." [1] The establishment was known as Phin Mowrey's Tavern. In 1820, Donald McIntosh purchased the tavern from Mowery and changed the name to Cleveland House. The first railroad station is said to have occupied a barn on the grounds of the hotel. In 1845, the hotel was destroyed by fire, and in 1848 it was replaced by David Dunham and operated as the Dunham House until 1851. In 1852 the three-hundred-room Forest City House, a five-story "hollow square" structure was built in the "Anglo-Italian style." Additions were completed in 1866 and 1872, and on September 16, 1915, the Forest City House closed.

The Van Sweringen brothers hired Graham, Burnham & Company, the firm of the late designer of Cleveland's Group Plan, to design the twelve-story, one-thousand-room hotel that would be the first piece of what they planned to be Cleveland's Union Terminal complex. On the ground level were eighteen retail shops, eleven facing Superior and seven facing Public Square. Amenities included a grill, a lunchroom, a fifteen-chair barbershop, a hairdresser, a billiards parlor, and a café. On the second floor were a dining room and a ballroom for six hundred guests. The top floor featured two-room suites, including a bedroom and a "sample room" where salesmen, who traveled from city to city by train, displayed their wares and met with their customers. At a final cost of more than $4.6 million, the "E"-shaped hotel facing Superior Avenue opened on Monday, December 16, 1918, with a black-tie gala.

CLEVELAND UNION TERMINAL, 1923–1934

It was now time to address the question of a union terminal. If the brothers thought for a minute that gaining the necessary approvals would be anything like the experience they had had in obtaining the franchise for

Public Square as it looked in 2014.

Renaissance Cleveland Hotel, Graham, Burnham & Company, 1918.

the Cleveland & Youngstown Railroad, they could not possibly have been more wrong. There were those on Cleveland City Council who remembered well how they had been duped into approving the plans for the New York Central's freight station and who still held a grudge. Although the city council vote to put the issue on the ballot in 1915 had passed 19–6, it had not come without extremely contentious debate, and the nineteen "yes" votes had come from all but one of the Democrat members who were loyal to the brothers' friend, Mayor Newton D. Baker. The voters had spoken—the freight station on Orange Avenue had passed 62,836–23,631, and the mall location of the new union terminal had passed 68,357–17,153.

Now the time had come for the Van Sweringen brothers to unveil the $50 million plan for their Union Terminal, not on the north end of the mall as the voters had approved but facing the southwest quadrant of Public Square, where the brothers had always wanted it to be located. O. P. reasoned that while the voters had approved a new union terminal on the north end of the mall, they could likewise be asked to approve the relocation to Public Square. Once again, things quickly became contentious. Peter Witt, Cleveland's former railway commissioner, a vocal advocate for traction streetcars and an outspoken critic of steam railroads, made his opposition to the Van Sweringens' plan clear. Try though he might, "Billy" Stage, formerly a member of Cleveland mayor Tom Johnson's cabinet, was unable to change his former cabinet colleague's mind. Attorney John Cannon, in studying the city charter, realized that an ordinance could be put on the ballot with as few as five thousand signatures on a petition. That would bypass the possibly endless objections and amendments that were likely to result by going through city council.

To keep O. P.'s friend Newton D. Baker on his side, Stage and Cannon went to Washington to meet with the secretary of war and share with him a draft of the ordinance. With Baker's agreement in principle, on August 26, 1918, the brothers formed the Cleveland Union Terminal Company. The plan was that participating railroads would finance the cost of the land the brothers had acquired during the past ten years, and the brothers would then have the six and one-half acres of "air rights" above the underground station on which to build the office buildings that were a part of their plan. Consistent with O. P.'s thinking on a grand scale, the plans included fifteen tracks for steam trains on the lowest level, and fifteen more tracks for traction trains above them. There was room to increase to twenty-four on each level and even expand to thirty-two in the future if it became necessary.

Attorney John Cannon presented the plan to the city council on September 11, 1918. He explained the rationale for having taken the unusual approach of going to the public for signatures, based on the short time before the November election. He ended his statement by saying, "I want you to consider it just the same as if you were considering it here for the first time." The meeting was then open to questions from the members of the council.

The first question was with respect to New York Central's indirect ownership of the Nickel Plate, which Cannon summarily dismissed as unfounded and ridiculous. Questioning then turned to the Orange Avenue Freight Station. Cannon did his best to parry the questions as irrelevant, but they certainly could not have been unexpected. Two days later, O. P. met with the city council. He found the council members to be universally hostile, with the single exception of Jimmy McGinty, who was employed by the Van Sweringens as a land buyer for the Union Terminal project. O. P. had the gift of being disarmingly charming and friendly. The longer he talked, the less hostile and even more friendly some of the council members appeared to become.

As the meeting was coming to a close, O. P. reminded those in attendance that Cleveland had benefited greatly over the years from the work of the Van Sweringens, including the city's only high-level freight terminal; a rapid transit line, albeit interrupted by the unavailability of materials due to the war effort; a suburban development unrivaled anywhere in the country; nearly three hundred acres of parklands, donated to the city at no cost; and a magnificent new hotel that would soon open.

The meetings dragged on past the deadline for putting the issue on the November ballot, but it was ultimately approved and placed on the ballot for a special election to be held, along with a city bond issue, on

January 6, 1919. After the polls closed on that cold January day and the votes were counted, the Van Sweringens and the Cleveland Union Terminal had won, 30,731 to 19,859.

In the coming months, the completion of the Vans' rapid transit line was in sight, except for the last mile, which could not be completed until Union Terminal was completed as well. O. P. negotiated with Cleveland Railway to provide the rolling stock, the trainmen, and the power to service the Shaker Rapid Transit. Cleveland Railway was reimbursed based on a per-mile cost plus 10 percent of the profits (if any) and was reimbursed for any loss. It had been sixteen years since the dream of rapid transit had first occurred to O. P. On April 11, 1920, it was on the threshold of reality.

Cleveland was a city without a downtown. Certainly, Moses Cleaveland would have argued that the city center was Public Square, while Daniel Burnham would have argued that it was the Mall. Indeed, neither truly filled the bill for Clevelanders at the time. Some would likely have argued for Playhouse Square, where major department stores were located, magnificent theaters were opening, and modern new office buildings were being constructed.

After years of often-contentious debate, the public referendum in 1919 had cleared the way for Van Sweringen's Union Terminal. Demolition of more than one thousand mostly dilapidated buildings began in the early 1920s, and the massive excavation project began in 1923, leading to the most ambitious construction project in Cleveland in the 1920s. Once completed, Terminal Tower was the tallest building outside of New York City until the construction of Boston's Prudential Building in 1964, and it remained the tallest in Cleveland until the construction of Key Tower in 1991.

The Vans had hired the Chicago architectural firm of Graham, Anderson, Probst & White, successor to D. H. Burnham and Company and Graham, Burnham & Company, the architects of the Hotel Cleveland that would be integrated into the Beaux Arts Cleveland Union Terminal. The result was a fifteen-acre, seven-building complex hugging the southwest quadrant of Public Square, largely built on the air rights over the railroad terminal and tracks. The original design of the union terminal called for a fifteen-story office tower above the lobby of the passenger station. Soon that was replaced with a fifty-two-story, 708-foot tower, making it the third-tallest structure in the world at 771 feet—shorter only than Paris's Eiffel Tower and New York's Woolworth Building when it was completed.

To support the weight of the massive buildings that were planned for the site, eighty-seven wells measuring between four and more than ten feet in diameter were drilled into bedrock, some one hundred to two hundred feet below the track level. Concrete and steel piers were then created to a height of twenty-five feet above track level. The terminal concourse, consisting of the passenger waiting areas and ticket lobby, passenger amenities, and the building above, rested on top of the piers. The first steel girder was swung into place on October 18, 1926.

To accommodate automobile traffic, West Huron Road; West Prospect Avenue; and West 3rd, West 4th, and West 5th Streets are bridges above the tracks and passenger platforms. The massive high-level, four-track, 3,350-foot Cleveland Union Terminal Railway Bridge was completed in 1929, crossing the Cuyahoga River at Irish Town Bend and entering Union Terminal. Today, the bridge carries two tracks of railroad traffic and two tracks of rapid transit traffic.

As progress on the terminal complex continued, the brothers' attention was completely diverted to building their railroad empire. In the summer of 1927, progress on the terminal was slowing. O. P. asked banker Charles L. Bradley to head the project. The timing was right for Bradley, a vice president of the Union Trust Company. He had been hoping to be named president of the Union Trust, but infighting among the senior executives at the bank left him uncertain about his future. With Bradley on board, the pace of construction immediately picked up. The first Terminal Tower offices were completed, with tenants in place by December of that year.

The Van Sweringen corporate offices were housed on the thirty-second through the thirty-sixth floors. The upper three floors were accessible only through private elevators from the thirty-second floor. The

Terminal Complex as seen from Public Square, Graham, Anderson, Probst & White, 1930.

Facing, Terminal Lobby Public Square entrance.

thirty-sixth floor housed the brothers' offices, connected by a passageway, with a marble-lined lavatory between them. The office doors were said never to have been closed.

Two other equally sized offices were those of Charles Bradley, chair of the board of Erie Railroad and Cleveland Railway Company, and Darwin Barrett, director of Nickel Plate Road, the Erie Railroad, and the Missouri & Pacific; director and treasurer of Allegheny Corporation; and vice president of the Chesapeake & Ohio Railroad (C&O). Each of the offices had dark oak paneling and working marble fireplaces. The rest of the floor consisted of two small conference/waiting rooms and offices for secretaries.

The thirty-fifth floor included two executive offices like those on the floor above, for John Bernet, president of the C&O and the Pere Marquette, and for Benjamin Jenks, corporate counsel.

The twelfth through fifteenth floors of the Terminal Tower included the Greenbriar Suite, a private space where the Van Sweringens entertained guests in the two-story library and living room, with a magnificent fireplace and oak paneling from a single tree in England's Sherwood Forest. Meetings were conducted in the nearby conference room or dining room, each of which also had a working fireplace. Overnight guests stayed in one of the four bedrooms, two on the fourteenth floor and two on the fifteenth floor.

On October 23, 1929, the first train arrived in the terminal, carrying the Van Sweringens and officials of the Erie Railroad. The official opening of the terminal group, including the Guildhall, Republic, and Midland Buildings across Prospect Avenue, took place on June 28 of the following year, with Newton D. Baker as the master of ceremonies. Julius Howland Barnes, a grain exporter and shipbuilder, was the keynote speaker. Other speakers included the New York Central's Patrick Crowley, the Nickel Plate's Walter Ross, and Cleveland's mayor John D. Marshall. While twenty-five hundred guests, largely celebrities of the railroad world and local civic leaders and businessmen, gathered for the formal opening and most certainly a sumptuous luncheon, the Van

Terminal Tower elevators.

Facing, Private elevator to executive offices on the thirty-fourth to thirty-sixth floors.

Sweringen brothers—like Levi T. Scofield thirty-six years earlier—were nowhere to be seen. The brothers followed the proceedings by radio from the comfort and seclusion of Roundwood Manor at Daisy Hill.

Three lines—the New York Central, the Big Four (the Cleveland, Cincinnati, Chicago & St. Louis), and the Nickel Plate (the New York, Chicago, and St. Louis)—combined for more than seventy trains a day arriving and departing Cleveland's new union terminal. Final destinations included New York, Boston, Chicago, Cincinnati, and St. Louis. They were later joined by the B&O and the Erie Railroad. Only the Shaker Rapid Transit occupied the traction section of the terminal. The Vans had hoped that Cleveland's interurbans would share the traction section, but by 1926, only three remained in existence, and they were nearing obsolescence due to the efficiency of automobiles and buses.

On July 20, 1930, the Shaker Rapid Transit inaugurated the long-promised service directly into the terminal. No longer using streetcar tracks and competing with automobile traffic, the six-mile ride from Shaker Square to Public Square took just twelve minutes. The 8.8-mile trip to the Lynnfield terminal took just twenty-two minutes. Rush-hour express service from downtown to Shaker Square, eliminating any intermediate stops, took just ten minutes.

The concourse floors and walls, like the rest of the terminal building, were clad with marble. Under an ornamental plaster ceiling, the waiting room was fitted with highly polished mahogany benches, gleaming bronze chandeliers, railings, and trim that rounded out the utilitarian opulence of the space. The announcement of the arrival and departure of trains and the slapping of the split-flap Solari boards directed travelers and visitors to the stairways to access the trains on the track level two stories below or to meet arriving passengers. The twelve tracks of the steam section were accessed from the waiting room and ticketing area by seventeen stairways. The stairways were divided in the middle by decorative brass railings to accommodate arriving and departing passengers. The six tracks of the traction section were accessed by fourteen sets of stairs.

Creating an Empire

Former executive office on the thirty-sixth floor.

Corridor adjoining the brothers' offices.

Library and dining room in the Greenbriar Suite.

Conference room in the Greenbriar Suite.

Dining room in the Greenbriar Suite.

Paneled corridor in the Greenbriar Suite.

The brothers' private bedrooms on the fifteenth floor, awaiting restoration.

English Oak Room.

An original Solari board.

The Union Terminal Concourse, now known as Tower City Center.

On three levels, 175,000 square feet of amenities included a large drug and sundries store, restaurants, coffee shops, sandwich shops, a lunchroom, a twenty-two-chair barbershop, and a wide range of specialty retail shops. The crown jewel was the exclusive English Oak Room with its oak-paneled walls and elaborately decorated ceiling.

Other than New York, Cleveland's was the only terminal served exclusively by electric engines. Trains changed engines in the Collinwood yard on the east side and in the Linndale yard on the west side. With the introduction of diesel engines in the late 1930s and the replacement of steam with diesel power, changing engines was no longer necessary by the 1950s.

BUILDERS EXCHANGE, MEDICAL ARTS, AND MIDLAND BUILDINGS

The Van Sweringen brothers had been granted the air rights above Union Terminal tracks for development. That included the space between West Prospect Avenue immediately south of the terminal complex, further south to West Huron Road, and bounded by Ontario Street on the east and West Superior on the west. Once again the brothers engaged Chicago architects Graham, Anderson, Probst & White to develop a master plan for the space. The resulting plan included four eighteen-story interconnected office towers in the Art Deco style. The architects went forward with the design of the first three buildings, with a parking lot reserving the footprint for the fourth. On July 10, 1928, plans for the first two structures were submitted to the city building department for approval and the issuance of building permits.

The November 11, 1928, issue of the *Plain Dealer* announced that the Builders Exchange, a trade association for the exchange of information within the construction industry, would relocate from the Rose Building—at the intersection of East 9th Street and Prospect Avenue, where it had been for the previous ten years—to the eighteenth floor of the Transportation Building, where it remained until 1941. The building, where the architects redesigned the space to accommodate the Exchange's feature exhibit, "Home in the Sky," was renamed the Builders Exchange Building on July 1, 1929, when the ten-year lease went into effect. The modifications included the creation of a court on the seventeenth and eighteenth floors, measuring fifty-six feet long, fifty-one feet wide, and thirty-five feet high, by opening the ceilings of those floors. Within the court, a thirty-nine-foot-wide, thirty-five-foot-deep, and thirty-five-foot-high house in the popular colonial style was constructed and fully equipped with all the latest features.

The Builders Exchange Building, to be flanked by the Medical Arts Building to the northeast and the Midland Bank Building to the west, fronts Huron Road. The amenities in the building included the Guildhall, a restaurant complex consisting of two elaborate public dining rooms, the Tudor Room and the Colonial Room, a cafeteria, and two private meeting/dining rooms. Located on the tenth floor and directly accessible from the Midland and Medical Arts Buildings, the Guildhall was inspired by the fifteenth-century home of the guilds in London. The Cleveland Lumber Institute joined the Better Homes Association as one of the early tenants when it occupied space on the tenth floor in January 1930. In February the Electrical League moved into space on the eighteenth floor, having outgrown its space of fourteen years in the Statler Building on Euclid Avenue. Later, having again outgrown its space, it would move to the Midland Building. The Cleveland Builders Supply had offices and a display room on the fourteenth floor. The lower nine floors were indoor parking, with a capacity of fifteen hundred cars. After the Builders Exchange moved to East 18th Street and Euclid Avenue in 1941, the building was renamed the Guildhall Building.

Located at the southwest corner of the intersection of Ontario Street and Prospect Avenue, the second building in the planned cluster was the Medical Arts Building. The first tenants moved into the building on June 29, 1929, just eight months after the first spade full of dirt signaled the beginning of construction. Each level the nine-story garage in the Builders Exchange Building was accessible to occupants of the Medical Arts

Aerial view of Medical Arts, Builders Exchange, and Midland Buildings, now Landmark Office Towers.

Terminal Complex as seen from the Flats. Courtesy of Drone Ohio.

Building on a floor-by-floor basis. In May 1931, the Accident and Medical departments of the Cleveland Railway Company were relocated from the Hanna Building at East 12th Street and Euclid Avenue to the sixth floor of the Medical Arts Building. This signaled a consolidation of Cleveland Railway's personnel in various locations within the terminal complex. Eventually, the entire sixth floor of the Medical Arts and Midland Buildings would house the company's general office staff.

The population of Cleveland Heights and Shaker Heights combined to quadruple from 16,852 in 1920 to 68,728 in 1930. Likely due to the population shifts from urban to suburban, and therefore a preference for doctors and dentists in the suburbs, the Medical Arts Building experienced an exodus of tenants. In the autumn of 1935, Republic Steel signed a lease for the top four floors of the building, and reconfiguration of those floors from medical and dental suites to corporate offices began. As space became available, the move of the steel company's corporate headquarters from Youngstown, Ohio, to Cleveland began, and the structure's name was changed to the Republic Building. In 1984, when LTV Steel purchased Republic Steel, the building was once again renamed, this time to the LTV Steel Building.

In August 1929 the Terminal Tower's nearly 425,000 square feet of office space was more than 90 percent leased; the Medical Arts Building's nearly 165,000 square feet was 50 percent leased; the Builders Exchange Building's upper nine floors, with more than 175,000 square feet of office space, was more than 65 percent leased; and the parking garage on the lower nine floors was 100 percent leased to a garage operator.

Construction of the Midland Building was the last to be started. In 1928 O. P. paid more than $1.5 million for a 15 percent interest in the Midland Bank that would be the prime tenant, occupying the lower three floors and with its name on the building. The bank fell victim to the Great Depression and was liquidated in 1932. In October 1930 Standard Oil of Ohio (SOHIO) had moved hundreds of office employees from outgrown quarters in the East Ohio Gas Company Building to the sixteenth and seventeenth floors of the Midland Building and the thirteenth floor of the adjacent Builders Exchange Building, with panoramic views of the SOHIO refineries in the flats to the south. Following the liquidation of the Midland Bank, the Electrical League relocated from the Builders Exchange Building to occupy the bank's vacated space on the eighteenth floor.

Other early tenants in the Midland Building included the New York, Pennsylvania, & Ohio Railroad; the Cleveland Railway Company, the predecessor to the Cleveland Transit System, now the Greater Cleveland Regional Transit Authority; the New York, Chicago, & St. Louis Railroad Company; the Pere Marquette Railway Company; Medusa Portland Cement; and several law offices and investment firms.

A DEPARTMENT STORE ON PUBLIC SQUARE

The Van Sweringen brothers wanted the biggest name they could get to fill the retail space at the northeast corner of the terminal complex and entered into negotiations with Chicago's Marshall Field & Company. As an insurance policy, O. P. bought a department store of his own—the seventy-year-old Cleveland-based Higbee Company—to the tune of just over $7.5 million. Negotiations did break down with Marshall Field, and Higbee's moved into the new building in 1931, joining the May Company, which had built an eight-hundred-thousand-square-foot store designed by Daniel Burnham in 1915, just a short walk east along Public Square.

With the entire complex completed, the final price tag exceeded $127 million. While office and retail businesses along Euclid Avenue were unhappy with the new competition, the same could not be said for the people of Cleveland who saw the city's new downtown as a true showplace. Now it was time to fill Union Terminal Station with trains and passengers.

In 1934 one additional piece of the terminal complex was in place with the completion of the five-story US Post Office at 1500 West 3rd Street. The nearly one-half-million-square-foot building served as Cleveland's main post office until the late 1980s, when the facility was relocated to Orange Avenue. The new facility stands on the land once occupied by the New York Central's freight station—the one that led to the Van Sweringens' acquisition of the Nickel Plate Railroad so many decades earlier.

NOTE

1. W. R. Rose, "The Forest City House," *Plain Dealer*, March 19, 1915, 10.

The former Higbee's Department Store, 1931.

The former US Post Office, 1500 West Third Street, now Post Office Plaza Office Building, 1934.

FIVE

BUILDING A RAILROAD EMPIRE

RAPID TRANSIT WAS PERHAPS THE GREATEST SINGLE contributor to the Van Sweringens' successful development of Shaker Heights. It was sixteen years after the idea first occurred to O. P. that rapid transit service started between downtown Cleveland and his garden community in Shaker Heights. In the process, the brothers' business interests had expanded . . . dramatically.

Railroads had been largely unregulated local and regional entities, operating within the eastern, southern, and western regions of the United States. In 1862, Congress passed the Pacific Railway Act, providing federal subsidies in the form of land for rights-of-way and loans for the construction of a transcontinental railroad, designating the thirty-second parallel as the initial route. In 1869, with the completion of the first transcontinental railroad, the coast-to-coast trip was reduced from several months to one week. The role of the federal government in that effort foreshadowed the regulation that was to come. Given the lack of government oversight as the railroads gained increasing amounts of power, so, too, did the railroaders, who became guilty of increasing amounts of self-serving abuse. It had become a matter of what was good for the owners rather than for the common good. As the abuses grew, so did the political pushback, resulting in the passage of the Interstate Commerce Act and the creation of the Interstate Commerce Commission (ICC) in 1887. The driving force behind the act was the need to exert some control over a "public utility" that existed as a de facto monopoly in the medium- and long-distance transportation markets. The act recognized that railroads could remain as private enterprises, but at the same time, needed to be regulated to ensure that the pricing of their services was "fair and reasonable" and justified based on cost.

The ICC's authority was increased in 1889 with the passage of the Sherman Antitrust Act, increased further in 1906 with the passage of the Hepburn Act, and increased again in 1910 with the Mann-Elkins Act. The 1889 act addressed the practice, almost from day one of the railroad industry, of the merger of lines to gain an unfair competitive advantage over others. The 1906 and 1910 acts dealt with the ICC's authority to set maximum railroad rates. By 1902, consolidation within the industry had reached an all-time high with the attempted merger of the Great Northern and the Northern Pacific Burlington lines. A holding company, Northern Securities Company, had been created to control the combined lines. The government sued under the Sherman Antitrust Act and won, and the decision was upheld by the Supreme Court in 1904, changing the landscape for future railroad consolidations.

THE NICKEL PLATE, 1916–1922

To enhance the value of their investment in Shaker Heights, the Van Sweringen brothers created the Nickel Plate Securities Company to hold their shares of the 513-mile New York, Chicago & St. Louis Railroad. Under New York Central ownership, the railroad, known as the Nickel Plate Road, had consistently lost money. In 1914, with revenues peaked at $12 million, the Nickel Plate lost nearly $184,000. Under the Van Sweringens' ownership and John Bernet's leadership, the railroad's revenues surged to nearly $17 million in 1917, $22 million in 1918, and $23.5 million in 1919 and were on track to top $28.5 million in 1920. With increased revenues came profitability. Operating revenues had more than doubled while operating expenses had only increased by 25 percent. The railroad's stock had grown from $35 to more than $200 per share during the same period, and the company paid a dividend of 11 percent.

This success encouraged the brothers to expand their railroad holdings. Not content to own just a single railroad, O. P. purchased fifteen hundred eight-foot-by-ten-foot maps of the national railroad system, studying them as a general would study topography before going into battle. The Nickel Plate, lacking feeder lines, relied on other railroads for its freight. It soon became apparent that the Toledo, St. Louis & Western, better known as the Clover Leaf Route, and the Lake Erie & Western (LE&W) would extend the Nickel Plate to two important western gateways, and there was every reason to believe that the lines would be available. The Clover Leaf Route terminated in St. Louis, which served as an interchange point for southwestern and western railroads, and Peoria served as a bypass for overcongested Chicago.

World War I began in Europe on June 28, 1914. The United States maintained neutrality despite the sinking of the *Lusitania* that took nearly twelve hundred lives on May 13, 1915. On February 3, 1917, the United States severed diplomatic relations with Germany in response to the German sinking of American merchant ships around the British Isles and entered the war on April 6. The country's railroads quickly proved inadequate to supply the nation's war effort, and on December 26, 1917, US president Woodrow Wilson nationalized most American railways under the Federal Possession and Control Act, creating the US Railroad Administration. Wilson appointed his son-in-law, William Gibbs McAdoo, the secretary of the Treasury, to head the new agency. The New York Central's A. H. Smith was named director of all carriers in the eastern region.

Fighting on the western front ended with an armistice that went into effect at the eleventh hour of the eleventh day of the eleventh month of 1918. Fighting elsewhere continued until the signing of the Treaty of Versailles on June 28, 1919, exactly five years after the assassination of the archduke and his wife that led to the outbreak of the war. Because the United States was not a party to the treaty, returning the railroads to private ownership did not occur until Congress's passage of the Esch-Cummins Transportation Act in February 1920. The act gave the ICC the power to approve or reject railroad mergers, set rates, and approve or reject abandonments of service, and a variety of other oversight responsibilities. In return, the government made guarantees to the railroads to ensure their financial survival after the restoration of control.

By 1920 there were more than one thousand railroads of all sizes operating within the United States. One hundred eighty-six of those roads were designated Class I, with annual revenues exceeding $1 million. When it was established, the ICC had been designed to be reactive, responding to proposals and problems. Now the commission was charged with the challenge of proactively creating and implementing a plan to restructure the railroad industry. William Zebina Ripley, a Harvard economics professor and transportation expert, was hired to facilitate the design of a consolidation plan. As he began his work, Ripley entered into preliminary discussions with the senior management of the three leading eastern railroads: the Pennsylvania, the New York Central, and the Baltimore and Ohio. In November 1920, Ripley, likely at the suggestion of Mr. Smith, wrote a letter to O. P. soliciting his thoughts on consolidation. In the letter, Ripley said, "We should have to assume that the Nickel Plate system was actually independent of the New York Central and not connected with it by personal ties or stock ownership of other trunk line interests." O. P. forwarded the letter to Smith, who suggested that in reply, O. P. say that he had been considering extending his railroad into coal and had studied possible alliances. In addition, Smith suggested that O. P. might also include that he saw other possibilities for the Nickel Plate extending into Michigan.[1]

Later that month and again in December, O. P. went to Washington to meet with Ripley. During the meeting, O. P. asked that in his consolidation plan, Ripley assign nine railroads to the Nickel Plate. Specifically, he requested the Lehigh Valley and the Delaware, Lackawanna & Western for access to the New York Harbor area and the Wheeling & Lake Erie, the Pittsburgh & West Virginia, and the Western Maryland for access to the coal region. For Michigan, O. P. requested the Pere Marquette, and for the western reach, the Clover Leaf, for which the Van Sweringens were already in negotiations, and the Lake Erie & Western. Last on his list was the Cincinnati Northern that ran to Jackson, Michigan.

When Ripley submitted his report in early 1921, he recommended six of the nine lines, not including the Lehigh, the Pere Marquette, and the Cincinnati Northern, but he added the Buffalo, Rochester & Pittsburgh. In August, after the ICC had studied Ripley's recommendations, it released its tentative plan. The Van Sweringens were allocated six railroads: the Delaware, Lackawanna & Western; the Wheeling & Lake Erie; the Pittsburgh & West Virginia; the Clover Leaf; the Lake Erie & Western; and the Bessemer & Lake Erie.

There was still the matter of ICC approval for the Cleveland Union Terminal. In February 1921 the New York Central, the Big Four, and the Nickel Plate went to the ICC for a certificate of convenience and necessity. Standing in the way of the planned approach to the terminal was the Wheeling & Lake Erie's rickety wood and stucco passenger station. O. P. suggested that the terminal tracks could be relocated without affecting the Wheeling's passenger and freight facilities. His engineers, however, estimated that the cost for the necessary grading would add $10 million to the terminal project. The Wheeling filed an intervening petition with the ICC, arguing that the terminal would destroy its passenger station.

On April 19, 1921, Colonel William Ainslie Colston, the finance director of the ICC, convened a hearing in Washington. The Wheeling & Lake Erie's chair and President McKinley's nephew, William McKinley Duncan, and attorney William C. Boyle represented the railroad's interest. G. E. Cowse, attorney for the Pennsylvania Railroad, was in attendance to oppose the terminal. In addition to the Van Sweringen brothers, proponents included Mr. Smith and A. S. Ingalls of the New York Central and the Central's attorney, F. L. Jerome; Cleveland mayor William F. FitzGerald; and Joseph Nutt and Warren Hayden. Attorneys for the Vans' interests included Newton D. Baker and William H. Boyd, representing the Cleveland Union Terminals Company; H. D. Howe, for the Nickel Plate; and Cannon and Stage.

As Baker began his testimony, the brothers' nemesis and uninvited witness Peter Witt entered the hearing room. Baker completed his testimony to no cross-examination, and Witt began his bombastic questioning of Baker despite Colston's repeated cautions about his outbursts. Witt is said to have said, "What I want to show is that the whole thing is fraudulent. . . . The interests of the Van Sweringen company are to make good on the millions of dollars of land which the people foolishly gave them for the station on Public Square. The interest of the banking fraternity which also is here represented is to add further protection to their loans."[2]

The proponents presented their case—essentially the same arguments they had presented to Cleveland City Council—before the hearing was adjourned for the night. O. P. took the train to New York to persuade the Rockefellers, owners of the Wheeling & Lake Erie, to withdraw the railroad's objections. When the hearing resumed the next morning, following Bernet's testimony, Witt presented two volumes of reports that had been prepared by the Pennsylvania. A settlement was reached with the Wheeling and presented in the hearing the following day, stipulating that "any ICC order in the case would not prejudice any Wheeling legal right, and that if the terminal should encroach on Wheeling property and court 'fixed the mode and manner of such crossing,' all expenses would be borne by the terminals company."[3]

Witt defiantly marched to the front of the room, saying, "When the corporation steps out the citizen steps in." He then called one witness, Clarence Dykstra, the executive secretary of Cleveland's Civic League. Dykstra testified that after the Pennsylvania Railroad announced that it would not participate in Union Terminal, Cleveland City Council opposed the construction of the terminal. Further, it was not until after Mayor Davis reported that he had the personal assurances of the six railroads that they would participate in Union Terminal that the city council approved the ordinance.

It was now time for a summation. Each side had two hours to make its case. Jerome, representing the New York Central, got so bogged down answering questions of the ICC's finance division that there was no time left for the eloquent Newton D. Baker. Witt argued for the opposition. The ICC's decision in August was a setback for the Van Sweringens and Union Terminal. The greatest concern centered on the cost of the project. Witt had had his way, winning the battle, but in the end, he did not win the war. And the Vans had more than half a million dollars in debt service annually on their $10 million investment in the land for the project—the same land that Witt had so erroneously claimed had been given by the people.

The brothers would soon face another setback when J. J. Albright, a substantial Van Sweringen investor, cosigned debt for the Locomobile Company, a Cleveland automobile manufacturer of which his brother-in-law was president. The troubled company had reorganized, and although Albright was unscathed, he failed to heed the advice of one of his bankers and guaranteed $4 million of additional Locomobile debt, posting his share of the Vans' Terminal Properties Company as collateral. This time he was not so lucky. The Van Sweringen brothers were seen as the likely purchasers of the securities. They agreed to make good on Albright's $4 million debt, plus interest. At the same time, the ICC decision had put them in a tenuous position. O. P. determined that the only solution was a rehearing before the ICC. Failure was not an option.

On September 20, 1921, with Commissioner Johnston B. Campbell presiding, the rehearing opened in a federal courtroom in Cleveland. Witt took aim at Smith with his sharpest attack yet. When it was O. P.'s turn, he reiterated his position that all railroads serving Cleveland would use the terminal "in due course." The commissioners toured the lakefront and Public Square locations. Witt, who was committed to a survey in Seattle, Washington, requested a continuance. The commission granted a short postponement, but when the hearings resumed, Witt was still in Seattle. Without him, there was no opposition. On December 6, the commission reversed its earlier decision, saying, "There is no evidence of bad faith or unfair advantage which might work to the disadvantage of the carriers." The ICC approved the station. Commissioner Joseph Bartlett Eastman, who had been impressed by Witt during the original hearing on the union terminal, saw him as being "keenly and immaculately honest." Eastman was "sharply critical" of the brothers, and his was the only vote against the terminal project.

With the Cleveland Union Terminal a reality, O. P. turned his attention to the acquisition of the Lake Erie & Western Railroad. Mr. Smith, now back at his desk at the New York Central, was beginning to think about what offensive and defensive steps the New York Central might consider regarding the new ICC powers. The LE&W, acquired by J. P. Morgan in 1898, had proved itself both redundant and a financial drain. Smith was only too happy to have Albert H. Harris, the Central's vice president of finance, enter into negotiations with O. P., and within three months, a deal was completed. The acquisition of the Lake Erie & Western Railroad on March 11, 1922, united the Nickel Plate with the railroad it had been built to complement forty years earlier.

It took a little longer to negotiate the acquisition of the Toledo, St. Louis & Western Railroad, also known as the Clover Leaf, for two reasons. First, the largest shareholders in the railroad were the estates of two deceased investors. Second, the company's president, Walter L. Ross, demanded that he receive an executive employment agreement of five years or until the road was corporately merged. The Clover Leaf became part of the Nickel Plate on December 28, 1922.

THE "NEW" NICKEL PLATE, 1922–1926

On January 9, 1922, envisioning more acquisitions to follow, the brothers established the Vaness Company to replace the Nickel Plate Securities Corporation. The brothers shared 60 percent of the common stock, and Joseph Nutt, Charles Bradley, Warren Hayden, and Otto Miller shared the remaining 40 percent. Two subsidiary holding companies were then created—the Clover Leaf Company, to hold the stock of the Toledo, St. Louis & Western Railroad, and the Western Company, to hold the stock of the Lake Erie & Western Railroad. The Toledo, St. Louis & Western added 454 miles of track and gave the Nickel Plate access to St. Louis. Joint ownership of the Detroit & Toledo Shore Line with the Grand Trunk Western Railroad gave the Nickel Plate access to Detroit and the automobile industry. The Lake Erie & Western added 719 additional miles. In December 1922, the Nickel Plate, the Clover Leaf, and the LE&W were merged. The Nickel Plate, 513 miles when the brothers purchased the railroad, was now a 1,696-mile road.

The Transportation Act of 1920 specified that the ICC, based on its consolidation plan, had the responsibility to approve the issuance of new securities and the authority to approve consolidations consistent with the commission's plan. As the commission did not anticipate the completion of a consolidation plan for several years, the Van Sweringens decided to solicit approval of the merger from all the states in which the railroads operated. With the approval of each of the states, the application was filed on April 28, 1923, and on June 18, the commission voted its approval. Although the vote was not unanimous, the Van Sweringens were victorious—once again, despite the dissent of Joseph Eastman. The "New" Nickel Plate common and preferred stock was issued.

The Vans paid a combined $21 million for the three railroads. They sold $17.1 million of unneeded stock they received as a result of the merger and received $6.7 million in railroad dividends. The bottom line? The Van Sweringen brothers had a net gain of nearly $3 million and still owned 54 percent of the New Nickel Plate voting stock. Between their 506 locomotives and 20,372 railroad cars, and all the other cars that rolled over their track, nearly $51 million in revenues generated close to $5.5 million in profit, and John J. Bernet was president of a network now approaching seventeen hundred miles of track, greatly extending the Van Sweringens' and Cleveland's reach.

The sale of 150,000 shares of Nickel Plate preferred stock to a syndicate headed by the Guaranty for more than $12 million brought the syndicate a gross profit of nearly $1 million. The brothers then sold some additional shares of preferred and common Nickel Plate stock to the Guaranty, bringing their proceeds from the sale of stock in 1923 to more than $17 million, which was immediately applied to their growing debt, leaving less than $4 million from the purchase of the Toledo, St. Louis

& Western and the Lake Erie & Western Railroads. That was more than offset by the nearly $6.75 million they or their companies would receive by the end of 1923. Now the brothers set their sights on the next big prize.

To grow the Nickel Plate, the Vans turned their attention to West Virginia, Michigan, and the East Coast. The attraction of West Virginia was coal, and two railroads served the coalfields in the Pocahontas region—the Norfolk & Western and the C&O. The Norfolk & Western was owned by the Pennsylvania Railroad, which was unwilling to sell it, leaving the 2,550-mile C&O. The C&O ran from Newport News to Richmond and Washington DC and then to Cincinnati and Chicago. A subsidiary, the Hocking Valley Railroad, connected Louisville and Toledo. Nearly 80 percent of the road's freight was bituminous coal, which was hauled east to the docks in Newport News and north to the Great Lakes and the Midwest, to supply industry.

Three railroads reached into Michigan—the Michigan Central, Canada's Grand Trunk, and the Pere Marquette. The Michigan Central was owned by the New York Central, who, like the Pennsylvania, had no interest in selling. That left the 2,262-mile Pere Marquette. A combination of three railroads, the Pere Marquette was a Michigan-based road serving the timber industry. One of the lines connected Chicago and Buffalo, but unlike the Nickel Plate, the route was north of Lake Erie, in a straight line to Grand Rapids and then on to Chicago. The second line connected Grand Rapids and Bay View, north of Charlevoix and Petoskey. The third line connected Toledo and Bay City/Saginaw; it intersected with a line from Port Huron to Ludington, where it connected with ferries to cross Lake Michigan to Milwaukee.

The Nickel Plate only went as far east as Buffalo, and the brothers wanted to extend their reach to the Eastern Seaboard. Again, there were three railroads to consider: the Delaware, Lackawanna & Western; the Lehigh Valley; and the Erie. The first two were perfect fits because they terminated in Buffalo, and each extended into New England. The price for the Lackawanna was well above that which the brothers were prepared to pay, and the Lehigh Valley's board was unwilling to engage in discussions.

The decision was made to concentrate on the first two priorities—the C&O, south into coal country, and the Pere Marquette, north into Michigan. Negotiations began with Henry and Arabella Huntington, who owned 12 percent of the C&O stock and held seven of the nine seats on the board. Mrs. Huntington was sentimental about the stock that had been left to her by her husband, Collis P. Huntington. The company was a direct descendant of the James River Company, founded by George Washington in 1785. C. P. Huntington had built up the C&O following the Civil War and established Huntington, West Virginia, in the process.

In May 1921 O. P. had made up his mind. He wanted to add the C&O to his growing railroad system. On the open market, the stock was selling in the range of $72 to $75 per share. The Vans entered the negotiations willing to pay $90; the Huntingtons held out for $105. The brothers, who were no strangers to juggling, devised a solution. To avoid a shareholder revolt and possibly some action by the ICC by paying a premium for the Huntingtons' C&O stock, the Nickel Plate purchased 96 percent of the stock at $80 ($5.6 million) and the Nickel Plate Securities Corporation purchased the remaining 4 percent ($1.4 million) at $566.67 per share. The Huntingtons got their $7.3 million, and O. P. got his railroad, but he did not yet have control. Over the next year, the Nickel Plate purchased additional shares of the C&O at an average price of $76 ($6.5 million), and Vaness, the brothers' holding company, bought another 23 percent of the C&O's stock for $93 per share, giving them comfortable control of 43 percent. With their railroad network now consisting of more than four thousand miles of track, three more railroads were within O. P.'s sights—the Hocking Valley Railway (881 miles), the Pere Marquette Railway (2,262 miles), and the Erie Railroad (2,700 miles).

To extend their network to the East Coast, the Van Sweringens had twice attempted to acquire the Lehigh Valley in 1922, with no success. The logical alternative was the twenty-seven-hundred-mile Erie, which

The Van Sweringen Business Empire, 1922

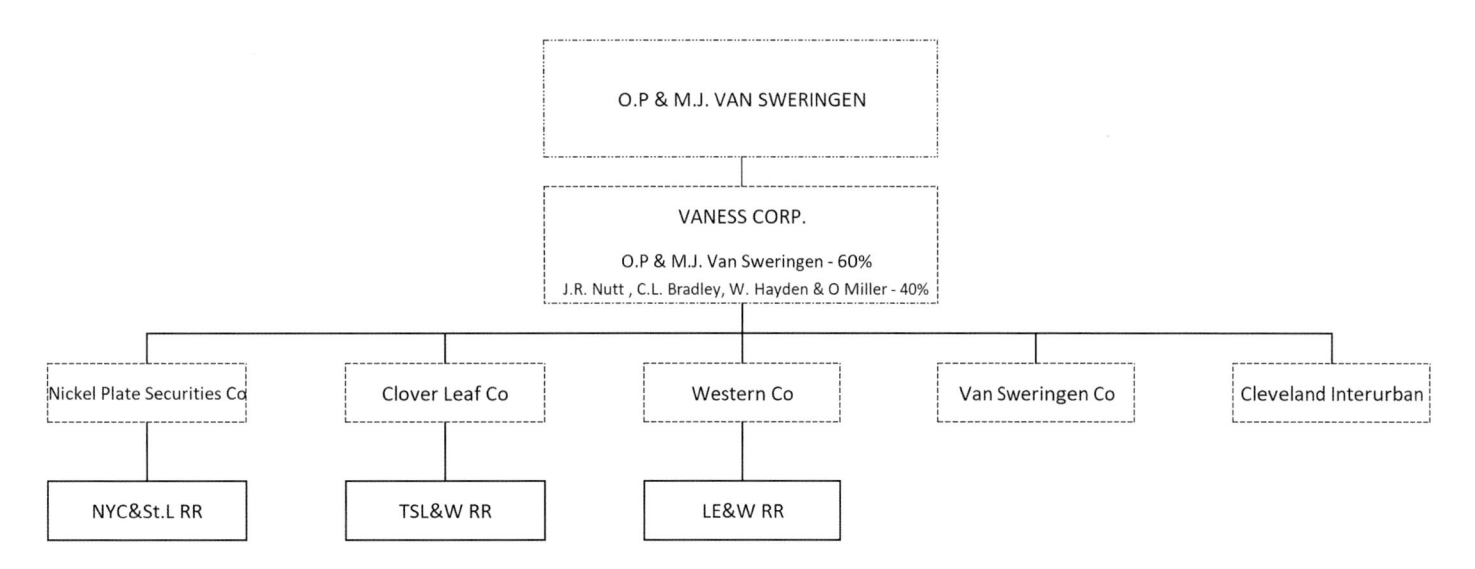

```
                    O.P & M.J. VAN SWERINGEN
                              |
                        VANESS CORP.
            O.P & M.J. Van Sweringen - 60%
      J.R. Nutt, C.L. Bradley, W. Hayden & O Miller - 40%
                              |
   ┌──────────────┬───────────┼───────────┬──────────────┐
Nickel Plate   Clover Leaf   Western    Van Sweringen  Cleveland
Securities Co     Co           Co            Co        Interurban
     |             |            |
  NYC&St.L      TSL&W RR     LE&W RR
    RR
```

was already connected to the Nickel Plate in Buffalo, Cleveland, and Chicago, among other locations. The Erie was a long-haul railroad, with the longest through route between New York and Chicago. Westbound, the Erie hauled coal from the anthracite fields near Wilkes-Barre, Scranton, and Carbondale, Pennsylvania. Eastbound the freight was perishable—fruit and vegetables from the West Coast and meat from the Southwest—through connections in Chicago.

Discussions began in early 1923 with a member of Erie's board of directors. In November, having accomplished little, the discussions ended and resumed with George F. Baker, cofounder of the First National Bank of the City of New York and an influence in the affairs of the Erie Railroad. By mid-1925, control of the Erie, including its subsidiary, the Pennsylvania Coal Company, was completed, but not without masterful juggling and not without concern that the ICC might find a violation of antitrust regulations. The Van Sweringens now returned their attention to the Pere Marquette. The brothers had become interested in the 2,262-mile railroad early in 1921, but they had been unable to come close to an agreement. In April 1924, with George Baker, the brothers launched a campaign to acquire two hundred thousand shares, giving them 30 percent ownership, but it was not until 1929 that the brothers gained operational control of the company.

The brothers had acquired the Nickel Plate in 1916. In 1922 they began to expand, and in less than four years, the Van Sweringens had built the fourth-largest railroad system in the east. With a network of more than ten thousand miles, they were in the same league as the Pennsylvania, New York Central, and the B&O. The Vans' success came from their commitment to improving the financial condition and updating the rolling stock and real estate of the acquired companies, but this commitment came at a steep price. The recent spate of acquisitions added more than $30 million of debt to the brothers' balance sheet. A plan was conceived to restructure their holdings, issuing various classes of stock that could be sold to fund the repayment of their debt.

If assembling the fourth-largest railroad in the east had required all of O. P.'s energy and most of his attention, he did not do so at the expense of the development of Shaker Heights and the rapid transit and certainly not at the expense of his vision for Public Square and his Union Terminal. Shaker Heights's population, which had stood at 1,616 in 1920, was approaching 18,000 in the 1930 census. The appraised value of the Van Sweringens' Shaker Village development stood at more than $29 million in 1925. Even though the rapid transit from Shaker Heights still operated over city streets for the final two miles to Public Square, ridership in 1925 was approaching two and a half million and would reach three million by 1930.

Public Square was abuzz with streetcar and interurban traffic. Among the bustle were the cars of the Cleveland Railway; the Lake Shore Electric, with stops in Rocky River, Bay Village, and Avon, en route to Toledo and Detroit; the Cleveland Southwestern, to Medina, Wooster, Mansfield, Bucyrus, and Oberlin; the Northern Ohio Traction & Light Company, to Akron with connections to Canton, Massillon, New Philadelphia, Uhrichsville, Ravenna, Warren, and Alliance; the Cleveland and Eastern, servicing Gates Mills, Chardon, and Middlefield; and the Cleveland, Painesville & Eastern, to Willoughby, Mentor, and Painesville. The Cleveland & Chagrin Falls connected with the Shaker Rapid at the end of the Moreland (Van Aken) line at the Lynnfield Road terminal.

Understandably, the Vans saw potential tenants for their Union Terminal, eliminating the long slow grind of those last miles over city streetcar tracks and eliminating the clutter and confusion on Public Square. Undoubtedly, the brothers saw acquisition opportunities as well, and in 1930 they acquired the Cleveland Railway Company. It was operated as a part of the Van Sweringen empire until 1937, and in 1942, it became the municipally owned Cleveland Transit System, today the Greater Cleveland Regional Transit Authority.

CONSOLIDATING THEIR RAILROAD EMPIRE

In March 1924, O. P. suggested to Mr. Smith that the four largest railroads in the east get together and work out a consolidation plan that might satisfy the ICC. Smith replied saying, "Van, you don't know what you're up against." O. P. suggested that Smith lay out his thoughts for each of the four systems while O. P. did the same. Smith was impressed when they put their plans side by side to see how very similar they were. Two days later, O. P. had convinced the leaders of the other two railroads to meet for a four-party conversation. After work on Saturday, March 8, 1924, Smith went to Central Park for a horseback ride. At dusk, a woman rider crossed in front of Smith, causing him to suddenly rein in his horse. Smith fell to the ground. His neck was broken; he was dead by the time he reached the hospital. O. P. had lost a great mentor, confidant, supporter, and friend.

In the spring of 1924, the ICC completed hearings for the consolidation of the eastern railroads. It was now time to create the final consolidation plan. The commissioners knew that no matter what they decided, the result would be met with considerable controversy. On May 8 Samuel Rea, the president of the Pennsylvania Railroad, and William Wallace Atterbury, who would succeed Rea as president on October 1, 1925; Patrick Crowley, Smith's successor as the president of the New York Central, and vice presidents Albert Hall Harris, George Hoadley Ingalls, and George Alexander Harwood; Daniel Willard, the president of the B&O, and George McLean Shriver, Willard's second-in-command; and the Van Sweringen brothers and John J. Bernet met in the Pennsylvania's offices—something utterly unthinkable just a few short months earlier.

After unrolling his maps on the table, O. P. opened the session with a brief review of all that had transpired leading to the tentative plan that was on the table in front of them. Two major points of contention surfaced immediately. First, the Pennsylvania and B&O argued that all the New England lines should be put together under the joint ownership of the four big trunk lines. The Central, which had leased the Boston & Albany since 1900, strenuously objected. Second, they contended that the Reading and the New Jersey Central, both shown on the preliminary plan as under the joint ownership of the four trunk lines, offered the only route for the B&O from Philadelphia to the New York Harbor. The New York Central was equally interested in the route because its route from the Great Lakes to the New York Harbor was far less direct. With freight rates being calculated on a point-to-point basis, the more direct the route, the more profitable it was.

To move beyond the New England disagreement, it was decided that the subject would be put to the side until it was clear that agreement could be reached on the other points. The New York Harbor question, however, needed to be addressed. Before his death, Smith's priority had been the Jersey Central, with its 700-mile main line linking Scranton and Wilkes-Barre with the New York Harbor. Crowley, Smith's successor, strongly preferred the 1,450-mile Lehigh Valley and the 950-mile Lackawanna. As the discussions continued, the New York Central claimed the Lehigh Valley, leaving the Lackawanna to the Van Sweringens.

As summer progressed, so did the meetings. The New York Central and the B&O compromised on the Reading-Jersey Central. The Central would get trackage rights over the Reading's Catawissa branch for its new through-route connection with the Lehigh Valley, operating virtually at will, while the ownership of the entire Reading and the Jersey Central went to the B&O. There were still some bumps in the road that needed to be ironed out, but it was clear that against all odds, O. P.'s hard work was beginning to pay off. The New York Central, the B&O, and the Van Sweringens were close to creating total harmony. Then, the Pennsylvania's Rea ended the July 9 meeting under a cloud, saying that he would state his position at a later meeting.

Later in July, the Pennsylvania's representatives voiced objections out of left field, putting all the progress that had been made heretofore in doubt. The long and often-contentious session spilled over into the next day, ending with the decision to present the plan to the ICC in hopes that some unofficial suggestions might serve to restore harmony. As the participants left the room, O. P. held back to speak with General Atterbury. He had an uncanny ability to read people, and what he read in Atterbury's face and voice was not the least bit reassuring. When he returned to his suite at the Commodore, a messenger delivered a note of encouragement from Willard. It read, in part:

> While I had hoped that we might be able to reach a complete understanding this morning, I do not think you should feel at all discouraged because we stopped somewhat short of doing so. The progress that has already been made along lines which you have advocated is far beyond anything that has ever been accomplished before, either in a voluntary way or at the suggestion of any governmental body, and to me it seems most encouraging that three out of four principal interests have been able to reach an understanding that is generally satisfactory. You have much reason to feel gratified by what has already been done, and I think there is still hope for a satisfactory outcome.[4]

O. P. responded to the note from his office the next day, as follows: "I will confess I was somewhat disappointed, [sic] because I had not expected quite the turn matters took. I am not discouraged. I shall try to have a talk with Mr. Rea and General Atterbury before the next meeting to check over the final maps in the hope that the situation may be clarified somewhat in their direction."[5]

But that was not to be. Three meetings were held in September. Rea and Atterbury objected to virtually all the progress that had been made. They objected to the Lehigh going to the Central; they objected to the Reading-Jersey Central going to the B&O; they objected to the Virginian going to the Van Sweringens; they objected to the Van Sweringens' refusal to give the Pennsylvania trackage rights on the Nickel Plate from port to port along the Lake Erie shore; they objected to the Lackawanna going to the Van Sweringens, contending that at least half should have gone to the Pennsylvania. In short, they objected and were objectionable.

To compromise, the Van Sweringens offered to consider permitting the Pennsylvania to distribute empty cars from port to port by using the Nickel Plate. The Pennsylvania was not about to cooperate with the other three. A meeting was arranged in the ICC's Washington headquarters on October 11, 1924. The Pennsylvania was an uncooperative participant.

The plan that was presented to the commissioners gave the Virginian, the Lackawanna, and the Bessemer & Lake Erie to the brothers. It also included formal recognition of the acquired but yet unmerged Nickel Plate system. The New York Central received the Lehigh Valley; the New York, Ontario & Western; and most of the Buffalo, Rochester & Pittsburgh. The B&O was given the Reading-Jersey Central; the Western Maryland, Monon & Ann Arbor; the Cincinnati, Indianapolis & Western; and the Wabash, east of the Mississippi River. Jointly, the four systems were given the Wheeling & Lake Erie, the Pittsburgh & West Virginia, and the Chicago & Eastern Illinois, and other smaller railroads were allocated among the four parties.

Willard stressed his regret that all four of the systems were not in agreement but was gratified that three were. Crowley expressed his full endorsement of the plan. Bernet stressed that the plan would preserve competition. O. P. stated that he would proceed with the plan as far as it applied to him. Rea read a fifty-five-hundred-word recitation of the Pennsylvania Railroad's objections. Commissioner Hall said that the consolidations committee of the ICC would consider the suggestions and schedule another meeting. In the meantime, he suggested that the four-party discussions continue. In the next meeting of the leaders of the four railroad systems, figures were presented showing that Rea's plan would increase the Pennsylvania's track mileage to 19,385; 15,166 for the Central; 12,586 for the Van Sweringens; and 11,364 for the B&O. Under the agreed-on plan by the other three, the Pennsylvania would increase to 16,237; the Central to 15,745; the Van Sweringens to 13,056; and the B&O to 13,465, with property investment and operating revenue in a similar ratio. All efforts to persuade Rea to join the other three went for naught. This was the same Rea and Pennsylvania Railroad that would have nothing to do with the Van Sweringens' Union Terminal. Following a meeting of the four on December 30, Willard said that the three might move ahead with their parts of the plan. Rea responded that he had expected as much.

On January 26, 1925, the four met again with the ICC. Willard read a prepared statement saying that their plan made for "rough equality in eastern railroading; that such equality was in the public interest; and that the disproportion of the Penn, already the largest system, should not be increased." The Pennsylvania pleaded that it lacked sufficient time for preparation and was granted more time to reply, which it did not do. The ICC appealed to Congress to relieve it of the responsibility of creating a plan of consolidation, saying, "Results as good, and perhaps better, are likely to be accomplished with less loss of time if the process of consolidation is permitted to develop under the guidance of the commission, in a more normal way."[6]

The four parties abandoned their efforts. The other three, now known as the "Triple Alliance," stuck together. Discouraged but not defeated, O. P. drove ahead. He already had his eyes on his next potential acquisitions—the Boston & Maine, the Chicago & Eastern Illinois, the Wheeling & Lake Erie, and the Virginian. But first, the brothers felt it was past time for the unification of the Nickel Plate, the C&O, the Hocking Valley, the Pere Marquette, and the Erie into a single network to compete with the giant New York Central and Pennsylvania Railroads.

The brothers proposed the creation of a new company to acquire control of the equipment and facilities of the five railroads, either by a long-term lease or the purchase of most of the outstanding stock. The company (the New York, Chicago & St. Louis Railway Company), with assets of $1.4 billion, would operate over more than 11,750 miles of track from New York and Newport News, Virginia, to Chicago, Peoria, and

St. Louis. The brothers' vision was a network to transport automobiles, auto parts, and chemicals from Michigan; steel from the Mahoning Valley and rubber from Akron; bituminous and anthracite coal from northern Pennsylvania and bituminous coal from Ohio, West Virginia, and Kentucky; and agricultural products, milk, meat, and fresh fruit and vegetables from the West and Southwest to the booming metropolitan New York area.

On January 20, 1925, the articles of incorporation of the New York, Chicago, & St. Louis Railway Company had been drawn up under the laws of the State of Ohio. The application was filed with the ICC on February 19, 1925, and in March and April, stockholders of each of the affected railroads ratified the plan. An acrimonious all-night vigil was held in Richmond, Virginia, the night before the C&O shareholders voted. Rea had cautioned O. P. that he had heard "that the C&O stockholders have been dealt with less favorably than the others." O. P. replied that they had tried to be fair to all the interests involved but that it was natural that there would be a few dissenters.

Many of the C&O shareholders came from prominent Richmond families, who felt the control of the railroad was arbitrarily being taken to the north. They feared that the C&O would be relegated to a "shadowy subsidiary." They were being offered 115 shares of the new preferred stock for every 100 shares of C&O preferred stock, and 55 shares of new common stock for every 100 shares of C&O common stock. When the votes were counted, the result was 506,543 shares in favor of the plan and 152,818 in opposition. The count of the non–Van Sweringen-held shares was much closer: 176,742 in favor and 152,818 opposed. The Scott Committee, formed by George Cole Scott and other minority shareholders, engaged Colonel Henry W. Anderson as counsel to "fight the invaders from the north."

Another obstacle, from an entirely unexpected quarter, was taken personally by the Van Sweringens. Their good friend and ally Daniel Willard, the president of the B&O, objected to the unification that would make the "New" Nickel Plate twice the size of the B&O. The New York Central was showing no willingness to sell half of the Reading-Jersey Central to the B&O, which would have given the two systems joint control until the Pennsylvania agreed that the Central would have the Lehigh Valley. Willard made it clear that he would testify at the ICC hearings that the Van Sweringens' plan amounted to consolidation and not unification.

The hearings on the unification of the New Nickel Plate were opened on April 15, 1925. The Scott Committee was unrelenting in its opposition to all things Van Sweringen. Anything and everything were viewed by the opposition as fair game. The extent of the details led the brothers to question whether the committee had help from one or more of their rivals. Perhaps Witt, who was a belligerent opponent? Or Rea, who was a C&O shareholder and eastern region rival? They were attacked on the most minute details of their real estate business and the terminal. They were attacked on the employment contract that had been given to Walter Ross as a part of the acquisition of the Clover Leaf. They were attacked on the dividend that was paid once the brothers acquired control of the Clover Leaf and the lack of dividends since. Attack, attack, attack.

In response, O. P. created a lengthy statement explaining in detail their complicated, interrelated business enterprises. When he was finished, his advisers declared it nearly perfect. Colonel Colston added a page and a half, while the eloquent orator Newton D. Baker made only a few very minor changes. On May 28, six weeks into the hearing, it was O. P.'s turn. He read the statement in a conversational tone, beginning as follows:

> First, my brother, M. J. Van Sweringen, and I have believed from the very beginning that we are engaged in a constructive undertaking that will promote the public interest. We have done the best we know how to be fair to every interest involved in the proposed unification. It does not matter in the comparison how small or how large any stockholder's [holding] is, or how

long he has held it. All should be justly dealt with, and we want to feel when this case is over, that this commission has either found our proposal fair to all or has so modified it that the most obscure and unrepresented stockholder in any of these properties will have been as fairly treated as larger interests which are here to represent themselves.

He went on to describe their earliest railroad ventures; the Nickel Plate consolidation of 1922 that brought the Nickel Plate, the Lake Erie & Western, and the Clover Leaf together; and the issuance of nonvoting preferred stock by the enlarged Nickel Plate:

> We were not speculating in shares. We were upbuilding a railroad, and we wanted to know that our policies would prevail in its development, and this aided in that assurance.
>
> We had a feeling, and still have, that one of the most unfortunate conditions in the railroad world is the absence of parental interest, guidance, and encouragement—someone to be responsible for the policies and pursuits of the company through having the major stock interest. If we could not control the properties to the extent necessary to assure continuity of policy, we did not want to be interested in them. We have tried to look into the future and be progressive, and we wanted a free hand in doing so.

He then went on to address the matter of interlocking directorates.

> It is our aim to control by ownership a majority of the common stock of the corporations for the success of which we are responsible. These railroad operations have become our principal occupation. Much has been said in this hearing about interlocking or common directors in the Nickel Plate, the Hocking Valley, and the Chesapeake & Ohio, but we make no apologies for wanting to control the policies of the properties for whose management we are responsible, and in which we have a larger investment than any other stockholder in the shares which are the first to suffer by reason of a mistake in policy, an error in judgment, or a mismanagement of the company. All other classes of shareholders and investors have their investment and their income protected ahead of our position. Should we not then, have this determination of policy in our hands, subject only to the failure to carry out our obligation?[7]

Having spoken his piece, O. P. Van Sweringen sat back, waiting for the inevitable assault. At one point his retort to his attacker was, "This is not a police state. I speak to you as a gentleman, and I expect to be spoken to as one."

Colonel Anderson, on behalf of the Scott Committee, had expressed great interest in Vaness Corporation, the holding company underneath which several other holding companies sat on the organization chart. The questioning centered on how the brothers', and particularly O. P.'s, compensation was derived and the matter of a trust in which the brothers' stock was held. In the margin of his unpublished manuscript, Raymond F. Blosser handwrote the question, "Who was helping Anderson on such matters, supposedly secret ones?"

During the second day of O. P.'s testimony, Anderson asked whether there was a trust agreement under which key Vaness stock was held. O. P. replied that he believed there was, but he wanted to check to be sure. Two months later, Anderson reminded O. P. during questioning, who affirmed that it had been in process at the time of Anderson's question and was now in place.

Under continued questioning, O. P. described the trust as being in place to ensure the perpetuation of the control of the company. The brothers were bachelors, and as such, their 80 percent interest in the company would ensure its future. Anderson read it differently. His interpretation appeared to be that the purpose of the trust was for the benefit of the Van Sweringens in perpetuity.

The Van Sweringen Business Empire, 1925

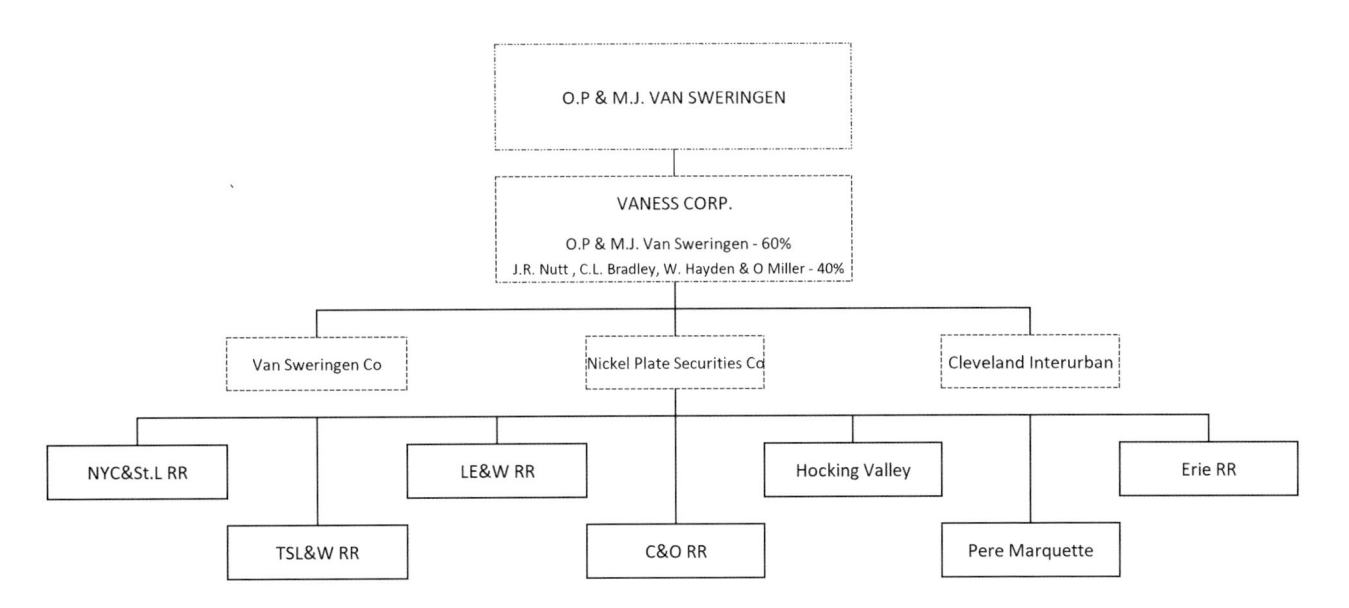

```
                    ┌─────────────────────────────────┐
                    │   O.P & M.J. VAN SWERINGEN      │
                    └─────────────────────────────────┘
                                    │
                    ┌─────────────────────────────────┐
                    │         VANESS CORP.            │
                    │                                 │
                    │  O.P & M.J. Van Sweringen - 60% │
                    │  J.R. Nutt, C.L. Bradley,       │
                    │  W. Hayden & O Miller - 40%     │
                    └─────────────────────────────────┘
                                    │
           ┌────────────────────────┼────────────────────────┐
   ┌───────────────┐       ┌─────────────────────┐    ┌──────────────────────┐
   │ Van Sweringen │       │ Nickel Plate        │    │ Cleveland Interurban │
   │ Co            │       │ Securities Co       │    │                      │
   └───────────────┘       └─────────────────────┘    └──────────────────────┘
        │                           │                           │
   ┌─────────┬──────────┬────────────┬──────────┐
┌──────────┐    ┌─────────┐    ┌──────────────┐    ┌────────┐
│ NYC&St.L │    │ LE&W RR │    │ Hocking Valley│    │ Erie RR│
│ RR       │    │         │    │              │    │        │
└──────────┘    └─────────┘    └──────────────┘    └────────┘
     │               │                  │                │
  ┌─────────┐   ┌─────────┐    ┌──────────────┐
  │ TSL&W RR│   │ C&O RR  │    │Pere Marquette│
  └─────────┘   └─────────┘    └──────────────┘
```

There was no resolution in sight, and the brothers needed to satisfy their mounting debt. They did so by selling 63 percent of their holdings in Erie common stock, generating more than $9.5 million, and $13 million of Erie preferred stock over the next six months. They were later able to buy back those shares and more, giving them absolute control of the Erie Railroad.

The uproar of the C&O opposition raised concerns with William Ripley, the Harvard professor who had been hired by the ICC to create the consolidation plan. He was worried that the brothers' setback might doom any possibility of a four-party plan. After conferring with Daniel Willard, Ripley facilitated a conversation between O. P. and Frederick Scott, the brother of the C&O committee's chair. Ripley, Scott, and O. P. met on September 18. According to Van Sweringen's notes of the meeting, Mr. Scott said that "preferentially they would not have united the property and that none of the Virginia people had been conferred with about the matter but that the plan had gone forward without discussions with them, and everyone had rushed into a lawsuit about it." Scott suggested that the Van Sweringens could mitigate the situation by buying the dissenting shares, but O. P. was not ready to talk price. Testimony lasted ten months, and on March 2, 1926, the ICC issued its 7–1 decision denying the Vans' application and dealing the Van Sweringen brothers a big blow, in large measure due to the minority shareholders of the C&O.

The brothers set to work to address the concerns that the ICC had cited in their decision. But first, they had $35 million due to banks and brokerage houses. They obtained a loan for Vaness and sold some more stock in the Erie Railroad with which they paid the debts that were due. With the pressure of the debt removed from their shoulders, the brothers could address the ICC's concerns.

Building a Railroad Empire

The first concern of the Commissioners was that the Vans were attempting to control the system without owning a controlling interest in the voting stock. The brothers launched a stock-buying campaign throughout the remainder of 1926 and early 1927 to acquire substantial amounts of stock in the C&O, Erie, and Pere Marquette. The second concern was described by the commissioners as the "utter lack of independent and impartial representation of all the stockholders." This was resolved in May 1927 when the voting trust agreement with two of the brothers' longest and most loyal supporters was dissolved.

More difficult was the commissioner's concern that the stock-exchange ratios between stockholders of the smaller companies be "just and reasonable." The brothers formed a special committee comprised of five C&O directors to meet with representatives of each of the five railroads to discuss modifications to the terms of the merger and in the process to develop a new unification plan. All agreed to extend voting privileges to all shareholders, but the ratio on which the shares of the various roads would be exchanged remained unsettled.

A suggestion, based on two of the commission's observations, was presented by one of the members of the special committee after five months of negotiations. The commission had observed that the combined C&O and Hocking Valley were among the most efficient coal carriers and that those two roads "would constitute the backbone of the proposed system." Further, they observed that the savings that were justification for the proposed unification could be achieved through stock ownership and contracts allowing for the use of joint facilities.

ACQUISITIONS AND RESTRUCTURING, 1927–1930

On February 11, 1927, O. P. returned to the ICC, seeking authority to acquire control of the Erie and Pere Marquette Railroads by issuing some $59.5 million of C&O common stock at $100 per share. Newton D. Baker led a stable of lawyers representing the Van Sweringens' interests. Colonel Anderson represented the opposition. The brothers' debt had surged to a staggering $85 million. The prior October, the C&O and Virginia Transportation Corporation—a holding company subsidiary of the C&O—began to buy back all the Erie stock that the brothers had sold to settle their debt the year before, and even more, depleting the C&O's cash resources and incurring $4.5 million in debt for Virginia Transportation. The Nickel Plate, through a subsidiary holding company, the Special Investment Corporation, took on $34.5 million in debt. The hearings opened in May 1927 and closed in June. The commission released its decision the following May, approving the acquisition of the Pere Marquette, but not the Erie.

The Erie Railroad had to pull its own weight. The decision was made to replace Frederick Underwood, who had been the Erie's president for the past twenty-five years. Bernet had worked miracles with the Nickel Plate and was asked to do so now for the Erie. Underwood retired, Bernet was named president of the Erie, and Walter Ross was named president of the Nickel Plate. Bernet called a meeting and told some two hundred "traffic men" that it was their job to get $10 million in new business by year's end. It took a bit more than a year, but the Erie added 65 percent of the goal. Charles E. Denney was moved from the Nickel Plate to become the Erie's operating vice president. Otherwise, replacements were made from within the Erie.

The Erie's equipment was outdated, making the line inefficient and costly to operate. O. P. immediately approved Bernet's requests, which included the replacement of 427 locomotives and 8,000 boxcars. Coal consumption dropped by 50 percent, as did other operating costs. With the foundation built, Bernet handed the railroad to Denney, assuming the presidencies of the C&O and the Pere Marquette in May 1929 and reacquiring the presidency of the Nickel Plate with Ross's retirement in 1933.

The Van Sweringens had insisted on the diversity of traffic, but now their empire had become too heavily coal oriented. To balance the diversity, they turned to the Missouri Pacific Railroad (Mo-Pac), which, combined with the Texas & Pacific and the New Orleans, Texas & Mexico, included nearly twelve thousand miles of track, plus another twenty-five hundred miles in the Mo-Pac's half interest in the Denver & Rio Grande Western. Instead of coal, freight included oil and oil products, agricultural products, fruit, vegetables, and manufactured goods.

On May 8 of the following year, a decision on the consolidation request was announced. No consolidation would be approved until the commission had established their long-awaited consolidation plan. The C&O could acquire the Pere Marquette, but not the Erie. Of the eleven commissioners, Commissioner Porter stood alone in support of the control of both roads; Commissioners Campbell and Eastman opposed; and seven others voted for the prevailing decision. Commissioner Woodlock concentrated on the financial implications. The opposition to the acquisition of the Erie was based on the feeling that the Erie would be an important component of any ICC-approved consolidation plan.

Witt's ally Eastman could be counted on to oppose everything that the Van Sweringens proposed. In a scathing barrage, he charged that the brothers' projects "have been characterized by the creation and use of a maze of dummy corporations," which he called "legal perversions, commonly used for the purposes of concealment or evasion." Eastman saw two purposes for the brothers' strategy: "to facilitate shoestring financial operations on a very large scale, [and] to escape supervision by this [ICC] commission." In fact, the extent to which the brothers had of necessity gone was a matter of the ICC's own making. The commission's inability, turned unwillingness, to bring forth a workable consolidation plan had triggered the brothers' actions.[8]

The Van Sweringens, while disappointed by the commission's ruling, were neither surprised nor unprepared. After extensive consultation with J. P. Morgan and Guaranty officials, the brothers created yet another entity—the Chesapeake Corporation—controlled directly by Vaness Corporation, the brothers' holding company. Bonds were issued to fund the purchase of six hundred thousand shares of C&O common stock held by Vaness and the Nickel Plate's subsidiary, Special Investment Corporation. J. P. Morgan issued $48 million of twenty-year 5 percent convertible collateral trust bonds, guaranteed by Chesapeake Corporation's C&O common stock. The issue opened at ten o'clock in the morning on May 11, 1927, and closed almost immediately, with a more than $213 million oversubscription. The sale netted Chesapeake Corporation nearly $43.5 million, which was immediately turned around to meet the debt for the C&O stock.

The success of the Chesapeake Corporation's money-raising strategy caught the eye of the Pennsylvania Railroad and Vice President Albert John County, who wrote to President Leonor F. Loree of the Delaware & Hudson Railroad as follows: "General Atterbury would like your views on a holding company similar to the Chesapeake Corporation recently formed by the Van Sweringens. It would put the stocks in one company and the sale of collateral trust notes secured thereby would provide additional funds which would prove useful. I admit that it could not be so profitable as the Chesapeake holding company."[9]

In the absence of a defined ICC plan, railroad-buying warfare amounting to nearly a half-billion dollars broke out between the giants of the eastern region. The Pennsylvania, the outsider in the four-party meetings, still sniped at what had become the Triple Alliance. In the face of the alliance's opposition, Atterbury was quietly goading the outsiders to argue for a five-system solution that would have primarily benefited one road, the Pennsylvania, and Pennroad Corporation, its Van Sweringen–like holding company.

Often challenged by Rea, followed by Atterbury and more recently by Willard, except for Witt, the Van Sweringens were largely unchallenged at home in Cleveland, but that would change with the appearance of another set of brothers, Frank Elijah and Charles Farrand Taplin. The 512-mile Wheeling & Lake Erie Railway, connecting the Ohio coal fields near Wheeling, West Virginia, with the important Lake Erie ports of Cleveland and Toledo, became a point of contention between the two pairs of brothers. The Van Sweringen brothers had shown initial interest in the Wheeling & Lake Erie in the early 1920s because its passenger and freight facilities were blocking the brothers' route to their proposed Union Station. The Taplin brothers were the sons of Charles G. Taplin, a vice president at Rockefeller's Standard Oil Company. The older of the two brothers, Frank, went to work as a clerk in the tank wagon department in 1893. In 1900, Frank joined the Pittsburgh Coal Company in sales, later becoming sales manager of the Youghiogheny & Ohio Coal Company.

In 1913, Taplin formed the Cleveland & Western Coal Company and began to acquire coal properties in Ohio, West Virginia, and Pennsylvania, resulting in his becoming the largest coal shipper on the Great Lakes. His younger brother, Charles, followed a different path, becoming a prominent attorney before joining his brother in the coal business. Frank felt that the Pittsburgh & West Virginia was discriminating against him when it came to supplying empty cars for transporting his coal. Charles made a name for himself by filing and winning reparation suits before the ICC, and the brothers became interested in acquiring the line. In 1923, the Taplins obtained an option on a substantial block of Pittsburgh & West Virginia stock and formed a syndicate for the purchase. The railroad owned the Pittsburgh Terminal Railroad & Coal Company, which was combined with the Taplins' other properties in 1925 to form the North American Coal Company.

The following year, Taplin offered to sell the Pittsburgh & West Virginia to the Triple Alliance at an unrealistic price of $200 per share, which the alliance rejected. Rebuffed by the alliance, Taplin decided on a different tactic. Coal was a mature industry, and Taplin saw a greater future in railroading. The Wheeling & Lake Erie, and later the Western Maryland, could follow. The Taplins reached out to the Rockefellers, who owned all the 7 percent preferred shares in the Wheeling & Lake Erie, but the Rockefellers showed no interest in selling to the Taplins, and the alliance, wanting to block a fifth system, made its move.

With O. P. taking the lead, in two weeks the alliance purchased 181,000 shares of common stock and 6 percent preferred stock in the Wheeling & Lake Erie. They then purchased more than 115,000 shares of the Rockefellers' 7 percent preferred stock. In addition, the B&O purchased nearly 145,000 shares of Western Maryland preferred. The result was that the alliance had, if not blocked, at least forestalled any hope that the Taplin brothers might have had for a fifth system, and it inadvertently cornered the market on Wheeling & Lake Erie in the process. On September 5, 1929, General Atterbury agreed that Pennroad Corporation would purchase the nearly 223,000 shares of the Pittsburgh & West Virginia stock held by the Taplin brothers. Included in the agreement drafted by Charles Taplin was the stipulation that Pennroad would sell the shares back to the Taplins—who remained at the helm of the railroad—should he succeed in putting his fifth-system plan in place.

On January 26, 1929, the Van Sweringen brothers incorporated the Alleghany Corporation in the State of Maryland. Two days after the incorporation, the Morgans agreed to buy and float an $85 million issue of a variety of Alleghany securities, including $35 million in bonds, $25 million in cumulative 5.5 percent preferred stock, and $25 million in common stock. Of the proceeds, Alleghany received nearly $83 million. The holding company was funded with 100,000 shares of Nickel Plate common stock and a little more than 440,000 shares of Chesapeake Corporation common stock, with a combined value of $48 million. The Van Sweringens received 2.25 million shares of Alleghany common stock and warrants to buy another 1.725 million shares at $30 per share, along with Alleghany's assumption of $1,029,000 of debt. In return, Alleghany paid $37 million to various Van Sweringen companies for additional shares of Chesapeake Corporation stock and shares of the C&O, the Erie, and the Buffalo, Rochester & Pittsburgh. Through this elaborate series of transactions, Alleghany Corporation now directly or indirectly controlled the entire Van Sweringen railroad empire.[10]

Alleghany securities were first sold under a private offer to a select list of two hundred clients and friends, in blocks of one thousand to ten thousand shares at $20 per share. When it was introduced on the New York Stock Exchange, the shares sold in the range of $35–$37. The stock hit a high of $56 in 1929 before dropping to a low of $0.375 in 1932.

To further diversify the empire, Vaness Corporation, through one of its holding company subsidiaries General Securities Corporation, bought more than $13 million of common and preferred shares of United States Distributing Corporation. Itself a holding company, United States Distributing controlled ownership of companies in the distribution of ice, coal, and building products, as well as trucking and warehousing companies. The Van Sweringens felt comfortable that they had overcome the objections and concerns voiced by the ICC.

NOTES

1. Blosser, 93.
2. Ibid., 96.
3. Ibid.
4. Ibid., 123.
5. Ibid.
6. Ibid., 124.
7. Ibid., 133–134.
8. Ibid., 161.
9. Ibid., 164.
10. Ibid., 195–197.

SIX

THE DOMINOES FALL

THE GREAT DEPRESSION

In early 1929, the Federal Reserve Bank of New York and the Federal Reserve Board agreed that the Wall Street boom needed to be put in check before a serious relapse occurred. Though they agreed, they were far apart on the solution. The bank wanted to raise the rediscount rate—the rate charged by the Federal Reserve banks for rediscounting commercial paper for member banks—to make credit expensive and speculation unprofitable, impacting both businesses and the stock market. The board remembered the uproar in 1921 and wanted to tighten credit for the stock market and remain reasonable for business.

In February 1929, the Federal Reserve Board warned its member banks against borrowing from the Federal Reserve Bank for speculative loans. Although the Federal Reserve Bank of New York opposed the action, it increasingly showed signs of effectiveness. The cost of dollars available to brokers for short-term purposes, called "call money," began to climb. In March, the money in the call market began to dry up, interest rates climbed to 20 percent, and stocks began to fall.

The National City Bank of New York defied the board, borrowing $25 million for the call market, and other New York banks followed suit, prompting the market to return to its bullish climb. This encouraged O. P. to increase his position in the Missouri Pacific by $19 million, to $32 million. In a defensive move, the Missouri Pacific issued $43 million in bonds, convertible to common stock at the purchaser's option.

In the summer of 1929, O. P., suffering from low blood pressure, experienced several heart attacks. The stress was showing on his face. Friends began to prod him to take some time to relax. M. J., who had put on a good deal of weight and was suffering from high blood pressure, had been suggesting to his older brother that it was time for them both to slow down. One morning, instead of riding to the office with Benjamin Jenks as was his custom, M. J. stayed behind at Daisy Hill, waiting for his brother. As they rode downtown, M. J. turned to O. P. and said, "Let's call it all off and sell out!" Only his deep silence indicated that O. P. had heard. After several minutes, he broke the silence, asking, "What would we do if we did sell out?" M. J. replied, "It's a good day to get out while we are up." Quick calculations had shown that they could get out and that their holdings would unquestionably bring them well over $100 million. O. P. thought about it that morning, and again after going to bed that night. He would not or could not get out. There was still so much left to be done.[1]

The decade of the roaring twenties had been a period of incredible social and economic growth after the eighteen-month depression that had followed World War I. The stock market was long overdue for a correction. On March 25, 1929, after the Federal Reserve Bank warned about excessive speculation, the market dropped, but it recovered when New York's National City Bank provided $25 million in credit. The market dropped again in May, but by June, the surge continued and investors were borrowing money to buy on margin. By August, brokers were lending small investors as much as two-thirds of the purchase price. Between June and early September, the stock market gained more than 20 percent. The market reached a high of 381.17 on September 3, 1929, before losing nearly 90 percent and reaching a low of 41.22 on July 8, 1932. It would not be until November 23, 1954, that the market would again see the high of that day after Labor Day 1929.

The stock of Van Sweringens' Alleghany Corporation had soared to a high of 56⅜ per share on September 5 before settling back down to around 50 later that day and then dropping to 18⅛ on October 29. The Van Sweringens took advantage of drops to buy more shares, adding the Chicago Great Western to their inventory of railroads. Alleghany stock was recovering to 32 and the Union Trust, Cleveland Trust, and Guardian Savings and Trust Company gave Vaness a $9 million loan. O. P. continued to buy Missouri Pacific stock, bringing his holding of the Mo-Pac to just over $100 million by May 1930. The Chicago & Eastern Illinois, with its desirable direct route between Chicago and St. Louis, was on O. P.'s radar.

Had the memory of the 1919–1920 depression been blurred by the raucous revelry of the twenties, or was it the supreme confidence of the enterprising spirit that led so many to leave everything on the line without any defensive measures?

On December 9, 1929, the ICC finally delivered what it called the final consolidation plan, completing the task that had begun eight years earlier. The ICC's inaction had left the Big Four to their own devices, and left alone, they had gone about their acquisition plans unabated.

The resulting ICC plan left the B&O only moderately happy; the New York Central, less happy; the Van Sweringens unhappy; and the Pennsylvania, with only itself to blame, very unhappy. Had it not been for the Pennsylvania's refusal to cooperate with the other three, likely, a fifth system would never have factored into the ICC's plan, but they did, and it did.

The Taplin brothers, the Van Sweringens' Cleveland-based nemeses, had proposed the acquisition of the Wheeling, the Western Maryland, the Lehigh Valley, and the Wabash as a fifth system. Professor Ripley, who had worked so hard to develop a plan for the commissioners' consideration, was summarily unimpressed. The ICC narrowly approved the creation of a fifth system—on paper. The B&O was given the right to the Reading and the Jersey Central; the Alton; the Buffalo, Rochester & Pittsburgh; and others. The New York Central gained the rights to the Virginian. The Van Sweringens retained control of the C&O, the Hocking Valley, and the Nickel Plate. The Erie, which had previously been opposed by the commission, was finally approved, and the Van Sweringens gained the rights to the Lackawanna and other smaller railroads. The Chicago & Eastern was designated to one of the small Midwestern groups. The Pennsylvania received no rights due to its existing dominance, and the Norfolk & Western; the Lehigh Valley; the Wabash; the Pittsburgh & West Virginia; the Seaboard; and the Detroit, Toledo & Ironton were assigned to the fifth system. The New Haven and the Boston & Maine were redesignated as principal railroads of a New England region.

In early March 1930, the Van Sweringens took control of the voting stock of the Missouri Pacific Railroad. In the process, it was discovered that the brothers had failed to obtain the permission of the Missouri Public Service Commission before acquiring more than 10 percent of the Mo-Pac stock. The commission held a hearing at which there was virtually no opposition. They announced their approval on May 6, and O. P. Van Sweringen was elected to succeed Williams as chair of the board. As ICC regulations prohibited his serving as chair of both an eastern and western region railroad, he resigned his chairmanship of the C&O, and M. J. stepped in to succeed him.

The Missouri Pacific outbid the Burlington to acquire properties that meatpacking giants Swift & Company and Armour & Company had been ordered to divest themselves of in an antitrust suit. O. P. believed they would be a perfect fit for future development of the Mo-Pac and that the meatpackers would route more of their traffic over other of his roads. O. P. created a new subsidiary, Terminal Shares, Incorporated, to hold the shares.

With the acquisition of the Missouri Pacific Railroad, the Van Sweringens' ultimate prize, a coast-to-coast railroad was only six hundred miles away. There were two properties of interest to O. P.—the Western Pacific and the Denver & Rio Grande Western. Acquiring the Western Pacific would give him half ownership of the Denver & Rio Grande Western as well. Arthur Curtiss James controlled the Western Pacific Railroad Corporation, which in turn held the stock of the Western Pacific Railroad Company. Without saying so explicitly, James made it clear he had no intention of selling.

As the nation and the world slipped deeper into the Great Depression, the Van Sweringens had one more major financing project—to ensure the financial future of the thirty-five-acre, $70 million terminal complex. It consisted of Union Terminal, topped by a fifty-two-story office tower, flanked on one side by a one-thousand-room hotel, on the other side by an equally large department store, and to the rear by three eighteen-story office buildings. In addition, there were the rapid transit system with its planned extensions and the 6.32-square-mile Shaker Heights development with its rapidly growing population that would more than double over the next three decades.

O. P. estimated that debentures in the amount of $60 million would be needed. J. P. Morgan & Co. declined on the basis that they did not sell real estate–based securities. The Guaranty Company also declined. Its greatest concern was that of the nearly fourteen thousand acres of land that the brothers had purchased, almost nine thousand acres remained unsold. The Guaranty finally agreed to a $30 million issue when the brothers removed the Shaker real estate from the package. The Van Sweringen Corporation was formed to hold the downtown real estate, while the Van Sweringen Company held the Shaker properties. The brothers posted five hundred thousand shares of Alleghany common stock at fifty cents on the dollar. If the pledged securities fell below one-half of the face value, the Van Sweringens were required to deliver sufficient collateral to make up the shortfall within twenty days.

Pyramiding, which had been so profitable during the runaway increases in the bull market, was disastrous as the bear market continued its steep decline. In mid-June, Alleghany, which had sold at 32 on April 26, hit 18 under a new wave of panic selling in the market. In September 1930, the market suffered another wave of selling, with nearly half of the listed stocks falling to new 1930 lows. O. P. continued to do whatever he could to try to prop up Alleghany's common stock. Still, the Van Sweringens would not walk away. On October 14, O. P. deposited another 150,000 Alleghany shares. He had no more to put in. With another drop in the market, Alleghany fell to 14. Following a phone call by O. P. to the Morgan partners and officials at Guaranty, John Murphy, Darwin Barrett, and William Wenneman joined the brothers in O. P.'s private railroad car. On October 23, 1930, while the others had meetings in New York, O. P. and Wenneman went on to Boston to argue that they should buy just one more railroad. He had his eye on the Boston & Maine. Alleghany dropped to 10¼. The Van Sweringen brothers were finished.

When O. P. finished his meeting, he called New York and was faced with the news of the morning's crash, and an emergency meeting was called with the bankers that evening. The brothers were threatened with the loss of control of their empire. O. P. solemnly and unemotionally outlined the reality of their situation. Cleveland Terminals Building Company owed more than $15.5 million; the securities collateralizing the $18.8 million stood at only 20 percent, not the required 25 percent; O. P. needed $5.75 million to make good on his pledge to the Van Sweringen Corporation; and a substantial interest payment was due to Van Sweringen Corporation noteholders in just over a week.

The representatives of Morgan and Guaranty agreed that the answer was not to let the Van Sweringens collapse. The prestige of Morgan and

Guaranty was at stake. They and other banks and brokers had handled close to $440 million in financing the Van Sweringens' railroad and real estate projects over the years. If the empire was allowed to collapse, there was no telling what effect that would have on the fragile market. Certainly, when the situation improved, there would be more of the Van Sweringens' profitable business. The bankers calculated that a $40 million loan would see the brothers through the next four and a half years, the period the bankers anticipated the Depression would last.

J. P. Morgan partner Thomas Lamont called Albert H. Wiggin, chair of the board of the Chase National Bank. Wiggin had been a member of the Van Sweringen's Glenville Syndicate in 1913 and committed $5 million unhesitatingly, which it increased to $5.5 million. The Morgan and Guaranty each committed to $11 million, National City and George Baker Jr. committed to $4.5 million each, and Banker's Trust committed $3 million. In one week, $39.5 million had been assembled and secured by $40 million in marketable securities and a like amount of real estate. The Van Sweringen brothers raised an additional $2.1 million—$1.5 million from the New York Trust Company and $600,000 from the Midland Bank. Although none of the bankers was on the Van Sweringen boards, O. P. did pledge to keep them apprised of any major commitments in the future.

O. P. agreed that he would liquidate the one remaining Paine Webber brokerage account by selling one-fourth of the Missouri Pacific securities as well as some stock in Chesapeake Corporation and the Kansas City Southern. On the home front, the brothers took on a mortgage of more than $535,000 from the Union Trust Company for the construction of the Farm Group of buildings at Daisy Hill. Wages for the Daisy Hill staff were cut by 15 percent. Executive salaries were reduced, as were the wages of the railroad and real estate workers. Service charges were levied on the individual railroads to offset the holding companies' routine expenses.

As the Depression deepened, a second round of wage reductions went into effect at Daisy Hill—this time 25 percent—accompanied by a reduction in the number of staff. The brothers also economized, giving up their saddle horses and stepping down from Lincolns to Buicks. In mid-1929, the brothers had stopped drawing salaries from the railroads, living instead on dividends. As business declined, the payment of dividends ended, and their income was limited to the $250,000 paid by the Cleveland Railway Company stock. Their expenses included $30,000 for general living expenses; $25,000 for Edith and Carrie, including upkeep on the town home; $20,000 for upkeep on Daisy Hill; $20,000–$25,000 for taxes; and $25,000 for insurance. Not included were the mortgage payments. Occasionally, M. J. was able to come up with $250–$300 to help the servants who had been let go and had not yet found new jobs.

The four-party conferences on railroad consolidation had resumed because President Herbert Hoover believed that an agreement between the lines had the potential of stimulating the economy. The Pennsylvania was in a mood to make concessions, and the other presidents had been sobered by the impact of the Depression. Eventually, the Pennsylvania made a major concession: it would sell the Lehigh Valley to the Van Sweringens in return for access to Bethlehem, Pennsylvania. Negotiations, often contentious, continued for several months. On October 3, the four parties—the Pennsylvania, the New York Central, the B&O, and the Van Sweringens—submitted their proposal to the ICC. The four would carve up the holdings designated for the fifth system. To the Van Sweringens went the Lehigh Valley and part of the Pittsburgh & West Virginia. They would retain the Wheeling & Lake Erie and the Indiana stem of the C&O and share the Virginian with the Pennsylvania, while having all the Chicago & Eastern.

After nine months of consideration, the ICC categorically rejected the proposal. In its place, the ICC consolidation plan gave the Virginian in its entirety to the New York Central. The ICC also formally approved the Van Sweringens' entire eastern system and added the Lehigh Valley. After eight years, the brothers had all they had initially requested and more. Perhaps, had the Pennsylvania cooperated and the ICC approved the early consolidation plan, the Van Sweringens would have been in a much stronger position to weather the storm of the Great Depression. Early on, the impact of the Depression had been on the holding companies, as the value of their stocks plummeted. Then, with industrial output stalled, the impact extended to the operating companies as well. National railroad freight revenues were at 80 percent of the 1927–1929 averages by the end of 1930; 60 percent by the end of 1931; and 45 percent by the end of 1932.

As the Depression deepened, finger-pointing increased. The House Interstate Commerce Committee launched investigations into stock ownership by railroads in general and the Van Sweringens and their holding companies in particular. Investigators spent four months on the thirty-fourth floor of the Terminal Tower. The *Cleveland Press* reported that "not through direct ownership but through control of thirty-two holding corporations, the Van Sweringens have come to occupy a dominating position in the affairs of the greatest transportation system ever welded together by a single group, involving 28,411 miles of railroads."[2]

On September 5, 1931, the Guaranty Trust Company seized technical control of the Alleghany Corporation. The Guaranty labeled the Van Sweringen Corporation—the holding company for the brothers' downtown real estate—as in a "bankruptcy and reorganization situation."[3]

Notes were due. The Guaranty calculated that the total value of everything the brothers owned would amount to only $8 million. Alternatively, the brothers could offer $500 in cash, plus twenty shares of Van Sweringen Corporation common stock. In doing so, the Van Sweringens were saved from the impossible situation of having to face the November 1 interest payments, which would have resulted in bankruptcy. *Fortune* magazine called it the "smartest deal in depression history."

In July 1931, Patrick Joyce, the president of the Chicago Great Western Railroad, proposed the acquisition of O. P.'s stock in the Kansas City Southern. The brothers were under a great deal of pressure from the New York banks to liquidate some of Alleghany's "fancy investments." Within two months, an agreement was consummated, and the Chicago Great Western acquired the Van Sweringens' Kansas City Southern stock for double the market price, netting the brothers $3.135 million, with the option to buy back up to half of the shares within two years. That was still nearly $7 million less than the Van Sweringens had originally paid for the stock. Alleghany considered selling its bonds and preferred shares in the Missouri Pacific if it could be done without too great a loss.

In January 1932, Congress approved the establishment of the Reconstruction Finance Corporation. It was clear that private banks could not lend the amount of money necessary to avoid industry-wide bankruptcy. The "super-bank" opened its doors in February and in short order the Missouri Pacific, the Erie, the Nickel Plate, the Chicago & Eastern Illinois, and the Rio Grande had received $20 million. By the end of 1934, the Van Sweringens' railroads received more than $75.6 million, making them the Reconstruction Finance Corporation's biggest railroad client, followed closely by the B&O.

In February 1932, Alleghany Corporation successfully liquidated its Paine Webber brokerage account by selling its shares in the Pere Marquette, the Erie, and the Nickel Plate to the C&O.

THE DOMINOES CONTINUE TO FALL

Beginning in January 1933, one by one Wall Street bankers and leading financiers appeared before the Senate Banking and Currency Committee to defend themselves and their actions. One of the primary targets was J. P. Morgan, and on June 5, O. P. appeared before the committee. He began his statement by recounting the years from the acquisition of the Nickel Plate to the present with the acquisition of the Missouri Pacific and ending with his optimism for the future of his railroad. O. P. planned to be generally uncooperative and make the committee's counsel work for every answer. On the third day, the strategy was changed. O. P. was his usual detailed self, as he was on the fourth and final day. The hearings lasted another year. When they concluded, they became the foundation for the Banking Act of 1933, the Truth-in-Securities Act, the Securities and Exchange Commission Act, and the Public Utility Holding Company Act.

The Van Sweringen Business Empire, 1934

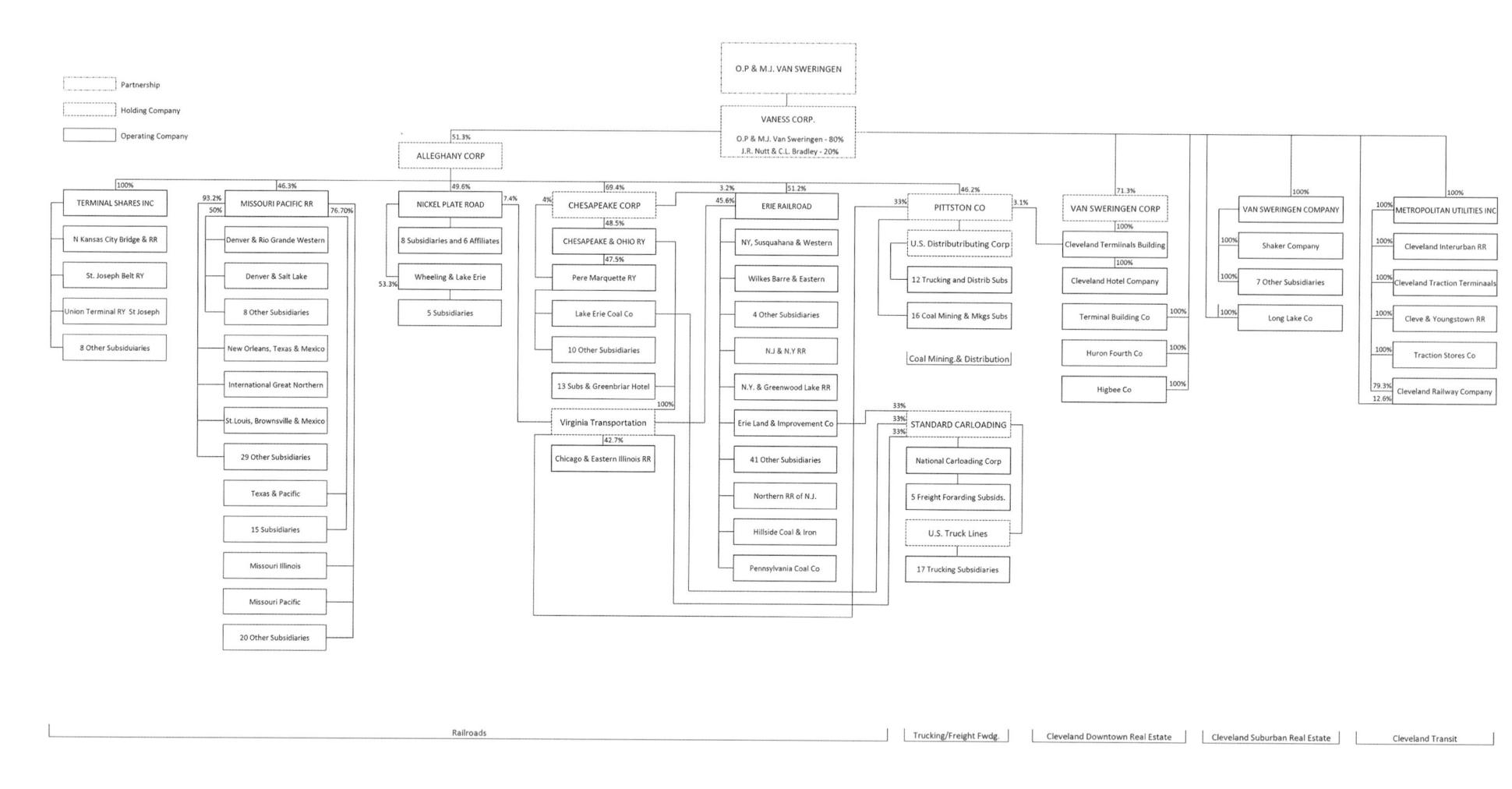

┆┄┄┆	Partnership
┌╌╌┐	Holding Company
▭	Operating Company

O.P & M.J. VAN SWERINGEN

VANESS CORP.
O.P & M.J. Van Sweringen – 80%
J.R. Nutt & C.L. Bradley – 20%

ALLEGHANY CORP (51.3%)

- **TERMINAL SHARES INC** (100%)
  - N Kansas City Bridge & RR
  - St. Joseph Belt RY
  - Union Terminal RY St Joseph
  - 8 Other Subsiduiaries

- **MISSOURI PACIFIC RR** (46.3%, 93.2%, 50%, 76.70%)
  - Denver & Rio Grande Western
  - Denver & Salt Lake
  - 8 Other Subsidiaries
  - New Orleans, Texas & Mexico
  - International Great Northern
  - St. Louis, Brownsville & Mexico
  - 29 Other Subsidiaries
  - Texas & Pacific
  - 15 Subsidiaries
  - Missouri Illinois
  - Missouri Pacific
  - 20 Other Subsidiaries

- **NICKEL PLATE ROAD** (49.6%, 7.4%)
  - 8 Subsidiaries and 6 Affiliates
  - Wheeling & Lake Erie (53.3%)
  - 5 Subsidiaries

- **CHESAPEAKE CORP** (69.4%, 4%)
  - **CHESAPEAKE & OHIO RY** (48.5%, 47.5%)
    - Pere Marquette RY
    - Lake Erie Coal Co
    - 10 Other Subsidiaries
    - 13 Subs & Greenbriar Hotel
    - Virginia Transportation (100%)
      - Chicago & Eastern Illinois RR (42.7%)

- **ERIE RAILROAD** (3.2%, 45.6%, 51.2%, 33%)
  - NY, Susquahana & Western
  - Wilkes Barre & Eastern
  - 4 Other Subsidiaries
  - N.J & N.Y RR
  - N.Y. & Greenwood Lake RR
  - Erie Land & Improvement Co
  - 41 Other Subsidiaries
  - Northern RR of N.J.
  - Hillside Coal & Iron
  - Pennsylvania Coal Co

- **PITTSTON CO** (46.2%, 3.1%)
  - U.S. Distribututing Corp
  - 12 Trucking and Distrib Subs
  - 16 Coal Mining & Mkgs Subs
  - Coal Mining & Distribution

- **STANDARD CARLOADING** (33%, 33%, 33%)
  - National Carloading Corp
  - 5 Freight Forarding Subsids.
  - U.S. Truck Lines
  - 17 Trucking Subsidiaries

- **VAN SWERINGEN CORP** (71.3%, 100%)
  - Cleveland Terminals Building (100%)
  - Cleveland Hotel Company (100%)
  - Terminal Building Co
  - Huron Fourth Co (100%)
  - Higbee Co (100%)

- **VAN SWERINGEN COMPANY** (100%)
  - Shaker Company (100%)
  - 7 Other Subsidiaries (100%)
  - Long Lake Co (100%)

- **METROPOLITAN UTILITIES INC** (100%)
  - Cleveland Interurban RR (100%)
  - Cleveland Traction Terminaals (100%)
  - Cleve & Youngstown RR (100%)
  - Traction Stores Co (100%)
  - Cleveland Railway Company (79.3%, 12.6%)

Legend (bottom): Railroads | Trucking/Freight Fwdg. | Cleveland Downtown Real Estate | Cleveland Suburban Real Estate | Cleveland Transit

---

The Ohio state senate opened hearings on Cleveland's closed banks, focusing on the loans to the Van Sweringens by the Union Trust Bank and the Guardian. They revealed to the public that the brothers had paid nothing for two or three years on mortgages, with the Union Trust on Daisy Hill totaling more than $535,000. The brothers had become the object of scathing, mean-spirited attacks in national magazines and Cleveland's *Plain Dealer*.

In 1933, both the Guardian Savings and Trust and the Union Trust Company, the brothers' primary banking relationships, closed... never to reopen. The Guardian, founded in 1894, had purchased the New

178 *Empire Builders*

Guardian Building, 619 Euclid Avenue.

Citizens Building, 840 Euclid Avenue.

Union Trust (Union Commerce Building), 925 Euclid Avenue.

England Building at 619 Euclid Avenue in 1914. Built in 1896, the fifteen-story New England Building was the tallest in Cleveland until the Rockefeller Building was completed in 1905. The Guardian Bank enlarged the building in 1916, renaming it the Guardian Building. Following the closing of the Guardian, the National City Bank leased the banking spaces in the Guardian Building, purchasing the building in 1944 and renaming it the National City Bank Building in 1949.

The Union Trust Company, founded in 1920 with the merger of twenty financial institutions, was originally housed in the Citizens Building at 840 Euclid Avenue, adjacent to the Schofield Building. In 1924, the bank moved to its new twenty-one-story headquarters at the northeast corner of the same intersection. At the time, the Union Trust Building was the second largest building in the world, with more than thirty acres of floor space, and it contained the world's largest banking floor. Following the closing of the banks, the State Banking Department managed the affairs of the Union Trust until the formation of Union Properties, Incorporated, in 1939, to liquidate the bank's assets, including some two thousand real estate properties. A new bank, the Union Bank of Commerce, was established in the Union Trust Building in May 1938.

The spring of 1934 was not kind to the brothers, who were unable to pay the property taxes on their extensive suburban real estate holdings. Alleghany had slid to the point that reorganization appeared the only option, and unfounded rumors circulated that they had defaulted on the loans from the syndicate of New York banks. By May of the next year, the rumors turned into reality. O. P. seemingly had learned his lesson. He criticized himself for the pyramid of companies he had created. When all was good, it was particularly good, but when things turned bad, the empire of holding companies turned very shaky in no time at all. He confided that if he ever got back on his feet he would rebuild very differently. Reflecting on their age, O. P. admitted that he never thought they would be in that position again. If only he had stayed east of the Mississippi and west of Green Road.

On March 15, 1934, O. P., with no dollars for interest payments, offered bondholders new priority preferred stock instead of interest for the next five years. That summer, Congress adopted an amendment to the bankruptcy act, allowing all bondholders to be bound to the plan with two-thirds in agreement. Three-quarters approved, and despite objections, the Van Sweringens' plan was upheld on December 29.

MORE GREAT LOSSES

On July 5, 1935, John Joseph Bernet, who had come to be known as the "Doctor of Sick Railroads," died at the age of sixty-seven and was buried in Cleveland's Calvary Cemetery. His poor eyesight as a child had made following in his father's footsteps as a blacksmith impossible, so he went to the Lake Shore & Michigan Southern Railroad, where he started as a telegrapher and began to learn railroading from the bottom up. What Bernet brought to the Van Sweringens is virtually incalculable. Not once but twice Bernet took run-down railroads and re-created them to stand among the leaders in the railroading industry, and in the process, he developed executive talent capable of succeeding him in his absence, among them, Charles E. Denney, who had succeeded him as president of the Nickel Plate in 1929 and who would now succeed him as the president of the C&O.

The Van Sweringen empire was built on a fragile foundation, relying on cash flow to meet the ever-growing obligations of day-to-day operations as well as the financial demands of an overwhelming appetite for growth. Always before, O. P. had found a solution, but now it was like pulling a rabbit from his hat. The rabbit came in the person of George Ashley Tomlinson, president and chair of the board of Great Lakes Towing Company. On August 10, O. P. sat with Tomlinson in the latter's Terminal Tower office and confided that he was stopped and did not know where to turn.

The two had met a dozen years earlier when O. P. approached Tomlinson to purchase the *Plain Dealer* for him. Although that acquisition had failed to materialize, the two came to know each other better when the brothers acquired the Wheeling & Lake Erie Railroad, where Tomlinson had been a director for five years. When it became apparent that the Van Sweringens were on the verge of acquiring the Missouri Pacific, Tomlinson had expressed his desire to serve on that board. As the Depression deepened, conversations between O. P. and Tomlinson turned increasingly to the topic of finding new money. At one point, Tomlinson indicated that if O. P. had nowhere else to turn, he might be able to help. O. P. was in conversation with several wealthy Clevelanders and was hopeful that his immediate need would be met.

When O. P. walked into Tomlinson's office that day in early August 1935, Tomlinson and his wife were about to leave for a long-overdue vacation in Colorado. But O. P. suggested that they could drive to Muncie, Indiana, the next day to meet with George Ball, of glass fruit jar fame, who shipped forty cars a day on the Nickel Plate, earning him a place on that road's board. Although M. J. had been ill of late, he insisted on driving, much to the objection of Daisy Jenks. The next morning, the brothers got into the front seat, with M. J. behind the wheel, and headed for Wade Park Manor in Cleveland's University Circle to pick up the Tomlinsons. They arrived in Muncie in midafternoon, and while the wives visited at the Ball's home, the others met with Ball at his office.

With all his charm, O. P. walked Ball through the history of the brothers' empire, before confiding that the financial need was critical. He explained that the banks, holding various securities as collateral, would soon begin to sell to cover notes they held. Ball had but one question—would O. P. stay with the companies and manage them? O. P. assured Ball that he had no intention of walking away from his life's work. Ball suggested to Tomlinson that if he would advance one-third, and O. P. would do the same, Ball would as well. This was shared with O. P. the next day. When O. P. was unable to cover the remaining third, Ball agreed to pick that up as well.

With the brothers' immediate crisis resolved, an even greater one took its place. Although O. P. had always had low blood pressure, M. J.'s blood pressure had always been high, and the pressures of recent events, likely including the strain of the Muncie trip, exacerbated the latter's condition. He entered Hanna House of Lakeside Hospital, where he was diagnosed with kidney damage in addition to high blood pressure. Following a week in the hospital, M. J. was sent home to recuperate.

The position in which the brothers found themselves was critical. It is unlikely that M. J. did much resting because, by September 21, the Vans had created the Midamerica Corporation, with a board of directors consisting of O. P. as president; M. J. as vice president; their business associate Charles Bradley as vice president; and George A. Ball, George A. Tomlinson, and F. B. Barnard as directors. The first meeting of the Midamerica Corporation was called to order in the Van Sweringens' suite at the Ambassador Hotel in Manhattan at nine o'clock on September 30. The deadline for making qualifying deposits for the afternoon's auction was just two hours away. There was some gossip that Leonor F. Loree, president of the Delaware & Hudson Railroad who had bought 10 percent of the New York Central; Frederick H. Prince, a stockbroker, investment banker, and financier; or perhaps even the Rockefellers would be in attendance to bid on the Van Sweringens' empire. Among those who had traveled to New York with the brothers that day were Ball and Tomlinson, who were prepared to bid as much as $3.5 million. Following lunch at the hotel, M. J. remained in the suite as the others went to 18 Vesey Street in Manhattan's Tribeca neighborhood to learn their fate.

Only the two Georges—Ball and Tomlinson—and F. A. O. Schwartz, the attorney representing George Whitney and the interests of J. P. Morgan, had posted qualifying deposits. At 3:30 p.m., the auctioneer began the proceedings. All that the brothers had worked so hard to create was about to be auctioned off. First, one hundred thousand shares of Alleghany stock went to Schwartz for $50,000. Bids were then taken on fifty-eight parcels of land that were then bundled into the four big groups that would follow. Then it was time for Group One. Schwartz bid $2,802,101. Leonard P. Ayers, a member of the Van Sweringen staff, responded with $2,803,000. There was no response from the Morgans. The gavel went

The Van Sweringen Business Empire, 1935

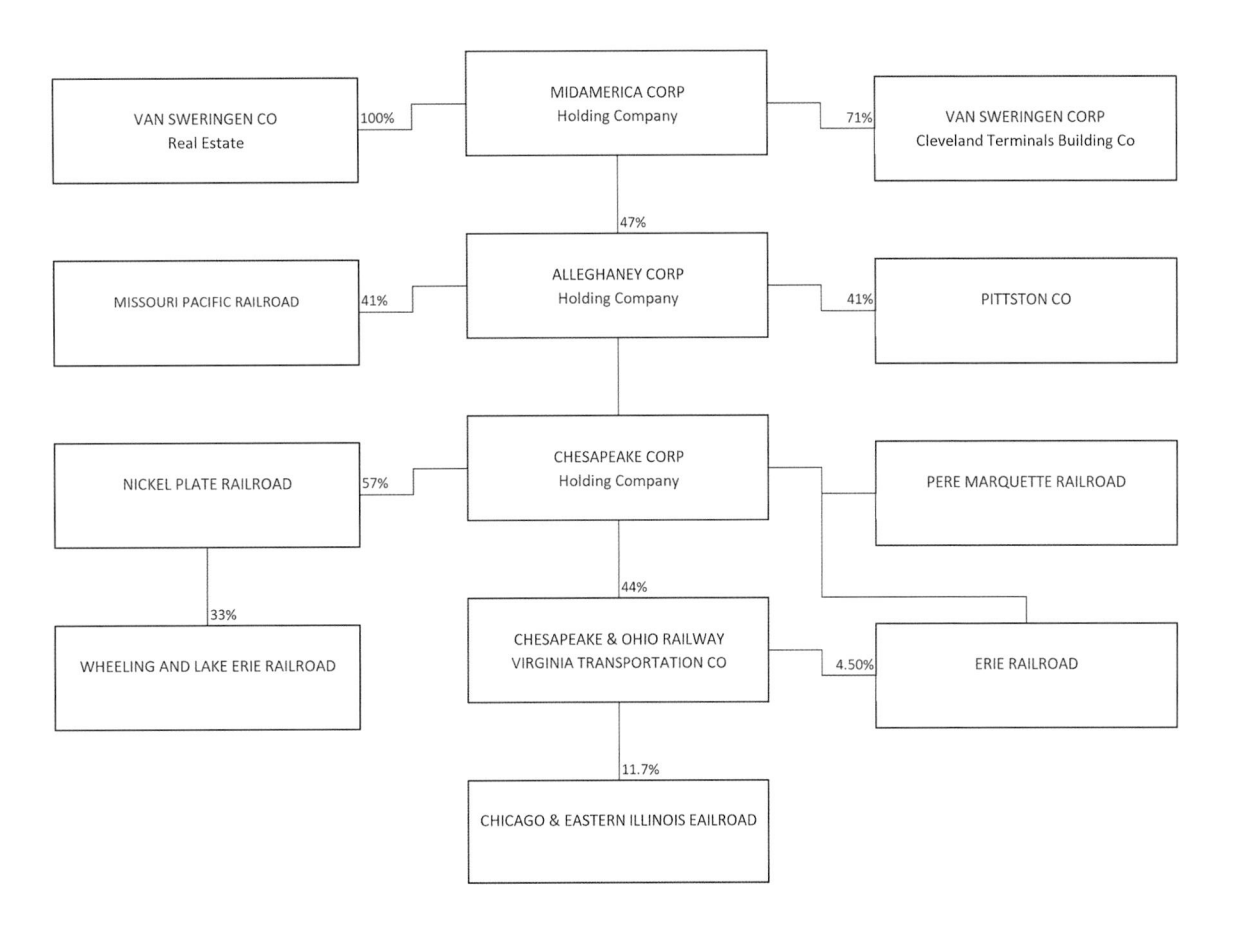

```
                          ┌─────────────────────┐
                          │   MIDAMERICA CORP   │
                          │   Holding Company   │
                          └─────────────────────┘
┌──────────────────┐ 100%  │                │ 71%  ┌──────────────────────────┐
│ VAN SWERINGEN CO │───────┤                ├──────│   VAN SWERINGEN CORP     │
│   Real Estate    │       │                │      │ Cleveland Terminals Building Co │
└──────────────────┘       └─────────────────┘     └──────────────────────────┘
                                    │ 47%
                          ┌─────────────────────┐
                          │   ALLEGHANEY CORP   │
                          │   Holding Company   │
                          └─────────────────────┘
┌──────────────────────┐ 41%  │            │ 41%  ┌──────────────┐
│ MISSOURI PACIFIC RR  │──────┤            ├──────│  PITTSTON CO │
└──────────────────────┘      └────────────┘      └──────────────┘
                                    │
                          ┌─────────────────────┐
                          │   CHESAPEAKE CORP   │
                          │   Holding Company   │
                          └─────────────────────┘
┌──────────────────────┐ 57%  │            │     ┌──────────────────────┐
│ NICKEL PLATE RAILROAD│──────┤            ├─────│ PERE MARQUETTE RR    │
└──────────────────────┘      └────────────┘     └──────────────────────┘
         │ 33%                      │ 44%
┌──────────────────────────┐ ┌──────────────────────────┐ 4.50% ┌──────────────┐
│ WHEELING AND LAKE ERIE RR│ │ CHESAPEAKE & OHIO RAILWAY│───────│ ERIE RAILROAD│
└──────────────────────────┘ │ VIRGINIA TRANSPORTATION CO│      └──────────────┘
                             └──────────────────────────┘
                                    │ 11.7%
                          ┌─────────────────────────────────┐
                          │ CHICAGO & EASTERN ILLINOIS EAILROAD │
                          └─────────────────────────────────┘
```

down, and the proceedings continued with Groups Two, Three, and Four. Group Three went to Midamerica, and Groups Two and Four, consisting of industrial stocks, went to New York investment bank Hallgarten & Company. The banks recovered just over $5.5 million. When it was all over, O. P. admitted that it had been a great strain, saying, "I'm sorry it had to be done this way. I'd rather have paid the bill." Much of the Van Sweringens' $3 billion empire was recovered by the brothers for less than $3 million.

Following the auction, the brothers took a long-overdue, much-needed, and richly deserved trip together. With the chauffeur at the wheel of the twelve-cylinder Lincoln sedan, they first drove to Wooster, Ohio, to visit their birthplaces. Undoubtedly, they reflected on their impoverished early years—the farm that their father had tried to work and failed; the family's home, Dwelling Number 473 in Chippewa Township; and their home and the school that their siblings had attended on Rogue's Hollow Road. From Wayne County, they headed to the Bluegrass country of Kentucky, stopping at horse-breeding farms before returning to Daisy Hill. M. J. seemed improved after the relaxing drive and returned to his office in the Terminal Tower for an hour or so while O. P. set about reconstructing the brothers' empire.

THE GREATEST LOSSES OF ALL

On October 17, saying that he was "going to the hospital for a little physical checkup," M. J. drove himself from Daisy Hill to Lakeside Hospital near University Circle. First reports suggested that he was resting, then that he was suffering from intestinal influenza, complicated by kidney damage and high blood pressure. By early December, M. J. was diagnosed with hypertensive myocarditis and lapsed into semiconsciousness. At 7:15 a.m., on December 12, 1935, with his beloved brother holding one hand and Daisy Jenks holding the other, Mantis James Van Sweringen took his last breath.

On M. J.'s will, which he had signed on March 20, 1922, he had written: "I desire that my brother, Oris P. Van Sweringen, in the event that he receives my property by this will, support and maintain our sisters in the same manner as we have heretofore done, but this provision in my will is intended only as an expression of confidence in his willingness to carry out my wishes and is not to be regarded as a charge upon my brother."

Each of the brothers had left the entirety of their estates to the other. An inventory of M. J.'s wealth at the time of his death amounted to $3,067.85, including seven horses valued at $1,400; $1,666.85 in a commercial account with the Cleveland Trust Company; and the beneficial interest in the common stock of the Vaness Company, $1.00. An inventory of the brothers' joint property showed a value of $199,851, including parcels on South Park Boulevard and Sedgewick Road with an aggregate value of $121,000. Two unsecured claims were shown: one against the Van Sweringen Company in the amount of $237,881.41 was appraised at $25,000; the other against the Vaness Company in the amount of $50,668.18 was appraised at $1.00. Other jointly shared assets included a variety of classes of stock in the Chesapeake & Ohio Railroad Company; Chesapeake Corporation; New York, Chicago, & St. Louis Railroad; Hilltop Realty Company; and Pere Marquette Railroad, with an aggregate value of $11,952.35. No appraised value was included in the inventory for Roundwood Manor, but its contents were appraised at $33,490, and possessions in the South Park mansion were valued at $5,490. A joint commercial account at Cleveland Trust held a balance of $2,917.75. According to the inventories submitted to the court and later received by the *Plain Dealer*, this represented the appraised value of the brothers who owned more railroads (the system contained 29,704 miles of track) than any other one group in the world.[4]

Allowing for the deduction of loans, M. J.'s insurance policies paid $554,000 to O. P., his sole heir. Because of O. P.'s borrowing, his insurance policies would pay less than $500,000.

After his brother's death, O. P. tried to go on, but it was difficult for him without M. J. at his side, where he had always been since his earliest memories. During the morning ride to the office, when O. P. had customarily carried on a conversation with the chauffer, he sat in silence, only breaking the silence to exclaim, "God, how I miss that brother of mine," and wondering aloud if he had worked M. J. too hard. When he arrived at the thirty-sixth-floor executive offices, O. P. entered his brother's office each morning to switch his desk lamp on, and each evening he returned to switch it off.

The surviving brother began to acquire stock in the Western Pacific, to complete his coast-to-coast system once the western railroads emerged from reorganization. Although the Missouri Pacific was in the process of reorganization and out of his control, he was able to participate in the reorganization as a majority shareholder. On February 1, 1936, the combination of cash and securities that served to collateralize Alleghany's senior bond issues was above the 150 percent requirement. O.

P. no longer needed the approval of Guaranty to control the Alleghany Corporation and its subordinate railroads. Clearly, except for the Erie, there was light at the end of the railroad tunnel.

But there was bad news as well. Shaker Heights real estate was not selling. Taxes were mounting, as were interest costs. On February 3, the Van Sweringen Company was forced into reorganization. On October 13, with office and retail space in the terminal complex unoccupied, the Van Sweringen Corporation and Cleveland Terminals Building Company joined Van Sweringen Company in reorganization. The Van Sweringen name and the Vaness Company would not be freed from the control of the court and the supervision of a special master until October 29, 1951, when probate court judge Nelson J. Brewer made the final journal entry, "N. J. B.—O. S. J."—the first three being the judge's initials, followed by the abbreviation for the legal term "order see journal."

The Senate Interstate Commerce Committee had been charged with the responsibility of conducting a broad investigation of railroad financing, including the use of holding companies, and ICC commissioner Joseph B. Eastman, long an admirer of the contentious Peter Witt and a Van Sweringen nemesis, was directed to select railroads for investigation. He promptly turned his focus to the Van Sweringen system. Investigators swarmed throughout the Van Sweringen Terminal Tower offices. The chair of the Senate committee, Burton Wheeler of Montana, complained that the investigators were being obstructed in carrying out their work in the Van Sweringen offices. If there was anything that was not contentious, the adversaries found a way it could be made so.

By August 1936, O. P. was sorely in need of a vacation, so he and the Jenkses took a several-day trip on a Great Lakes freighter. It was enough to make O. P. feel somewhat rested and ready to get back to work. With the nation showing some degree of recovery, Van Sweringen was able to settle some $15 million of his debt. In the meantime, his mind continued to churn as he wrestled with the changing business landscape. Trucking was cutting into the less-than-carload business. He decided to offer compartmentalized fractions of a freight car to shippers who did not need a full car. He planned to erect cranes at strategic rail yards to unload the compartment—known today as a container—from the truck and load it onto a flatbed railcar, reversing the process at the other end.

It was time to go to New York for more meetings. At six o'clock on the evening of November 22, 1936, O. P.; William Wenneman, O. P.'s secretary; and Herbert Fitzpatrick, vice president and general counsel of the C&O, boarded the Van Sweringens' private car on the Erie Railroad train, bound for a meeting in New York the next day. The train was in the yard at Scranton at four in the morning. As a switch engine was in the process of cutting a dining car out of the train, there was a collision. Although the car in which O. P. was traveling was not bumped directly, the impact was sufficient to break the sill, a heavy steel beam running the length of the car and causing O. P.'s heart to race madly. He assured everyone that he was unhurt, and he and his companions were moved to another car.

Following breakfast, O. P. complained about not feeling well and returned to his compartment to rest. At about 11:40 a.m., Wenneman went to awaken him and found him unconscious. A doctor was summoned, and a few minutes after noon on Monday, November 23, 1936, Oris Paxton Van Sweringen was pronounced dead at the age of fifty-seven. The official cause of death was coronary thrombosis.

Among the tributes over the following days—of admirers and detractors alike—were these:

> Opinions may differ in their estimate of Mr. Van Sweringen's work, but certainly in the railroad world, he was a leader of vision and force. We came to have great respect for his energy, character, and high purpose. —Thomas W. Lamont, J. P. Morgan & Co.

> An extraordinary episode. The Van Sweringen personality contrasted absolutely with that of the traditional "company promoter" . . . their holding-company device had been pushed to the limit, even before the depression was in sight. —*New York Times*

They made their mark in the railroad field. They had the sagacity to pick able railroad operators and give them a free hand. They left their railroads better agencies of service than they found them. —*Wall Street Journal*

It is my opinion that time will vindicate his judgment.
—William J. Hanrahan

The death of O. P. Van Sweringen is so great a tragedy that we shall not know how great it is for some time to come. This can be said of few men in the world today. —*Cleveland News*

Cleveland will remember the Van Sweringens as modest gentlemen whose retiring disposition and interminable industry set them apart from other men, who won great renown from small beginnings and died long before their work was finished.
—*Plain Dealer*

His real stature will be fully realized in the years to come. Everyone privileged to know him admired him for his great talent.
—George A. Ball, Ball Brothers Company

On Wednesday, November 25, 1936, with more than six hundred in attendance, a service was held in the Ship Room at Roundwood Manor. Reverend Charles H. Myers, founding pastor of Plymouth Church of Shaker Heights, officiated, as he had at the time of M. J.'s death less than one year earlier. He described O. P. as follows:

> He was a builder. He wanted everything that he touched to be finer and nobler and more splendid. The life of this great city, therefore, moved with a quickened tempo because of him. Upon the monument of Sir Christopher Wren, it is inscribed, "If you seek a monument. look about you."
>
> So, we say, as our eyes survey this beautiful suburb, the great structures of the Terminal area, and the vast railroad enterprise—"If you seek a monument, look about you." Yet O. P. Van Sweringen was in his personal life a very humble man. He loathed ostentatious and unseeming display. He was simple, almost austere, in his habits. He possessed humility, which is always a concomitant of greatness. He made mistakes and often failed. But it must be said that big mistakes were those of high courage rather than timidity. For such men, the realization of hope never comes, for one hope succeeds another and one aspiration grows out of another.

That same day, at a joint meeting, the Cleveland Advertising Club and the Rotary Club of Cleveland adopted a memorial to Mr. Van Sweringen that said the following:

> One could go on indefinitely recounting the practical and material benefits to which we citizens of Cleveland have fallen heir. But these men bequeathed us more than winding boulevards, new skylines, and great transportation systems. They were men of character, and their personal lives and business ethics are something for us to emulate.
>
> In this publicity-seeking age, their simple lives remind us that modesty is still a virtue—that good personal habits and clean living are still admired—that industry and honesty still remain the royal road to success, and their rise from humble beginnings shows our young people that opportunity for the individual is still alive in America.

O. P. was buried in the Van Sweringen family plot in Lake View Cemetery next to M. J., beneath a single stone with the simple epitaph "Brothers."

NOTES

1. Blosser, 203–204.
2. Ibid., 238.
3. Ibid., 239.
4. *Plain Dealer,* August 4, 1936, 1, 2.

Van Sweringen family plot, Lake View Cemetery—family marker.

Van Sweringen family plot, Lake View Cemetery—the brothers.

Van Sweringen family plot, Lake View Cemetery—the Van Sweringen family

Van Sweringen

Orin Paxton	Mantis James
1879-1936	1881-1935

Brothers

James Tower	Jennie Curtis	Carrie Blanch	Edith Elizabeth	Herbert Curtis	Mabel Adams
1832-1903	1844-1886	1872-1940	1874-1945	1869-1942	1869-1947

SEVEN

AFTER THE VAN SWERINGENS

THE BROTHERS' ESTATE

Following the death of his brother, O. P. had put his own insurance policies in a trust administered by three friends, John Murphy, Joseph Anzalone, and John Fackler, with instructions that the proceeds were to go to his sisters, Carrie and Edith; his brother, Herbert; and Benjamin and Daisy Jenks. He further instructed that if none of the five survived him, the principal would be payable to the Jenkses' son, David, or David's heirs.

The brothers' personal real estate in Shaker Heights included the mansion and gatehouse on twelve acres of land and their brother's former home at 2931 Sedgewick Road. In Hunting Valley, they owned the 660-acre Daisy Hill Farm, which included the fifty-four-room, ninety-thousand-square-foot Roundwood Manor and garages, as well as a gatehouse and the cluster of buildings known as the Farm Group. All of the property was seized by the Union Trust Company.

The contents of the Van Sweringens' Roundwood Manor were auctioned by Hiram Parke, president of New York's prestigious Parke-Bernet Galleries. The 225-page catalog listed some 1,250 "important pieces" of "period furniture, early American and Oriental rugs, world-famous silver and rare old china, glass, and figurines," including the chair used by Charles Dickens when he was the editor of the *London Daily News*; an oak stool from Dickens's home, Gad's Hill; and an eighty-four-legged banquet table to seat forty guests. The collection was expected to bring $1 million during the three-day auction—October 25–27, 1938. The auction was preceded by a three-day preview exhibition. On October 29, the *Plain Dealer* reported that the auction had brought in only $89,282.

With the death of the brothers, control of their empire passed to George A. Ball of Muncie, Indiana, and George A. Tomlinson of Cleveland. It was they who had come to the brothers' rescue and funded the successful bids that allowed the brothers to retrieve their empire in September 1935. Following M. J.'s death, Tomlinson had taken the younger brother's place at the foot of the conference table for the daily luncheon meetings with key members of the Van Sweringen staff. Attorney Herbert Fitzpatrick, general counsel of the C&O, was elected to serve as president of Midamerica Corporation. John Patrick Murphy, who had come to Cleveland in 1920 to serve as the brothers' lawyer and who represented them in their real estate development and the creation of their railroad empire, was named executor of the Van Swering estate.

The End of an Era

Although Ball was approaching seventy-four years of age, he had committed to helping the brothers in any way he could in the background. He had no interest in the day-to-day operations of the Van Sweringen empire. On April 26, 1937, Ball sold his interest in the Midamerica Corporation to Robert R. Young and Frank F. Kolbe—New York Stock Exchange brokers—and Allan R. Kirby, of Wilkes-Barre, Pennsylvania, heir to the F. W. Woolworth retail store fortune. The sale price was $6.375 million, $4 million of which went to the George and Frances Ball Foundation to fund education and youth, civic enhancement, arts and culture, and nature and historic preservation. Herbert Fitzpatrick remained the operating head of Midamerica.

During his tenure as majority owner of the Van Sweringen empire, Ball had begun to streamline the corporate structure, moving Alleghany Corporation to the position of control that Vaness had held before the creation of Midamerica Corporation. In May 1937, Charles L. Bradley was elected president of Alleghany Corporation, and Robert Young was elected to the newly created position of chair of the board. In addition, later that month, Young was elected chair of the board of the C&O. Also in May, Tomlinson was reelected to the position of chair of the board of the Missouri Pacific and chair of the International-Great Northern Railroad Company. Young then began to show signs of his intention to elevate the Chesapeake Corporation to replace Alleghany Corporation at the top of the organizational chart.

If Young thought he was going to experience better treatment at the hands of the Senate committees and the ICC than had been accorded the Van Sweringens, he was badly misinformed. Young pointed to this restructuring in meetings with the Senate Interstate Commerce Committee and the Senate Railway Finance Committee, saying that he intended to eliminate all the holding companies. He did not want to be associated in any way with the Van Sweringens. Senate committee investigators argued that his reorganization plans would be detrimental to the C&O, stripping it of needed assets. They reminded him that the management team was largely a holdover from the Van Sweringen organization and that his personal investment of $255,000 in the $3 billion corporate empire was nothing more than business as usual. New York Stock Exchange experts testified that the new holding company, Chesapeake Corporation, would have no present assets and could not, therefore, be listed on the stock exchange.

Young's testimony occurred before the Senate Railway Finance Committee had completed its eight-month investigation. Young expressed that he would welcome the regulation of holding companies and that he was looking forward to working with the ICC to make that happen. On August 11, 1937, the Federal District Court in Baltimore issued a temporary injunction against the merger of the Alleghany and Chesapeake holding companies. August 13 was the date for a further hearing to decide whether the injunction should be made permanent. On August 12, the ICC ordered an investigation into the finances of the empire.

Although the matter of the merger of the two holding companies remained unsettled, an examiner for the ICC did recommend the approval of the consolidation of the Nickel Plate and Erie Railroads into the C&O. The ICC gave its final approval of the consolidation plan in mid-December. The consolidation gave the C&O direct control of the two railroads, over which it had formerly had indirect control through holding companies. Thus, the consolidation plan initiated by the Van Sweringens years earlier became a reality.

In November, Frank Kolbe, citing the sharp drop in the value of the shares, sold his investment in the syndicate, leaving Young and Kirby in control. Anita O'Keefe Young—wife of Robert Young and sister of famed artist Georgia O'Keefe—acquired Kolbe's shares. In a turn of events, George Tomlinson, who had resigned following the acquisition by Young, Kolbe, and Kirby, was elected president of Alleghany Corporation in early January 1938. George Brooke, recently elected president of the C&O, was elected president of the Nickel Plate and the Pere Marquette as well.

It was becoming clear that Young was anxious to dissolve the Chesapeake Corporation, and on March 14, Charles Bradley announced a special meeting of the stockholders to be held on April 4. On March 17, the *Plain Dealer* published a front-page article under the headline, "Open C. & O. War on Young, Kirby," saying, "An apparent attempt to wrest from Robert R. Young and Allen P. Kirby control of the Chesapeake Corp. and, incidentally, the Chesapeake & Ohio Railway came to light yesterday, New York dispatches state, in the issuance to the New York Stock Exchange by John P. Murphy, secretary, of a call of a special meeting of stockholders April 4 to make changes in the directorate of Chesapeake Corp." The plan was to elect Kolbe's successor, increase the number of directors to seven, and remove any or all of the (then) present board.

To break the deadlock on the Chesapeake board created by Kolbe's resignation, which pitted Charles Bradley and John Murphy against Robert Young and Allan Kirby, Young signaled his interest in the election of Harris Creech, president of the Cleveland Trust Company, to fill the vacant seat. Creech had previously been invited to assume the seat vacated by the death of Frank H. Ginn but had declined at that time. Filling the seat would give one side or the other control over the election of seven of the nine directors at the annual meeting on April 19. There remained the question of the right of the Guaranty Trust Company of New York to vote proxies at the annual meeting. On April 1, federal judge Albert C. Coxe announced that he would reserve his decision to issue a preliminary injunction against the Guaranty's right to vote the Chesapeake stock that it was holding as trustee until April 4. The special meeting that had been scheduled for that day was then rescheduled for Friday, April 8. The ruling on Monday was that the Guaranty could vote the shares in trust. Young appealed to the US Circuit Court of Appeals in New York, and the decision of the lower court was overturned, blocking the bank. With further appeals pending, on April 15, the *Plain Dealer* reported that a truce had been reached between the warring factions and that both the special meeting and the annual stockholders' meeting had been postponed—the special meeting until April 16 and the annual meeting until May 4. Under the terms of the stipulation, neither Alleghany nor the Guaranty was permitted to vote their shares of Chesapeake stock. In the meantime, the Guaranty continued peace talks with Young, who could best have been described as uncooperative. Finally, a compromise was reached, to take effect following the adjournment of the often-rescheduled meeting on May 19. Young maintained his control of the C&O; the board was increased to nine members; and the Guaranty was given one seat that it filled with Earle Bailie, a Wall Street investment banker.

On June 10, 1938, the US Circuit Court of Appeals for the Second District of New York handed down its ruling, a unanimous decision denying a temporary injunction against the Guaranty Trust Company that would have prevented the bank from voting Chesapeake Corporation shares that it held as trustee for Alleghany Corporation. The *Plain Dealer* reported that under the ruling, if it chose, the bank could enlarge the board of the Chesapeake Corporation to the point that Young's control exercised through Alleghany could be nullified.

On June 16, the new board delayed Young's plan to dissolve the Chesapeake Corporation for thirty days and removed him from his position as the board's chair. Bradley, Murphy, Bailie, and John B. Hollister were designated to prepare a plan for the liquidation and dissolution of the holding company, to be submitted to the full board in thirty days.

In the meantime, a committee consisting of Joseph Nutt, Robert Young, Herbert Fitzpatrick, and George Brooke was assembled to develop a plan for managing the 6 percent Nickel Plate notes due to expire on October 1. The notes, originally valued at $25 million, had been due to mature in 1932 but were extended to 1938 and their value reduced to $15 million. Failing the development of an acceptable plan, the alternative would have been reorganization under bankruptcy protection. The committee, developing a plan for the dissolution of the Chesapeake Corporation, continued its work, but legal complications, including tax implications, were delaying its completion. Late in August 1938, Young was named to the dissolution committee, and a special committee of two, consisting of Young and Bailie, was formed to arrange for the sale of the Chesapeake's holdings, including nearly 60,500 shares of Chesapeake Ohio Railway preferred stock.

The Van Sweringen Company, now a part of the Terminal & Shaker Heights Realty Company, had reduced its obligations by $2 million through the transfer of undeveloped farmland back to the original owners, or by sale to new owners. Directors of the new organization included Harry B. Howells, an attorney representing the Cleveland Trust Company; James C. Logue, an attorney for a group of bondholders; Robert Young; J. J. Anzalone, treasurer of the Van Sweringen Company; and Frederick A. Henry, former circuit judge, as an impartial outsider. It was agreed that once the company's indebtedness was reduced, new directors would be chosen by the vote of the common stockholders to replace the appointees.

On November 28, following the stockholder's overwhelming approval of the dissolution plan, the Chesapeake Corporation approved the committee's plan to dissolve the holding company, handing Young a defeat. He was the one who had initiated the discussion of the elimination of the middle holding company but had changed his mind at the last moment, fearing that the liquidation would be detrimental to Alleghany's bonds. The next day, Young resigned as a director of Chesapeake Corporation. He vowed to continue his war with the banks, blaming the Guaranty for the defeat he had suffered, even though the result was consistent with where he had stood on the dissolution of the holding company all along.

In February 1939, John C. Myers, president of the Ashland-based pump manufacturer, resigned from the C&O board amid denial from Young that it signaled an escalation of the war between Young and the Guaranty over control of the $750 million C&O. Young was fast becoming known for his Wall Street battles, and battles raged within his organization as well. On February 21, directors of the C&O increased the board from ten to twelve directors, disregarding names proposed by Young. Added to the board were Homer L. Ferguson, president of the Newport News Shipbuilding & Drydock Company, and Ralph C. Gifford, president of the First National Bank of Louisville.

On April 14, the Guaranty resigned as trustee of two Alleghany Corporation bond issues. In response, Young demanded the resignations of Bradley, Murphy, Bailie, Dickinson, and Hollister as directors and trustees of the Chesapeake Corporation, and Bailie, Hollister, and Dickinson as directors of the C&O Railway. The friction between Young and the C&O board continued to play itself out on April 18, when the board, although keeping him on as a director, removed him from the executive and finance committees. On May 16, directors of the Nickel Plate Road elected its president George Brooke to the additional position of chair of the board, replacing Young and removing him from the executive committee as well. George Ball regained control of Alleghany Corporation, representing the interests of the George and Frances Ball Foundation when Young and Kirby defaulted on their obligation. George Tomlinson, the president of Alleghany Corporation, resigned, and the board named Allan Kirby, Young's partner in the 1937 purchase of the Allegheny, to the position of president.

On January 14, 1940, Herbert Fitzpatrick announced his retirement as chair of the board and vice president–law of the C&O, effective April 15. He had been a close associate of the Van Sweringen brothers, and his announcement set off speculation that the internal conflict was far from over. The announcement by Young on January 17 that Fitzpatrick had been pushed out as punishment for what Young called "loyalty to the C. & O. stockholders' interests against the selfish interests of a banking clique" suggested that speculation was correct.

Young and Kirby, who had been at odds with George Ball, charging breach of trust, filed a suit against Bradley and Murphy in the US District Court on May 28, 1940, to gain ownership of the Higbee Company.

Also named in the suit were George A. Ball and the George and Frances Ball Foundation. In the suit, Young and Kirby claimed that when they acquired the Alleghany Corporation from Ball, they also bid on the Higbee Company, "substantially in excess of $600,000, but Ball refused to accept their offer." Young and Kirby claimed that Ball urged them to "retain Bradley and Murphy in positions of responsibility and authority," saying that "Bradley and Murphy would be loyal and devote their efforts to the protection and enhancement of the interests." Young and Kirby went on to claim that "Bradley, Murphy, Ball, and Foundation . . . wrongfully and fraudulently entered into a conspiracy to deprive [Young and Kirby] of control of said corporation and others." They also charged that "in consideration of the collaboration by Bradley and Murphy with Ball in his efforts to obstruct [Young and Kirby] and prevent them from exercising their right to control said Alleghany Corp. and its subsidiaries and affiliated companies . . . on June 4, 1937, through his control of Foundation caused said Foundation to sell to Bradley and Murphy the aforesaid Higbee securities for a total purchase price of $600,000, upon terms and conditions which were very favorable to Bradley and Murphy."

In early March 1942, in partial settlement of the $8 million suit against him, Ball transferred the Higbee's securities to Young and Kirby. Ball had held the securities as collateral for a note made in 1937 by John Murphy, president of Higbee Company. Two remaining suits brought by Young and Kirby were dismissed, and the securities were advertised for sale on March 13. In return, Young transferred a key block of Alleghany shares to Ball. In preparation for the C&O's April 1942 annual meeting, the majority of the company's board stood with Young to replace all the directors whom Young had seen as loyal to the Guaranty Bank or George Ball, giving Young solid control of the railroad. Further, on March 9, Young made it clear that "anyone joining or assisting" Bradley and Murphy's efforts to retain control of the Higbee Company would be held "strictly accountable." The following day Murphy and Bradley obtained a temporary injunction preventing the Terminal & Shaker Heights Realty Company from selling Higbee's securities. Murphy and Bradley contended that they had paid $60,000 to the George and Frances Ball Foundation in 1937, that the remaining $540,000 was not due and payable until the completion of the Higbee reorganization, and that they were ready to pay the balance but that the reorganization was blocked by a suit filed by two preferred stockholders. On March 12, Judge A. G. Newcomb, of the Court of Common Pleas, ruled that the restraining order would remain in effect until further notice. Finally, on June 5, 1942, it was announced that Bradley and Murphy had paid Terminal & Shaker Heights Realty Company $566,290 in principal and interest to maintain control of the department store, thus dismissing the injunction. Judge Paul Jones of the Northern Ohio District Court found in favor of Murphy and Bradley. His decision was upheld by the Sixth US Court of Appeals and by the US Supreme Court on November 13, 1944, just months after Charles Bradley's death.

As the economy continued to improve, Alleghany continued to retire bonds. Since March 1938, three bond issues had been purchased for retirement in the principal amount of more than $5.1 million. The net income of the C&O reached an all-time high of nearly $45 million for the year ended December 31, 1941. For the same year, the net income of the Nickel Plate reached an all-time high of more than $12.5 million.

On December 29, 1942, the final liquidation of Chesapeake Corporation was completed. The Van Sweringen brothers had created the Chesapeake Corporation as a holding company in May 1927 to sell $48 million in bonds. Chesapeake had become the holding company for securities of the C&O, the Pere Marquette, and numerous other subsidiaries including the Greenbriar Resort in White Sulphur Springs, West Virginia. In advance of the April 1943 C&O annual meeting, Young announced that Cleveland industrialist Cyrus S. Eaton would be nominated to the company's board of directors.

The reorganization of the Missouri Pacific Railroad had ground on in the federal court in St. Louis for ten years. Young, representing the Alleghany Corporation's substantial interest, and John Stedman, representing the senior bondholders, had developed what they thought would be a satisfactory compromise to stay within the $560 million capitalization limit the ICC had established. Under the plan, stockholders that had been eliminated by the ICC plan would receive warrants for the purchase of new stock. The railroad's board chair J. S. Pyeatt deemed the compromise "far from fair."

Reminiscent of a decade earlier, the Nickel Plate applied to the ICC for approval to purchase sixty thousand shares of the Wheeling & Lake Erie Railway Company. The railroad, the object of contention between the late Frank Taplin and the Van Sweringen brothers, had paid dividends on its common stock in 1937—the first time in sixty-five years—and had continued regular dividend payments since. If approved by the ICC, the combined holdings of the Wheeling by the C&O and the Nickel Plate would approach 65 percent, up from the then-current 53 percent. In late September, the ICC denied the Nickel Plate permission to acquire the sixty thousand shares of Wheeling common stock, saying the opposition came on behalf of the Nickel Plate's shareholders because the railroad was in arrears on its 6 percent dividend. In response, Young indicated that C&O might purchase the stock.

In September 1943, the debate on competitive bidding on railroad financing—of which Alleghany's chair, Robert Young, was a leading proponent—took center stage on the floor of the ICC. Briefs were being prepared by the Investment Bankers Association, the National Association Security Dealers, the Savings Bank Association, life insurance companies, the C&O Railway, the Railway Executives Association, Otis & Company, and Halsey, Stuart & Company.

Competitive bidding was at the root of Young's war with J. P. Morgan and the Guaranty and a great deal of the cause for the split and ensuing battles between factions of the directors of the various corporations that made up the Alleghany empire. Young was a financial progressive at a time when most senior corporate executives, certainly in the railroad industry, were financially conservative. Discussion of competitive bidding had begun shortly after the Transportation Act of 1920 and gave the ICC authority over the issuance and sale of railroad securities. It was not until 1922, however, that the ICC had begun to hold hearings on the subject.

In 1926, the ICC announced a new policy for competitive bidding in the financing of railroad cars and locomotives. This was a departure from the status quo whereby banking houses like J. P. Morgan and Kuhn, Loeb & Company, the traditional bankers for the railroad industry, backed the railroad's notes at a stipulated price. Backed by the Van Sweringen brothers' nemesis, Joseph B. Eastman, the ICC set out to end the relationship between the railroad and its bankers that was compared to that of the family physician and his patient. In the New Haven test case, the railroad and the bankers agreed to let the ICC determine the fair minimum price. The result of competitive bidding was a significant reduction of bankers' commissions on equipment trust certificates but a less striking reduction on bonds.[1]

Beginning in 1922, the Van Sweringen brothers had developed their plan for the "New" Nickel Plate, only to be rejected by the ICC. The question of the consolidation of the C&O and its subsidiaries—the Nickel Plate, the Pere Marquette, and the Wheeling & Lake Erie—was once again on the table. The new plan, submitted to the ICC on October 16, 1943, called for $100 par preferred shares with 3.75 percent annual interest to be paid quarterly. The new shares were to be distributed on December 1, 1943, to common shareholders of record on November 1 and redeemable at $105 plus accrued interest. The plan further specified annual payment into a sinking fund beginning March 1, 1944, equal to 5 percent of the prior calendar year's net profit for preferred shares and 3 percent for common shares. The sinking fund was to be used to retire preferred shares. The greatest benefit would be to the Alleghany Corporation, holder of nearly 1.85 million shares of C&O common stock.

The shares of the Wheeling & Lake Erie previously purchased by the Van Sweringens and owned by the Nickel Plate and C&O Railroads had been ordered to be placed in a trust, prohibiting the shares from being voted. F. E. Williamson, president of the New York Central, indicated in a letter to the ICC that the Central opposed any consolidation of the C&O and its subsidiaries but would not object to the proposed purchase of Wheeling & Lake Erie stock. On November 17, the ICC approved the purchase of more than seventy-four thousand shares of Wheeling & Lake Erie. The next step was an appeal to the ICC to terminate the trusteeship.

Another case involving the former Van Sweringen empire was the question of Alleghany's compliance with Congress's 1940 ruling making it unlawful for a holding company to acquire control of a railroad without ICC approval. The ICC initiated an investigation to determine when Alleghany acquired control of the C&O. Young asserted that Alleghany had acquired the C&O in 1937 when he and Kirby purchased the holdings of the George and Frances Ball Foundation. George Leisure, attorney for Alleghany, asserted that the railroad had been acquired by the Van Sweringens in 1929. J. J. Doran, attorney for the ICC, contended that the acquisition was not until 1942.

On December 4, 1945, the Nickel Plate board declared a dividend of $3.00 a share on 6 percent preferred stock. This was the first dividend paid to Nickel Plate stockholders in more than fourteen years. The board also authorized the purchase of Wheeling & Lake Erie common stock at $70 per share, obtaining a one-year option on 115,369 common shares and 1,638 preferred shares, totaling nearly $19 million. The Pere Marquette board approved the C&O's offer to merge or consolidate and declared a $1.25 per share dividend on its preferred stock. Merger negotiations between the C&O and the Nickel Plate had terminated in October when it was clear that the latter's shareholders would not approve such an action. On February 19, 1946, directors of the C&O and Pere Marquette Railroads signed an agreement of merger, approving the terms and conditions of the merger pending a vote of C&O shareholders on April 23 and of Pere Marquette shareholders on May 7.

On January 12, 1947, the *Plain Dealer*'s business section featured the news that Robert R. Young, chair of the Alleghany Corporation board, had announced that the company had purchased 162,500 shares of stock in the New York Central. The Central, second in passenger business, mileage, operating revenues, and investment, was described as a sleeping giant compared to the C&O, the Nickel Plate, and the Pere Marquette. The announcement raised suspicion that Young might be planning to unload the Nickel Plate, whose directors had been strenuous in their objection to Young's terms to merge the Nickel Plate into the C&O.

Although the purchase of Central stock only represented 2.5 percent of the company's stock, it was a larger block than that held by any of the board's directors. By January 28, the C&O held 250,400 shares of New York Central stock—162,500 shares that it acquired from Alleghany and the remainder that it had purchased in the open market. The shares had been deposited in a voting trust with Chase National Bank of New York.

Aggressive buying of Central stock by the C&O continued, and on February 12, it was learned that the total had increased to 315,400 shares of common stock or about 4.9 percent. On March 18, subject to approval by the ICC, the Central's chair, Gustav Metzman; Harold S. Vanderbilt, Cornelius Vanderbilt's great-grandson; Robert R. Young, chair of the Alleghany Corporation and the C&O; and Robert J. Bowman, president of the C&O, were invited to seats on the New York Central Board. On March 21, Robert W. Purcell, vice president of the C&O, confirmed the report that the railroad had increased its ownership to four hundred thousand shares of New York Central common stock, for control of 6.2 percent. One week later, Purcell confirmed the speculation that the goal was the merger of the two railroads. He announced that the C&O would apply to the ICC to free the C&O's four hundred thousand shares of

Central stock from Chase National Bank, where it was held in a voting trust. The aggregate cost of the shares exceeded $7.5 million.

But first, on April 1, the ICC approved the merger of the C&O and the Pere Marquette, creating a five-thousand-mile system. Under the terms of the merger, holders of Pere Marquette preferred stock could exchange each share for eight-tenths of a share of 3.5 percent C&O preferred stock and four-tenths of a share of common stock, and holders of Pere Marquette common stock could exchange each share for one-half of a share of C&O common stock.

The same day, and presumably unrelated to the C&O's buying campaign, the New York Central System announced plans to build a $12–$15 million addition to the Terminal group of buildings in Cleveland. The eighteen-story office building would be built on the south side of Prospect Avenue, between West 2nd and West 3rd Streets, on a foundation that had been laid in 1928 to facilitate the future construction of another building. In the meantime, the site was being used as a parking lot.

The ICC's hearings on seats for Robert Young and Robert Bowman on the New York Central Board of Directors had concluded in September. Young had been straightforward in discussing his plans for the ultimate merger of the C&O and New York Central System. The Central, although a carrier of a significant tonnage of industrial goods, was one of the leading passenger lines in the nation. Young saw the merger as a good means of diversifying the C&O, which was largely a coal hauler. The forward-thinking Young had begun modernizing his passenger service with a major investment in new engines and cars, and he saw the Central as needing such modernization as well.

On December 10, 1947, C. E. Boles, an examiner for the ICC, recommended in no uncertain terms that the applications for approval of Young and Bowman as directors of both railroads be rejected. Boles was in doubt that the addition of the two to the Central's board would result in any benefits, financial or otherwise, to the Central. He saw the C&O's proposal as a violation of the Interstate Commerce Act and perhaps of the Clayton Antitrust Act as well. He went further, saying that Young and Bowman had demonstrated their willingness to take extreme risks with corporate funds speculating that they could take seats on the Central's board despite all ICC precedents and do a better job than the present management of the New York Central System. Boles's recommendations concluded by saying that the funds with which Young had acquired four hundred thousand shares of Central stock had come from the sale of the C&O's holdings in the Wheeling & Lake Erie. He described the Wheeling & Lake Erie as a high-grade investment with a recent history of regular dividends. The Central shares for which Young had paid more than $7.5 million now were valued at just over $5 million. He characterized Young's actions, including the willingness to dispose of the Nickel Plate, as driven by personal ambition and not by public interest. In early January 1948, the C&O responded to Boles's recommendation, saying that his report was "inaccurate and based on erroneous finding," and the tenor of the report "makes it clear that the examiner is against the petition and the petitioners." In April, Young said that he would request a congressional investigation if the C&O was denied the board seats.

In early January 1948, Gustav Metzman, president of the New York Central System, had announced that the railroad expected delivery of the first of its $60 million order for 720 streamlined passenger cars and that the order was expected to be completed by that October.

After a year of silence on the subject, speculation arose that Young was very much interested in gaining control of the New York Central. On April 29, 1949, *The Sun* (New York) suggested that Young was expected to relinquish the chairmanship of the C&O and to renew his pursuit of control of the Central through Alleghany Corporation.

In August 1949, Alleghany Corporation sold the last of its common shares of Nickel Plate stock. Speculation had arisen after Nickel Plate stockholders objected to Young's proposal to merge the Nickel Plate into the C&O, that the railroad might no longer have a place in the Alleghany portfolio of railroads. Alleghany had, however, increased its position in Nickel Plate preferred shares.

It had been three years since the C&O had acquired four hundred thousand shares of Central stock, and Young and Robert Bowman were invited to seats on the New York Central board, only to be rejected by the ICC. Young had announced plans for a series of conferences to renew his effort to acquire control of the New York Central System. On November 28, 1949, an article in the *Plain Dealer* reported Young's intention to "resign as chairman of the Chesapeake & Ohio Railroad and take active control of the New York Central System." Young had said that he intended to "install himself as chairman of the board of the New York Central and Allan Kirby, president of the Alleghany Corporation, which controls the C. & O., as the Central's president." He then tempered his intent through a statement released by Thomas J. Deegan, his public relations adviser, saying, "Mr. Young does not contemplate resigning as chairman of the board of the C. & O. He has frequently stated that this would be one of the courses he could follow if he were interested in accepting the invitation of the board of the New York Central to serve on that board." Two days later, testifying before the ICC in a hearing on the reorganization of the Missouri Pacific Railroad, Young described the Mo-Pac as having "a brilliant future, particularly if the hands of the New York Group can be taken off of it." Presumably, Young was referring to the large insurance companies that held a significant position in Mo-Pac bonds.

The C&O continued to increase its holdings in the New York Central System, and in 1953, the company announced that it owned eight hundred thousand shares of the railroad, approximately 12.5 percent of the outstanding shares. Combining the Central with the Missouri Pacific would nearly achieve his dream of coast-to-coast rail service.

The banner headline on the front page of the *Plain Dealer* on January 20, 1954, announced, "C. & O. Control Gained by Eaton." The front-page article headlined "Young Sells Stock to Clear the Track to Move In At N. Y. C." began as follows: "Cyrus S. Eaton, 70-year-old Cleveland industrialist, late yesterday added another peak to an already fabulous career in business and finance as he acquired working control of the Chesapeake & Ohio Railway and became its chairman. He now holds C. & O. common shares worth about $9,000,000."

Eaton, who had joined the C&O board in 1943, was best known in Cleveland for the consolidation of three steel companies in 1927—Bourne-Fuller Company, Central Alloy Steel Company, and Republic Iron and Steel—creating the Republic Steel Corporation, the third-largest steel producer in the United States behind US Steel and Bethlehem Steel. Like the Van Sweringen brothers, Eaton had amassed a substantial fortune that he lost in the Depression. Unlike the Van Sweringen brothers, Eaton lived to rebuild his fortune during the 1940s and 1950s and would live to the age of ninety-five. In his later years, Eaton turned his interest to world peace, transforming his boyhood home in Pugwash, Nova Scotia, into a "Thinker's Lodge" and funding and hosting the first Pugwash Conference of Nuclear Scientists in July 1957.[2]

To remove any objections that the ICC might have to Young's move to the New York Central System, all directors and officers of Alleghany Corporation sold their shares of the C&O. Likewise, all directors and officers of the C&O sold their holdings in Alleghany. In addition, all contracts, leases, and joint salary agreements between the two companies were eliminated. Officials of the New York Central System had no comment other than to say that there were no vacancies on their board of directors. On January 25, 1954, William White, president of the New York Central System, acknowledged Young's and Kirby's desire to become board members, indicating that the request would be taken up by the board at their next meeting on February 10. The headline of the *Plain Dealer* on Thursday, February 11, was clear—"N. Y. C. Rejects Young for Board," to which Young immediately threatened a proxy fight for control of the railroad.

Pointing to the Pere Marquette and Nickel Plate Railroads, Young told the Central's nearly forty-five thousand shareholders that the Central, which had paid a dividend of $1.00 per share in 1953, would be paying annual dividends in the $7–$10 range "if it had had the right kind of management." He prepared an alternate slate of directors for an "anti-Morgan, pro-New York Central" board. In mid-February, the Securities & Exchange Commission ordered an investigation into the trading of Central shares. The C&O had sold its eight hundred thousand shares of Central stock to Clinton W. Murchison of Dallas and Sid W. Richardson of Fort Worth, both friends of Young. The transactions net the C&O $2.4 million. While the shares were owned by the C&O, they were held in a voting trust, but once they were sold by the railroad, they were eligible to be voted. Young, Kirby, and Alleghany Corporation combined to hold 200,200 shares of Central stock. On March 3 the ICC was asked by the Central to investigate the roles of Cyrus Eaton, Clint Murchison, and Sid Richardson. The next day, Young filed a suit against all fifteen of the directors of the Central, asking that they be enjoined from spending railroad money and return any money already spent in the proxy fight to retain their seats on the board.

On April 7, the ICC turned down the Central's petition to investigate Robert Young. The Central set April 19 as the date of record of ownership for eligibility of shares to be voted. Of the nearly 6.5 million shares of outstanding common stock, the slate of directors proposed by Young—which included the first woman to be nominated to the board of a major railroad—owned nearly 1.1 million shares. Of those shares, just over one million were owned by Murchison, Richardson, Young, and Alleghany Corporation. An additional 30,000 shares were owned by companies that were controlled by a board nominee. Those shares combined to represent 17.4 percent. The slate representing current management combined to own a little more than 106,000 shares, or 1.6 percent. Three days before the April 19 date of record, the ownership of 800,000 shares had not yet been transferred to Murchison and Richardson, who filed a suit against the New York Central System in the New York State Supreme Court to compel the Central to complete the transfer of ownership of the shares they had purchased from the C&O.

The pace of charges and countercharges escalated between the two sides. On April 28, Harold S. Vanderbilt sought an injunction against the voting of the 800,000 shares owned by the two Texas millionaires, calling the "purported sale a sham and a device." The ICC scheduled a hearing on the Central's petition for May 14, just twelve days before the Central's annual meeting was scheduled to take place. The *Plain Dealer* reported that on May 25, the appellate division of the New York State Supreme Court had returned no decision on either the New York Central's petition blocking the two holders of the 800,000 shares of Central stock purchased from the C&O or the request that if the decision was delayed, the court order a postponement in the New York Central's annual meeting. Neither occurred, paving the way for the annual meeting to be held as scheduled and for Murchison and Richardson to vote their shares.

In anticipation of a victory, Young addressed attendees at the annual meeting, saying that because of the harsh treatment at the hands of Cleveland newspapers during the proxy battle, the headquarters of the New York Central System would remain in New York and not be relocated to Cleveland. As the vote counting droned on, it was becoming increasingly clear that any runaway victory for Young was unlikely, giving rise to the possibility of challenges and recounts dragging the process out even longer. On June 2, vote counters counted the 800,000 disputed shares, making a Young victory almost certain. However, William White made it known that a legal battle would ensue.

On June 12, the *Plain Dealer* announced that "Young Wins N. Y. C. Control by Over A Million Shares." The question of the 800,000 former C&O shares had become moot. The announcement of the results would be made official in Albany on June 15, and Robert Young would take his seat at the head of the table and seat his board of fourteen men and one woman. Thus would end the eighty-five-year control of the New York Central by J. P. Morgan and the Vanderbilt family. Young would nominate Alfred E. Perlman, the fifty-one-year-old executive vice president of the Denver & Rio Grande Western Railroad, to be the Central's new president. Young still held control of the Alleghany Corporation, and with it, the Missouri Pacific Railway. Finally, after twenty years of bankruptcy reorganization, the ICC would declare the Mo-Pac to have value.

The battle that had begun with the resignation of Robert Ralph Young as chair of the board of directors of the C&O on January 19, 1954, ended on June 15 when the directors of the New York Central System elected him chair of their board. The war had begun when Young and Frank Kolbe acquired the Van Sweringens' Midamerica Corporation from George Ball on April 26, 1937. What they had bought was the bankrupt skeleton of the largest privately owned railroad in the nation that the Van Sweringen brothers had only just begun to reorganize when first M. J. and then, in less than a year, O. P. had died. What was left after the C&O was removed from the control of the Allegany Corporation by the acquisition of the C&O by Canadian American investment banker, businessman, and philanthropist Cyrus Eaton was the Nickel Plate and the Erie Railroads, along with a scattering of other properties. But Young's victory would be short-lived. Having suffered from depression for some fifteen years, Young ended the war by ending his own life on January 25, 1958.

NOTES

1. Barclay J. Sickler, "History and Results of Competitive Bidding for Railroad Equipment Trust Certificates," *Journal of Land & Public Utility Economics* 5, no. 1 (1929): 71–78, https://doi.org/10.2307/3138513.

2. The purpose of the conference was to bring together leading scholars from around the world to discuss ways of reducing armaments and tempering the nuclear arms race.

EIGHT

AFTERWORD

THE BEGINNING OF A NEW ERA

Reminders of the Van Sweringen era and their incredible legacy include their extensive real estate holdings. Their personal real estate included the town estate at 17400 South Park Boulevard and its gatehouse at 17715 Shaker Boulevard and the magnificent country estate of Roundwood Manor at Daisy Hill in Hunting Valley, reminders of their lifestyle at the peak of their careers. Their commercial real estate included Moreland Courts on Shaker Boulevard, Shaker Square, and the Union Terminal complex on Public Square, a towering reminder of the brothers' railroad empire.

The Van Sweringens' debt to the Union Trust Company—largely responsible for the bank's closing—caused the seizing of the brothers' personal real estate and personal property. The town estate, including its twelve acres of land, was appraised at a value of $147,500—a little more than $3 million in 2022 dollars. In preparation for liquidation, the property was divided into salable parcels, reducing the mansion's frontage from 533 feet to 200 feet and its depth from 895 feet to 315 feet. The parcels created on either side of the mansion were acquired by Agnes and William Dunn in 1940. In 1945, Charles A. and Althea J. Fassen purchased the mansion and the 1.35-acre parcel on which it stands for $20,600 at a sheriff's sale. In a matter of months, they sold it to Robert R. and Leah M. Morrow, who made it their home for the next ten years, followed by William H. and Marion H. Spiller for the next seven. The most recent owners include Kevin P. O'Donnell (2000–2006) and Andrew P. and Robin D. Schachat (2006–present).

Later in 1945, the Dunns consolidated the deeds of the various parcels that had been a part of the Van Sweringens' Shaker Heights estate, which they had acquired during the prior five years. Their first purchase, from the Union Trust Company (in liquidation) in May 1940, was a long narrow parcel fronting Shaker Boulevard—now the right-of-way for the driveway leading to the gatehouse. Their second purchase in November 1943 was an interior parcel, also from Union Trust. In April 1944, the Dunns purchased three additional parcels, including the one on which the gatehouse stands, from developer and builder L. M. Gundersen. Finally, in May 1945, the five parcels were consolidated, forming a single 1.7-acre parcel that to this day is the footprint of the gatehouse property. It was not until 1958 that Phillip S. and Miriam B. Britton purchased and became the first occupants of the free-standing gatehouse at 17715 Shaker Boulevard. It is likely that the Brittons transformed two of the

Van Sweringen Mansion—17300 South Park Boulevard, rear elevation.

Van Sweringen Mansion, 17300 South Park Boulevard—living room.

Van Sweringen Mansion, 17300 South Park Boulevard—dining room.

Van Sweringen Mansion, 17300 South Park Boulevard—breakfast room.

The Van Sweringen Gatehouse, 17715 Shaker Boulevard—front elevation.

The Van Sweringen Gatehouse, 17715 Shaker Boulevard—rear elevation.

The Van Sweringen Gatehouse, 17715 Shaker Boulevard—servants' quarters.

The Van Sweringen Gatehouse, 17715 Shaker Boulevard—tunnel.

four garage bays into a spacious kitchen. In 1961, the Brittons sold the gatehouse to James F. Lincoln, chair of the board of the family's Lincoln Electric Company, as a home that he shared with his second wife, Jane D. White. After Lincoln died in 1965, his widow remained in the gatehouse until 1977, when she sold the property to Phillip M. and Alga M. Schloss. Alga remained in the gatehouse following her husband's death in 2000, until her own death in 2020. At that time, the property was purchased by Andrew Wolfort and Anna E. Strohl, who undertook a major renovation and restoration, including the conversion of the two remaining garages to a family room and the addition of a garage with guest quarters on the second floor.

In December 1939, realtor Clewell Sykes, who had been active in the development of Shaker Heights, began to market thirty-eight parcels on eighty acres of land acquired from the Daisy Hill Company, a subsidiary of Union Properties Company. George Burrows, well known for the homes he had designed in Shaker Heights, was already working on designs for seven clients in what Sykes was marketing as Deer Creek Colony. In February 1940, ground was broken on a two-and-one-half-acre parcel for the first home, with seven rooms, in the early American style.

In July 1940, Union Properties Company announced that Daisy Hill Farms would be divided into twenty-seven parcels of eight to twenty-five acres each. The sixty-five acres adjoining Roundwood Manor, comprised of eight parcels, were withheld from the market pending final determination by the probate court. By July 1942, more than half of the Daisy Hill lots had been sold, with homes completed and occupied on a large percentage of them. On New Year's Eve, the Daisy Hill Landowners welcomed 1943 with a gala in Roundwood Manor. Invitations were sent to 150 couples, who danced to the music of Jack Horowitz and his orchestra. The party was so successful that it was repeated to welcome 1944, with 300 couples dancing to the music of Mike Vitale's Orchestra.

On June 18, 1944, the *Plain Dealer* real estate listings included "Daisy Hill—Farm residence of the Van Sweringen brothers." It went on to say, "Plans have been prepared to reduce this fabulous house to a 5-bedroom, 3-bath size, usable by the average family. Included will be the 'Dickens' library and the usual other rooms—all spaciously laid out. A fine tile swimming pool and 7 landscaped, rolling acres will make this one of Cleveland's finest suburban homes in the most protected part of exclusive Hunting Valley Village." Follow-up advertisements indicated that "this beautiful home can be bought for a fraction of its value."

By mid-1946, thirteen families were living on 340 of the 660 acres of Daisy Hill. On July 28, 1946, the *Plain Dealer* announced that Mr. and Mrs. Gordon Stouffer had purchased the Van Sweringen mansion at Daisy Hill and were going to "remodel it on smaller dimensions to fit their own needs." As Philip Small had designed Roundwood Manor for the Van Sweringens, Stouffer hired the firm of Small, Smith, and Reeb as architects for the project. The result was the shortening of the east–west main block by removing the wings at each end, reducing the size of the Ship Room and the guest dining room, shortening the north–south guest wing by half, and reducing the number of guest suites from twenty-four to ten. The overall size was reduced from ninety thousand to fifty-five thousand square feet and the room count from fifty-four to twenty.

Gordon Stouffer was chair of the Stouffer Corporation, founded by his parents in 1922 as a stand-up milk counter in the Arcade on Euclid Avenue. Stouffer and his brother Vernon operated a chain of seven restaurants, including Stouffer's Tavern on Shaker Square. On September 14, 1947, Gordon and Mary Stouffer hosted the first social event at their newly remodeled home, with brunch, swimming, and tennis. Stouffer died on June 7, 1956, at the age of fifty-one. On January 14, 1960, Roundwood was transferred from his estate to his widow, Mary, who put the property on the market.

On September 13, Roundwood Manor was purchased by James A. and Mary R. Bohannon. He had been an engineer and vice president of the Marmon Motor Car Company in Indianapolis before moving to Cleveland in 1929 to assume the presidency of the Peerless Motor Car

Roundwood Manor, 3450 Roundwood Road—front from east.

Roundwood Manor, 3450 Roundwood Road—front from west.

Roundwood Manor, 3450 Roundwood Road—entrance hallway.

Roundwood Manor, 3450 Roundwood Road—ship room.

Company. Peerless closed in 1931, ending the era of luxury automobile manufacturing in Cleveland. Bohannon retained the building, forming the Brewing Corporation of America and brewing Carling ale and beer under license from the Brewing Corporation of Canada beginning in 1933.

When the Bohannons moved from their twenty-five-room Greystone Manor in Mentor to Roundwood Manor, among the eighteen vanloads of treasures were several pieces acquired at the October 1938 auction of the Van Sweringens' estate. Among the antiques making the return trip to Roundwood Manor were a French gold-inlaid credenza and wing chair and a Simon Willard grandfather clock. Bohannon's collection also included a massive hand-carved desk, a gift to Ambassador Myron T. Herrick from French president Raymond Poincare as an expression of gratitude to Herrick on behalf of the French people following World War I, Bohannon had purchased at the ambassador's estate sale. Following Bohannon's death on September 1, 1968, his widow moved to a three-bedroom suite in Bratenahl Place, overlooking Lake Erie.

The next two decades saw two occupants in the manor, including Carl Fazio, president of Fisher Foods, and his wife, Anita, followed by Joseph F. Hrudka, the founder of Mr. Gasket Company, a manufacturer of high-performance automotive gaskets. In 1989, Samir and Sylvia Korey acquired Roundwood Manor. Korey, a petrochemical engineering consultant with a degree in chemical engineering from Cleveland State University, and his wife, who held a degree in civil engineering, had lived in Kuwait, Dubai, and London before returning to Cleveland with their four children. The mansion needed a substantial amount of work to restore its original beauty, including the removal of wall-to-wall carpeting, revealing a layer of cement that had to be removed with a hammer and chisel to get down to the original slate floors throughout the first floor. By 2002, with the older children in college, it was time to downsize, and in June of that year, Roundwood Manor was once again on the market. By 2016, with no prospective buyers who would have been acceptable to the homeowners' association, Sylvia developed a plan to reconfigure the mansion for sale as condominium units. The Village of Hunting Valley opposed the plan, and Sylvia continues to live there.

Over the years, the buildings that comprised the gatehouse, built in 1927 at Roundwood Road and Shaker Boulevard, underwent several significant renovations. Following the settlement of the Van Sweringens' estates, in 1941, the gatehouse complex was purchased by Jason and Frances Crain, who made it their home until 1986 when it was purchased by Frank B. Carr. In September 1990, the property was once again sold, this time to Robert C. and Agnes M. Maynard. On August 2, 2021, the Maynards sold a 0.45-acre sublot known as 3045 Roundwood Road to William H. Lennon, and on February 11, 2022, the Maynards sold the remaining property to Joseph D. and Mary Sullivan.

Photographs of Daisy Hill Gatehouse.

On March 20, 1941, Carl H. and Gertrude L. Hanna acquired two sixteen-acre parcels from the Daisy Hill Company, one of which was known as the Farm Group and included the stables, a part of which had become the Van Sweringens' twenty-two-car garage. Located at 33919 Hackney Road, Hanna envisioned the garages as adjoined English garden court apartment suites. On April 7, 1947, having done little to the property, Hanna sold the Farm Group parcel to Francis J. and Anne H. O'Neill. O'Neill was known as Steve, in honor of his baseball hero Steve O'Neill, a catcher with the Cleveland Indians. O'Neill and his brothers were the founders of Leaseway Corporation. Anne died in 1971, and in 1974, he

Daisy Hill Gatehouse, 36040 Shaker Boulevard/3025 Roundwood Road.

Daisy Hill Gatehouse, 36040 Shaker Boulevard/3025 Roundwood Road.

Daisy Hill Gatehouse, 36040 Shaker Boulevard/3025 Roundwood Road.

33919 Hackney Road/Clanonderry Court.

33919 Hackney Road/Clanonderry Court.

Clanonderry, 33919 Hackney Road/Clanonderry Court.

Clanonderry, 33919 Hackney Road/Clanonderry Court.

married Nancy Marsteller. Following O'Neill's death in 1983, the Farm Group, by then known as Clanonderry, was transferred to Nancy, who sold the property to Richard and Anne Ames in June 2001 but who continued to live at Clanonderry until her death in 2005.

When the Ameses assumed its stewardship, it was clear that the Farm Group that had been designed by O. P. Van Sweringen's favorite architects Philip L. Small and Charles B. Rowley was in need of serious renewal. The Ameses engaged Cleveland architect David H. Ellison and New York architect Mark Ferguson to renovate and restore the many buildings and to add a new home in place of the former twenty-car garage, consistent with the historic character of the existing structures. Special attention was paid to the stone turrets and the bridges that span the creek that winds its way through the property, the work of the late Gates Mills mason George Brown.

Photographs of Daisy Hill Farm Group.

In a special issue of *Cosmopolitan* magazine in March 1963, an article entitled "The Good Life in Shaker Heights" proclaimed that Shaker was the wealthiest city in the United States in 1960, saying that "back-yard swimming pools are commonplace, nearly everyone belongs to a country club and most kids have new cars." If that was true—according to the US Census, the richest city per capita in America in 1960 was Detroit—it would not be for long. Shaker Heights was already a city in transition. The Van Sweringens' own real estate was not all that was changing. In the years following World War II, traditional Classical Revival styles gave way to modernism. Midcentury modern architecture and interior design (1945–1969) became more popular. The style was particularly more appealing to the younger home buyers than the classical styles of their parents' generation.

With the relaxing of the Van Sweringens' ridged architectural restrictions, the first home to break the mold in Shaker Heights was designed for Joseph and Virginia Jaffe by Robert A. Little, who would be the recipient of the 1965 Cleveland Arts Prize for Architecture, and son-in-law of Salmon Halle, for whom he had designed Halle Brothers' first suburban department store, near Shaker Square. Little's design for the Jaffe's home at 14306 South Park Boulevard was a significant departure from traditional Shaker Heights architecture. With no lack of perseverance, the design was finally accepted by the Architectural Review Board, and the building permit was issued on September 28, 1951. Construction was completed on October 30 of the following year. In June 1961, a permit was issued for the addition of a twenty-seven- by eighteen-foot family room. The house was the Jaffe's home until after Joseph's death. Virginia sold the property on February 2, 1985, to Michael J. and Gale V. Flament, who continue to make it their home.

In 1953, two building permits were issued for midcentury modern homes. One at 14907 Shaker Boulevard, designed by M. A. Norcross, was completed on June 17, 1954; the other, at 2529 Warwick Road, designed by Nathan Bernstein, was completed on December 16 of the same year. Midcentury modern, many with first-floor master suites, was becoming established in Shaker Heights, and architects were inspired to present even more modernistic designs. In 1968, two such homes were built at 2860 and 2900 Drummond Road. The home at 2860 Drummond was designed in 1966 by renowned Cleveland architect Fred S. Toguchi on a lot purchased by R. William and Joan W. Rosenfeld on October 29, 1965. Toguchi was also a recipient of the 1965 Cleveland Arts Prize for Architecture. Among his significant projects are the Burke Lakefront Airport Terminal, the Beck Center for the Arts in Lakewood, and the Lausche

Halle Brothers Store, 13000 Shaker Boulevard, Shaker Square, Robert A. Little

Jaffe House, 14306 South Park Boulevard, Robert A. Little.

McDonald House, 14907 Shaker Boulevard, designed by M. A. Norcross.

Biskind House, 2529 Warwick Road, designed by Nathan Bernstein.

Rosenfeld House, 2860 Drummond Road, designed by F. S. Toguchi.

Markey House, 2900 Drummond Road, designed by Morris and Dewalt.

Whitley House, 2963 Morley Road.

Reed/Leskosky House, 18523 Van Aken Boulevard.

State Office Building. The home at 2900 Drummond was designed for Dr. and Mrs. Richard Markey by another recipient of the Cleveland Arts Prize for Architecture (1983), William B. Morris.

In May 1972, Cleveland architect James M. Whitley purchased a lot on Morley Road, south of South Woodland Boulevard and west of Warrensville Center Road. Best known for commercial projects, including Cleveland's Tower City Center, Whitley set about to design a new home for his wife, Stella, and himself. In June 1974, the City of Shaker Heights issued a building permit for the modernist design he had created. Serving as general contractor, Whitley completed the house on December 1, 1975.

On September 29, 2016, architects Ronald A. Reed and Vincent M. Leskosky purchased a lot at 18523 Van Aken Boulevard, vacant since the 1951 four-bedroom colonial was demolished. At first glance, the house they designed and built might appear out of place in Shaker Heights, but upon reflection, elements of the house are drawn from the traditional houses on either side.

Photographs of Jaffe House.

The relaxation of restrictions was not limited to residential properties. In February 1958, a permit was issued by the City of Shaker Heights for the construction of an office building for the Allstate Insurance Company at 3605 Warrensville Center Road, south of Chagrin Boulevard on the east side of the street. The regional headquarters building was officially opened to much fanfare on February 4, 1959. In December 1971, the building was acquired by the architectural firm of Dalton-Dalton-Little-Newport, and its staff of 170 architects, engineers, and planners relocated from the Arcade on Euclid Avenue. (Little was the architect who designed the Halle Brothers store at Shaker Square and the Jaffe House on South Park Boulevard.)

Late in 1972, Shaker Heights City Council was asked to consider zoning changes that would permit the construction of a twenty-story high-rise office tower on the seven-acre site of the architectural firm's one-story headquarters. The following October, Dalton was granted permission to build an eighteen-story office building adjoining its existing building, with entrances on Warrensville Center and Northfield Roads, although the high-rise was never built. Today, the former Dalton building has been greatly expanded and is home to University Hospitals Management Services.

In 1968, building permits were issued for Tower East, a five-acre complex consisting of twelve-story and five-story office buildings and a seven-hundred-car parking garage at the southwest corner of the intersection of Warrensville Center Road and Chagrin Boulevard. The campus was designed by the world-famous Walter Gropius, founder of the Bauhaus school of design in Germany and founder of the international style, and this was the last project he undertook before his death on July 5, 1969.

Deed restrictions were relaxed as well. No longer was Shaker Heights open only to the white Anglo-Saxon Protestant upper class. As early Shaker residents who had raised their families and now found themselves empty nesters moved out, the next generation of new Shaker residents moved in to take their place, most seeking the high quality of Shaker public schools, and many came from the City of Cleveland, and an increasing number were African American. Today, Shaker Heights is proud of its commitment to a racially, ethnically, religiously, and economically diverse community.

With the growth of the suburbs in the 1950s and 1960s, and the development of Greater Cleveland's first large outdoor shopping center, Southgate Shopping Center in Maple Heights in 1955, and the area's first enclosed suburban shopping mall, Severance Shopping Center in Cleveland Heights in 1963, the city's downtown department stores fell out of favor. Higbee's, Halle's, and the May Company built anchor locations

UH Management Services Center, 3605 Warrensville Center Road.

Tower East, 3521 Northfield Road.

Public Square rededication on June 30, 2016.

in the suburbs. Taylor's department store, Sterling-Linder-Davis, and Bonds closed their doors. By the 1970s, the sidewalks that had bustled with shoppers and diners were rolling up even before the last office workers had boarded their bus or rapid for the trip home.

The 1980s marked the beginning of the renovation of the center city. In 1982, two historic landmarks were demolished: the Cuyahoga Building (1892), designed by Daniel H. Burnham and John W. Root; and the Williamson Building (1900), designed by George B. Post and where the Van Sweringen real estate empire got its start. This cleared the space opposite the Soldiers' and Sailors' Monument, between Superior and Euclid Avenues, for the construction of the SOHIO Building, later known as the BP Building, a modern office building located at 200 Public Square. Designed by Hellmuth, Obata + Kassabaum, the original plan called for a building that would be taller than the 52-story, 771-foot Terminal Tower, but popular opposition was so strong that city officials insisted that the plans be changed. Construction of the 47-story, 658-foot postmodern building was completed in 1985, and occupancy began two years later. In 1988, when construction of the Society Center (now the Key Tower) began adjacent to the historic Society for Savings Building, public sentiment had softened and the design by Argentine American César Pelli was approved for the 57-story (947-foot), nearly 1.25-million-square-foot building.

The city that was once home to the most beautiful street in America—the fifth-largest city with a population of more than 900,000 and with the fifth-greatest industrial output—now ranks fifty-fourth with a population of less than 375,000. The city's steel, chemicals, and manufacturing industries have largely been replaced by health care, biotech, and finance. Only Sherwin-Williams Company remains as a nod to

Right, BP Tower, 200 Public Square.

Facing left, Key Tower, 127 Public Square.

Facing right, Terminal Tower, 50 Public Square.

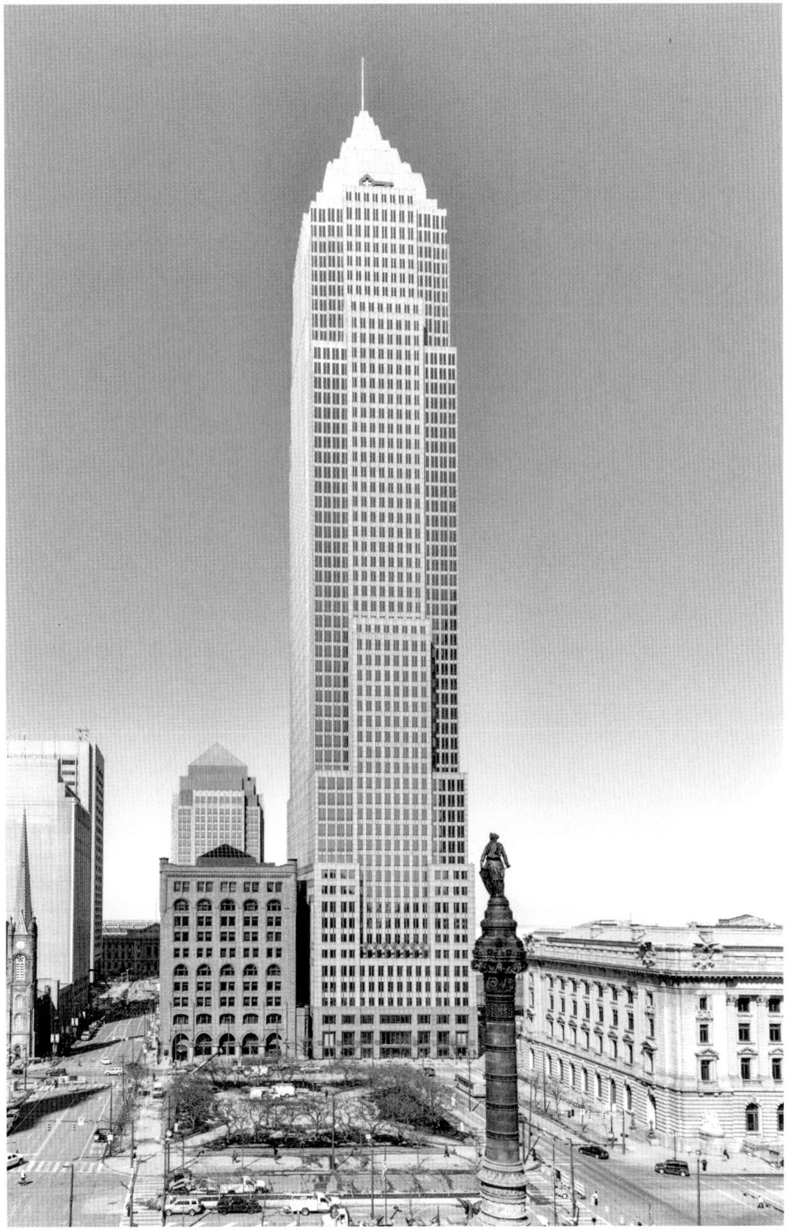

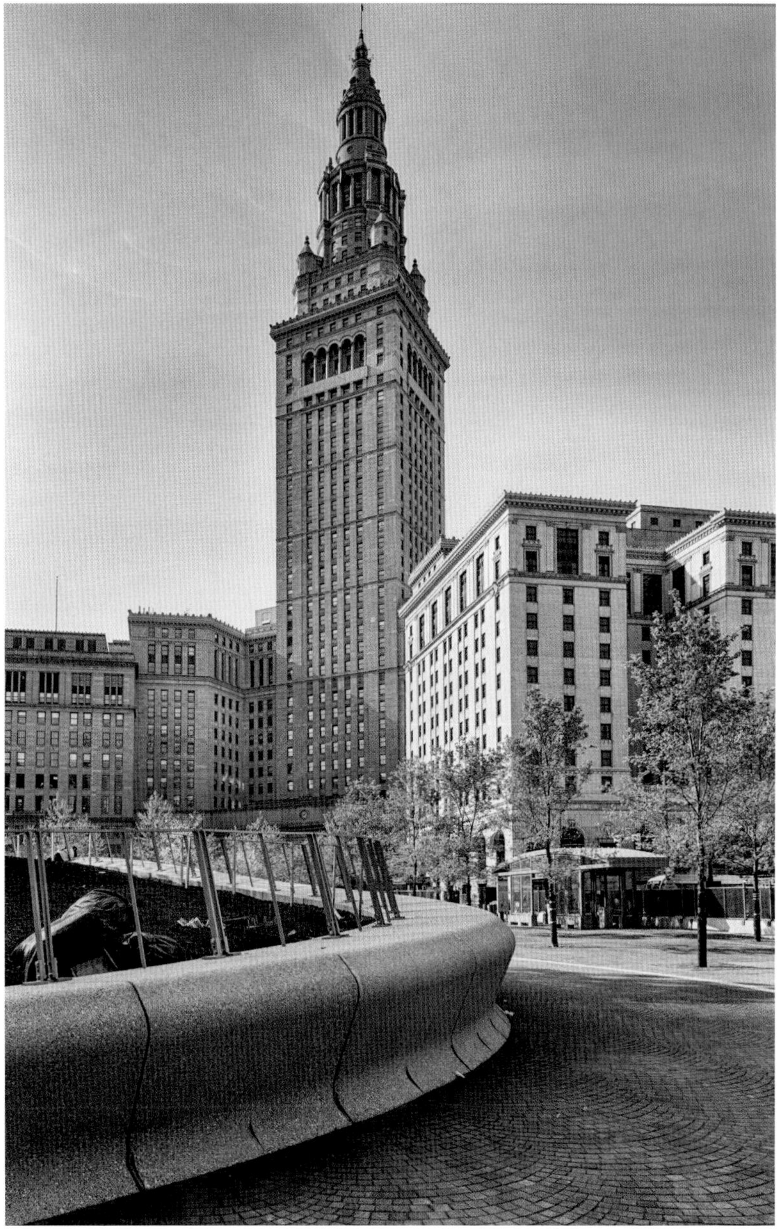

Cleveland's industrial past. It has been joined by the Cleveland Clinic, ranking second in the world with 22 hospitals and 275 outpatient facilities in locations around the globe. One by one, many of the city's downtown banks, office buildings, department stores, and industrial buildings have undergone renovation and repurposing, largely as residential properties to attract young professionals, empty nesters, and retirees to urban living. Among them are the former homes of the brothers' primary banks—the Guardian Savings and Trust Company at the northeast corner of East 6th Street and Euclid Avenue, the Union Trust Company on the northeast corner of East 9th Street and Euclid Avenue, and the Cleveland Trust Company on the southeast corner of the same intersection.

The Garfield Building was designed by Henry Ives Cobb and built on Bond Street (now East 6th Street) in 1893 by Harry Augustus Garfield and James Rudolph Garfield, the sons of President James A. Garfield. Below ground level, the space was designed for use as a bank, including meeting rooms, banking space, and massive vaults. The first occupant of the banking space was the Cleveland Trust Company, which moved in in 1895. On the first floor, Cleveland Trust created "club rooms," where male patrons could conduct their business in comfort, and a ladies' parlor and tearoom for its female patrons. The rapid growth of the bank prompted the leadership to consider a move to a larger space. The decision was made to build a new bank building on the southeast corner of East 9th Street and Euclid Avenue. Designed by George B. Post, Cleveland Trust moved into its new location in the Rotunda in 1908.

The New England Building had been built next door to the Garfield Building in 1896, on land purchased in 1894 from the heirs of Henry Chisholm, the founder of Cleveland Rolling Mill, which later became part of American Steel and Wire and, subsequently, US Steel. Designed by the Boston-based architectural firm of Shepley, Rutan and Coolidge, the New England Building, the city's first steel-frame office building, was the tallest building in Cleveland until the completion of the Rockefeller Building in 1905. In 1915, the New England Building was acquired by Guardian Savings and Trust, who hired the architectural firm of Walker and Weeks to transform the building into a bank, retaining the stately columns on the building's front on Euclid Avenue and renaming it the Guardian Building.

In 1918, National City Bank, founded in 1845 as the City Bank of Cleveland, purchased and moved into the Garfield Building. When Guardian Savings and Trust Company failed in 1933 and was ordered to liquidate, National City first leased and then purchased the Guardian Building from the liquidator in 1944, renaming it the National City Bank Building. By 1975, National City had its business functions scattered all around downtown Cleveland. To consolidate, in 1978, the bank acquired and demolished properties on the northwest corner of East 9th Street and Euclid Avenue, including the four-story Bond Clothing Company store built in 1946 in the Art Moderne style, and in their place built the thirty-five-story National City Center office tower. Construction was completed in 1980, and the building served as National City's headquarters. By 2003, National City was the nation's sixth-largest mortgage lender. With the subprime mortgage crisis beginning in mid-2007, by late 2008, National City Bank had been acquired by Pittsburgh-based PNC and the building became its regional headquarters.

In 2015, the former Garfield and New England Buildings, turned National City Bank Building, were acquired by Millennia Companies, who redeveloped the property, opening the Garfield Apartments in 2017. Today, the Garfield Building houses 123 luxurious apartments, ranging from one bedroom with one bath to two-floor apartments with two bedrooms and two baths; it also includes a fitness center and luxurious common spaces. The ground-level banking floor of the former New England Building was repurposed as an upscale restaurant and the vaults on the lower-level as private dining space.

In 1938, following the failure of the Union Trust Company in 1933, a new and unrelated Union Bank of Commerce occupied the former Union Trust Company Building at the northeast corner of Euclid Avenue and East 9th Street. Union Commerce hired Graham, Anderson,

Probst & White, the architectural firm engaged by the Van Sweringens to design the Cleveland Hotel on Public Square and the Terminal Tower. Construction began in 1922, and the twenty-one-floor, one-million-square-foot building with the largest banking floor in the world at that time, was completed in 1924. Following the Huntington Bank's acquisition of Union Commerce Bank in 1983, and until 2011 when the bank moved to the BP Building on Public Square, the massive bank and office building was known as the Huntington Bank Building. Like the Garfield Building in 2015, the 925 Building, as it was then called, was acquired by Millennia Companies and renamed the Centennial Building, with plans to transform it into 868 one- and two-bedroom below- and market-rate apartment units on seventeen floors, to appeal to Cleveland's downtown workforce, with four floors of office and retail space.

Directly across Euclid Avenue from the Centennial is The 9, in the former Cleveland Trust Company complex. In 1930, Cleveland Trust had joined with Guardian and Union Trust to loan $9 million to the Van Sweringens during the brothers' campaign to acquire the Missouri Pacific Railroad. In 1973, Marcel Breuer designed what was intended to be the first of two twenty-nine-story high-rise office towers.

In December 2012, the Geis Companies purchased the former Cleveland Trust complex, which had been vacant since 1996 after the bank's merger with Society National Bank. The adjacent P & H buildings on Prospect and Huron were demolished, and a new Cuyahoga County Administration Building was built in their place. The historic Rotunda and part of the first floor of the Swetland Building at 1010 Euclid Avenue—now known as the 1010 Building—were repurposed as an upscale Heinen's grocery store. The rest of the 1010 Building was repurposed as office space and market-rate apartments. The Breuer Tower, now known as The 9, combines 200 luxury apartments and 156 luxury hotel units, plus an array of drinking and dining venues and assorted amenities.

Nothing is more symbolic of the brothers' contribution to and impact on the City of Cleveland than the Union Terminal complex. Until 1967, the Terminal Tower was the tallest building in the world outside of New York City. Ten years later, with the end of the Erie Railroad's commuter service on January 14, 1977, the last passenger train pulled out of Cleveland Union Terminal. This gave rise to the purchase of the complex by Forest City Enterprises in 1980 and the opening of the three-story shopping mall and food court in 1990. The next year, two eleven-story office towers were constructed, flanking Tower City Center's skylight.

In 2014, Cleveland's Public Square, the front yard of the terminal complex, began a major transformation under the leadership of the "New Group Plan Commission" and LAND Studio. Originally a public grazing land and meeting place, the nine-and-a-half-acre New England–style Public Square took on many looks, but almost always with four distinct quadrants divided by two wide streets, in keeping with the 1796 plan. When Public Square was rededicated in June 2016, Ontario ended on the north and south sides of the Square, and Superior was narrowed from seventy-seven to forty-eight feet in width, open only to emergency vehicles and public buses. Only the Soldiers' and Sailors' Monument remains as a reminder of the Square's previous symmetry.

Also in 2016, Forest City sold its interest in the Terminal Tower to K & D Group, a leading real estate developer and property manager who has repurposed ten floors of office space into nearly three hundred residential units and common-space amenities. That same year, Forest City sold its interest in Tower City Center to Bedrock Real Estate Services, and in 2021, Bedrock announced plans to convert the indoor shopping mall into a "retail marketplace." The plan includes a blend of retail and entertainment, and later the connection of Tower City to the Cuyahoga River with staircases and terraces, including the redesign of Tower City Center to permit easy access between Public Square and the river. The Renaissance Cleveland Hotel, the Van Sweringens' first building of the complex, is under major renovation. The hotel will once again be known as the Hotel Cleveland, as part of Marriott's Autograph Collection to reestablish the hotel and restore Cleveland's status as a destination city.

As for the Van Sweringen railroad empire, the Nickel Plate, the Wabash, and several smaller railroads merged with the Norfolk & Western on October 16, 1964, which in 1959 had merged with the Virginian Railway and in 1982 would merge with the Southern Railway to form the Norfolk Southern Railway.

On October 17, 1960, the Erie Railroad and the Delaware, Lackawanna & Western Railroad merged to form the Erie Lackawanna Railroad, which was acquired by the Norfolk & Western Railway on March 1, 1968. Chessie would become known as CSX with its merger with the Seaboard Coast Line in 1980.

The C&O acquired the B&O in 1962. Chessie System was incorporated on February 26, 1973, and became the parent of the B&O, the C&O, and the Western Maryland on June 15 of that year.

The National Railroad Passenger Corporation (Amtrak) began service on May 1, 1971, after the passage of the Rail Passenger Service Act of 1970, to take over the intercity rail service formerly operated by private railroads, including the Penn Central. Nationalizing passenger rail service, Amtrak today operates more than three hundred trains daily over 21,400 miles of track to more than five hundred destinations in forty-six states and three Canadian provinces.

The Consolidated Rail Corporation (Conrail) was formed on April 1, 1976, to combine otherwise profitable freight lines of bankrupt carriers in the northeastern United States. Among the lines were the Penn Central (the result of the 1968 acquisition of the New York Central by the Pennsylvania Railroad), the Erie Lackawanna, and the Lehigh. In 1980, the Staggers Rail Act was signed into law to relax the government control over and restore profitability to the railroad industry for the first time since the formation of the ICC. That same year, Chessie merged with Seaboard Coast Line, forming CSX. In 1987, Conrail was privatized, having become profitable, and in 1997, the system was cut into two pieces, with CSX acquiring one and Norfolk Southern acquiring the other.

Alleghany Corporation, created by the Van Sweringen brothers on January 26, 1929, as a holding company for their railroad investments, had been acquired by Robert Young and Allan Kirby on April 26, 1937.

Following Young's suicide in 1958, Kirby succeeded him as chair of the board of directors, and Fred Kirby succeeded his father in 1965—a position that he would hold until 1992. In 1966, the company had sold the majority of its more than two million shares of New York Central stock, ending Alleghany's role in the railroad industry until the investment holding company reentered railroading in 1994 with the acquisition of a stake in the Santa Fe Pacific Corporation, which merged with the Burlington Northern the following year, becoming one of the largest railroads in North America. Alleghany Corporation's 2021 revenues exceeded $13 billion, and in October 2022, it was acquired by Warren Buffett's $530 billion Berkshire Hathaway, signaling the end of another era.

EPILOGUE

This is where the story of two boys, inseparable brothers born into abject poverty, who dared to dream and dared to act on those dreams, ends. Those dreams included a luxury garden community, with home and workplace connected by rapid transit. To provide the last few miles of the transportation they had promised, they acquired a 513-mile railroad that was in their way and built a $3 billion empire—the largest privately owned railroad system in America before it fell victim to the Great Depression.

What was it that drove the Van Sweringen brothers? Was it the failures of their alcoholic father? Was it the fear that they might repeat the failures of their early ventures? Was it the feeling that nothing was ever enough? Was it their failure to consolidate the "New" Nickel Plate? Were their sudden deaths attributable to the cumulative effect of the fear that drove them and the pace at which they appear to have been driven throughout their adult lives?

Even before the brothers entered the railroad industry in 1916, track in the United States had peaked at just over 250,000 miles. There were warning signs that the industry had reached its summit, and return on investment was on the decline. In 1890 the two leaders in the industry—the

New York Central and the Pennsylvania Railroad—had entered into a Community of Interest agreement to prop up the weak roads.

Certainly, the brothers did not anticipate the extent to which the ICC would regulate every aspect of their business empire. It is equally certain that they did not anticipate the severity of the Great Depression that followed the stock market's crash. And it is unlikely that they anticipated the changes in modes of transportation. In 1920, there were 7.5 million automobiles on America's roadways (14.14 people per car) and an additional one million trucks. Planning had already begun in Washington, DC, for a national highway system. By 1927, there were 27.5 million families in the United States; 55.7 percent of those families owned an automobile, and 10 percent of those were two-car families. By 1930, there were more than 23.1 million automobiles and 3.4 million trucks on America's roads and highways.

In July 1916, Congress passed the Federal Aid Road Act, the nation's first federal highway funding act. Although progress was interrupted by World War I, in November 1921, Congress passed the Phipps Act, the Federal Highway Act of 1921, to develop a massive national highway system. The first interstate highway, the 162-mile Pennsylvania Turnpike, from Carlisle to Irwin, was opened on October 1, 1940. The handwriting was on the wall for passenger railroad traffic.

The first scheduled passenger airline service began in the United States on January 1, 1914. The St. Petersburg–Tampa Airboat Line only lasted four months, making two flights a day, six days a week in two aircraft and carrying more than twelve hundred people during those four months. Although a failure, the service showed what was possible, and on May 23, 1926, Ben F. Redman flew from Salt Lake City to Los Angeles aboard Western Air Express Airline. The eight-hour trip signaled the beginning of a new era in travel—one that would blossom after World War II.

Why then, with significant progress being made in terms of both automobile and air travel, did the Van Sweringens invest so much into passenger routes and amenities for passenger travel in Cleveland Union Terminal?

How much different might things have been for the Van Sweringens if the New York Central had granted the brothers' request for an agreement to use the Nickel Plate right-of-way for their rapid transit? Would the Van Sweringen brothers have been content to concentrate their energies on the development of what we now know as Beachwood, Gates Mills, Pepper Pike, and Hunting Valley?

How much different might it have been if the ICC had approved the Vans' Consolidation Plan? Would the brothers have been satisfied with their railroad empire being one of the four largest in the nation? Might they have turned to philanthropy, perhaps to benefit those who, like themselves, were born into poverty?

If O. P. and M. J. had lived another twenty years, what might they have achieved? Would they have learned from their bitter experiences, making certain not to make the same mistakes twice? Knowing now what others were able to do with the Vans' Alleghany Corporation, what might the brothers have done?

While we will never know the answers to these questions and more, what we do know is that the brothers were only half without each other. O. P.'s enterprising spirit and M. J.'s devotion to his older brother combined to accomplish more, with less, than any other duo of their time, and perhaps of all time. The loss of M. J., O. P.'s "other half," was more than the older brother could bear. That the brothers shared a bedroom and a checkbook, and that the door to their adjoining offices was never closed, stands in strong testament to the uniqueness of their brotherly bond. Truly, the whole was far greater than the sum of each of its parts.

It was not ego but deep-seated insecurity that drove at least the elder brother, if not both of them. It was that insecurity that drove them to share a bedroom all their lives. It was that insecurity, compounded by the early loss of their beloved mother, that formed the bond with Daisy Jenks, the bond of mother and sons.

APPENDIX A

POPULATION OF THE WESTERN RESERVE

Year	Cleveland	Rank	Cuyahoga	CWR*
1800	7			1,500
1810	57		1,459	16,042
1820	605		6,328	56,889
1830	1,075		10,373	102,347
1840	6,071	45	26,507	229,467
1850	17,034	41	48,099	327,897
1860	43,417	21	78,033	385,660
1870	92,829	15	132,010	465,646
1880	160,146	12	196,943	588,571
1890	261,353	10	309,970	739,303
1900	391,768	7	439,120	934,870
1910	560,663	6	637,425	1,259,549
1920	796,841	5	943,495	1,912,440
1930	900,429	5	1,201,455	2,339,042
1940	878,366	6	1,217,250	2,401,575
1950	914,808	7	1,389,532	2,804,418
1960	876,050	8	1,647,895	3,523,843
1970	750,879	12	1,720,835	3,840,414
1980	573,822	19	1,498,400	3,690,144
1990	505,616	23	1,412,140	3,572,817
2000	478,403	33	1,393,848	3,661,048
2010	396,815	45	1,280,122	3,562,157
2020	372,624	54	1,264,817	2,683,780

Note: *Connecticut Western Reserve—Ashtabula, Cuyahoga, Erie, Geauga, Huron, Lake, Lorain, Medina, Portage, and Trumbull, and parts of Ashland, Mahoning, Ottawa, and Summit Counties.

Source: "U. S. Decennial Census," US Census Bureau.

APPENDIX B

GENEALOGY OF THE VAN SWERINGEN FAMILY

Relationship	Name	Birth	Death
5G GFather	Garrett van Sweringen	February 4, 1636	2/04/1698
	Barbarah de Barrette	3/01/1640	1670
4G GFather	Thomas Swearingen	1665	3/19/1710
	Jane Hyde Doyne	1669	1/06/1716
3G GFather	Van B. Swearingen	1692	8/27/1787
	Elizabeth Walker	1695	1767
2G GFather	Thomas Cresap Swearingen	1741	1808
	Mary Baker	1743	ca. 1800
G GFather	Samuel Swearingen	ca. 1770	7/10/1834
	Janetta Towar	5/22/1777	1/06/1857
GFather	Thomas Samuel Swearingen	10/22/1805	2/10/1855
GMother	Edith Beale	8/27/1800	7/3/1865
Father	James Tower Swearingen	2/10/1832	8/4/1903
Mother	Jennie Curtis	1844	1/18/1886
Brother	Herbert Curtis Van Sweringen	6/04/1868	1/5/1942
Sister-in-law	Mabel Adams	1869	7/26/1947

Relationship	Name	Birth	Death
Nephew	Raymond Adams Van Sweringen	9/27/1898	1/13/1968
Nephew's spouse	Grace G. Watkins	1895	1/24/1964
Grand nephew	James Paxton "Pax" Van Sweringen	7/31/1925	7/5/2020
Grand nephew's spouse	Barbara Jean Cailor	5/29/1928	9/2/2002
Grand niece	Edith W. Van Sweringen	1928	9/10/1937
Sister	Maud Alene Sweringen	6/6/1870	3/3/1871
Sister	Carrie Blanche Van Sweringen	4/24/1872	7/15/1940
Sister	Edith Elizabeth Van Sweringen	6/7/1874	7/19/1945
Self	Oris Paxton Van Sweringen	4/24/1879	11/23/1936
Self	Mantis James Van Sweringen	7/8/1881	12/12/1935

Genealogy of the Van Sweringen Family

APPENDIX C

REAL ESTATE STANDARDS

(Reformatted, but otherwise true to original wording and punctuation)

Shaker Village Standards, Second Edition, 1928
GOOD TASTE IN HOMEBUILDING

EVERYONE delights in the graceful lines of a beautiful residence.

The well-planned house and garden universally appeal.

Good taste calls for well-designed residences that combine the things that make for comfort and convenience with the things that make for beauty.

The beautiful home is proportioned to fit both site and surroundings.

The beautiful home suggests hospitality and friendliness tempered by dignity and reserve.

The most pleasing is never conspicuous—never flashy.

As the well-groomed man looks to becoming details in such things as hats, shoes, hose and neckties, so the well-built home shows harmony of style and construction throughout, including sides, rear, roof, treatment of doors, windows and the like.

Design of lawn and treatment of garden front and the relationship of the garage to the house are also important considerations.

These things hold good for both the small residence and the large estate.

Happily, a beautiful home is just as possible on a small parcel as on a large one.

It takes a good designer to fashion good clothes, a skilled architect to design attractive homes.

Without the guidance of a competent architect, imagination may easily run to the freakish in residences. It is not too far a cry to that Queen Anne era, when towers and arches were as numerous as the sacred niches of a Buddhist temple. Then, again, there are those horribly ugly examples of the Age of Cast Iron and the Brownstone Period, which should make the intending home-builder of today sufficiently wary.

The ugly residence injures surrounding property values, particularly with relation to possibilities of re-sale. This represents a damage for which there is no insurance coverage.

Against such occurrences the only safeguard is in creating definite standards for home construction. And this is practical only when land is extensively held under single control for a long period of time.

Shaker Village is the largest area for high-class residences under single control. Standards and protective restrictions have been applied there from the outset. Over 2600 homes have been built there. They cover a construction span of about twelve years. They represent a wide range of architectural treatment. Nevertheless, there is marked harmony.

The properly designed home "wears" well. The house of poor or mediocre design is sure to be a disappointment. To obtain pleasing results engage an architect. It is the wise thing to do from the economical, as well as the artistic standpoint, for when the house is properly designed at the outset it obviates the trouble and expense of redesigning or of building portions of it anew.

The architect selected should be a graduate architect, or one whose qualifications warrant and whose drawings express a thorough, technical knowledge of the highest and best in architecture, together with the ability to combine materials and prescribe color schemes that will proclaim the result the work of a trained and competent hand.

Before designing the house, the architect will require the deed showing the restrictions on the property. He should be told the number, size and desired arrangement of rooms. His advice in all matters of architecture and construction should be carefully considered thereafter.

Submission of drawings is a necessary preparatory step for approval of proposed construction. All drawings offered for approval, whether for new buildings, repairs or additions, should include all floor plans; all elevations; the color scheme in detail for the exterior; a complete section through the building showing the height of stories; and three-inch or full-size details of the front entrance, cornices and other special features that need to be detailed to insure the right result. A fully dimensioned plot plan on a scale of not less than one-eighth of an inch to the foot should be included among the drawings. The plan should show the driveway and the house and garage so located upon the lot as to avoid violation of the restrictions.

Submission of the plot plan is especially important for the reason that banks and insurance companies, before financing or re-financing property, require, in many cases, plot plans and certificates showing the house upon the lot free from violations of the restrictions.

All drawings should be new, complete, clear and clean. Unless expressly excepted, they should be drawn in ink or blue-printed from ink drawings. Complete specifications also should be submitted.

So that proper credit may be given to him, the architect's name should appear on all drawings along with such other necessary information as the lot number, street, and the name and address of the owner. A duplicate of the approved plans should be kept on the job at all times.

PLANNING THE HOUSE

The greatest care should be exercised in planning the house, for it is the plan that gives the house its character. It expresses the personality of the builder, and, if the house is sold, determines the personality of the purchaser. Nothing should be taken for granted. Doubt as to any detail of design or construction should be dissolved before actual work starts. A good vacant lot has great possibilities that may be destroyed by a poorly designed house.

Every house should be laid out by a competent surveyor or engineer. More than one person has dug a cellar on the wrong lot. It pays to be sure.

Before the house has been staked or any excavation started, the residence location should be compared with those of existing buildings on adjacent lots on the same side of the street.

Thus, it will be possible to determine before construction whether the proposed house lines up properly with the neighboring buildings. In this way, any discrepancy may be corrected without the need for ripping out work already done.

On lots with extra wide frontage and tapering sides, houses should conform with those on neighboring regularly-shaped parcels.

The best architects state that houses set close to the ground give a sense of beauty and coziness that they do not give when approached by a flight of steps. Hundreds of thousands of dollars have been spent by Shaker Village to place street sewers deep enough to permit the house being set close to the ground.

Only certain types of houses are suited to this climate. These types are well defined. The one selected should be followed closely without variations unless the changes be prescribed by a competent architect. Each house should be distinct in design and detail from every other house.

All deeds for Shaker Village property require that all houses shall be full two stories in height. This restriction excludes bungalows and other houses of a similar type. It ensures a greater harmony in size and character of houses in the community.

Enclosed vestibules and bays over one story in height should not encroach on the front building line. Open front entrance porches, one-story bays, not over three feet in depth, and chimneys, are sometimes allowed to encroach on the front building line, but not without written consent. Projecting vestibules should not be built on one-family or two-family houses of colonial or similar design. Houses of other designs that permit projecting vestibules should be set back so that the front of the vestibule will be on the prescribed front building line.

The regulation as to distances from the lot lines at which buildings are to be placed is intended to provide adequate light and air for each house. Therefore, it is recommended that the intending homebuilder avoid the construction of too large a house with relation to the size of the lot. By properly adjusting the dimensions of the residence to the size of lot, air, light and openness are assured and the rights of neighbors are safeguarded.

Careful thought should be given to the basement plan in laying out the house. Basements are usable in proportion to their light and air, and, in this connection, the installation of large cellar windows in areaways will be helpful. The coal bin should be easily accessible from the driveway. The furnace should be near the coal bin for convenience in firing.

Proper driveway location, with relation to house and to driveways on adjoining lots, is important. To insure conformity in the neighborhood in this respect, plans for drive location should be submitted for approval before building plans are finished.

The main entrance of the dwelling should be toward the street and on the front elevation.

The windows on side elevations in the principal rooms should be full-length windows rather than high-up windows or casement sash. The charm of a house is enhanced on approach by a glimpse of tapestry or other furnishings through the drapery framed vista of a full-length window.

The ridge line of the main part of the house should be not less than sixteen feet above the finished second floor, unless otherwise authorized in writing. The first-story height should be not less than eight and one-half feet, and the second story not less than eight feet in the clear.

The roof of the house has a value much greater than that given by its ability to shed water. It is the roof that is outlined against the sky. By its symmetry, its display of lights and shadows, or its contrast of color with the rest of the building, it promotes interest, arouses enthusiasm and suggests comfort and contentment.

Open sleeping porches are, as a rule, objectionable to adjoining owners. They may not be constructed unless approved in writing.

Porches that are enclosed are in all cases considered as a part of the house with relation to the front and other building lines and should not be permitted to encroach upon those lines.

All cornices should be closed. Galvanized iron cornices and exposed rafter ends require written consent.

The final grade of the lot is very important, for each lot has its own problems and each abutting land owner has certain legal rights which one is bound to respect. The grade of a lot may affect, or may be affected by, the grade of two or more abutting lots. The ideal grade for abutting lots is one that permits the flow of rain water in the natural direction and in the natural volume without abrupt differences in elevation at the meeting line.

The grade of any lot may not be changed with relation to the adjoining lots unless permission is granted in writing. In the event it is desired to change the natural grade, a plan should be submitted showing the effect desired with relation to all adjoining property.

To prevent possible damage to the owners of adjoining land, all surplus dirt should be removed from the lot at the time of excavation. Its distribution upon the lot, apart from causing additional expense, may bring complaints from adjoining owners.

Low land is subservient to higher land. It must take care of the water that comes to it naturally. This can be done by catch basins.

Either the deed for each parcel should contain all of the restrictions applying to the property or else these restrictions should be recited at length in the title papers. Otherwise the restrictions can only be obtained from the records at the Court House to insure against the possibility of mistakes.

Shaker Village houses have two or more "fronts" but no "backs." This is so because the wide, open spaces between the houses make each dwelling almost as visible from the next street as from that upon which the lot abuts.

Then, too, automobile traffic lessens interest in the street side of the house and suggests the privacy and safety of a well studied garden, behind the house, if you will, but not at the "back" of it. The "Garden Front" surrounded and beautified with flowers and mirrored in the waters of a limpid pool, has a charm and sacredness about it for your family and friends that the mere passerby on the street is not privileged to see or enjoy.

APPENDIX D

DEED RESTRICTIONS

(Reformatted, but otherwise true to original wording and punctuation)

"And the Grantee _____ for successors and assigns, in consideration of the execution and delivery of this Deed, hereby covenant and agree with and for the benefit of the Grant or, its successors and assigns, to hold said premises hereby conveyed, upon the following terms:

1. Said premises shall be used solely and exclusively for single family private residence purposes. No buildings or structures or any additions thereto or any alterations thereof shall be erected, reconstructed, placed or suffered to remain upon said premises unless nor until the architect therefor, the size, location, type, cost, use, the materials of construction thereof, the color scheme therefor, the grading plan of the lot, including the grade elevations of said buildings and structures, the plot plan showing the proposed location of said buildings and structures upon said premises, and the plans, specifications and details of said buildings and structures shall have been approved in writing by the Grantor and a true copy of said plans, specifications and details shall have been located permanently with the Grantor, and no buildings or structures, except such as conform to said plans, specifications and details shall be erected, reconstructed or suffered to remain upon said premises. No dwelling house being less than two stories in height shall be erected or suffered to remain upon said premises, and each and every said dwelling house shall be so planned and so placed upon said premises that the width of the front elevation thereof shall be greater than the depth of said dwelling house, except that if the entire available building space between the side lines of said premises be occupied by the front of said dwelling house, the foregoing restrictions as to the depth of said dwelling house shall not apply, and the front elevation and the front or main entrance thereof shall be towards the principal highway as designated by the Grantor, upon which said premises abut, nor shall said dwelling house be erected, placed or suffered to remain upon said premises within _____ feet of the side lines of any of the adjoining property, nor within _____ feet of _____ nor within _____ feet of any other highway or highways now existing or hereafter established. This restriction as to the distances at which said dwelling house shall be placed from the front and side lines of said premises shall not apply to, nor include porches, verandas, porches cochere or other similar projections of said dwelling house, except that said projections shall not be constructed or suffered to remain beyond the building lines hereinbefore established without the written consent of the Granter; provided, however, that if in the opinion of said Grantor, by reason of the shape, dimensions or topography of the premises hereby conveyed, or for any other reasons satisfactory to the Grantor, the enforcement of the foregoing provisions respecting the location of said dwelling house would work a hardship, the Granter may modify such provisions so as to permit a different location that will not, in its judgment, do material damage to any abutting or adjacent property. Unless expressly permitted otherwise in writing by the Granter, all driveways, except on

corner lots, shall be placed upon said premises at the left side of said dwelling house as viewed from the Street. The location of driveways upon corner lots shall be fixed by the Granter at the time of the approval of the plans and specifications for said dwelling house. No outbuildings, except for the exclusive use of the family occupying said premises and their family servants, shall be erected, placed or suffered to remain upon said premises, nor shall said outbuildings be erected, placed or suffered to remain upon said premises nearer to the side lines of any adjoining property or highways than the respective building lines hereinbefore provided in respect to said dwelling house; except, however, that where it would be impracticable to locate said outbuildings upon said premises without violating the foregoing provisions by reason of the dimensions of said premises, then said outbuildings may be located in such place upon said premises as the Granter shall direct; provided however that on corner parcels, the garage shall be made an integral part of said dwelling house, unless expressly permitted otherwise by the Granter.

2. No portion of the within described premises nearer to any highway than the building lines established under the provisions of the next preceding paragraph shall be used for any purpose other than that of a lawn; nothing herein contained, however, shall be construed as preventing the use of such portion of said premises for walks and drives, the planting of trees or shrubbery, the growing of flowers or ornamental plants or for statuary, fountains and similar ornamentations for the purpose of beautifying said premises, but no vegetable so-called, nor grains of the ordinary garden or field variety shall be grown upon such portion thereof, and no weeds, underbrush or other unsightly growths shall be permitted to grow or remain anywhere upon said premises, and no unsightly objects shall be allowed to be placed or suffered to remain anywhere thereon.

3. The premises hereby conveyed shall be used and occupied solely and exclusively by a single family, including their family servants, and not more than one dwelling house shall be erected or suffered to remain upon said premises.

4. No chickens or other fowl or live stock of any kind shall be kept or harbored on the land hereby conveyed, except by written consent of the Grantor, and said consent may be revoked by the Grantor at any time by giving 30 days' written notice to the occupant of said premises, and mailing a copy of said notice to the last known address of the said owner of said premises.

5. The premises hereby conveyed shall not be occupied, leased, rented, conveyed or otherwise alienated, nor shall the title or possession thereof pass to another without the written consent of the Grantor, except that the Grantor shall not withhold such consent if and after a written request has been made to the Grantor to permit such occupation, leasing, renting, conveyance or alienation by a majority of the owners of the Sub Lots which adjoin or face said premises upon both sides of the highway or highways upon which said premises front or abut, and within a distance of five Sub Lots from the respective boundary lines of the said premises, except transfer of title by way of devise or inheritance, in which case the devisee or heir shall take such property subject to the restrictions herein imposed, and except that said property may be mortgaged or subjected to judicial sale, provided in any such case that no purchaser of said premises at judicial sale shall have the right to occupy, lease, rent, convey or otherwise alienate said premises without the written consent of the Grantor first had and obtained in the manner above stated.

It being understood however, that the rights hereby reserved to the Grantor shall apply with equal force and effect to its successors and assigns, but in the event the ownership and control of the rights hereby reserved pass from the hands of the Van Sweringen interests, either by reason of the appointment of a receiver, assignment for the benefit of creditors, bankruptcy, by sale under legal process of any kind, by the transfer of the ownership of a majority stock to another than the Van Sweringen interests, or otherwise, the provision for consents by the Grantor in this Section No. 5 provided for shall be deemed to sufficiently obtained, if obtained from a majority of the owners of the said *five* adjoining and facing Sub Lots, and thenceforth the right to enforce the restrictions in this Section No. 5 of this Deed contained shall immediately pass to the owners of the said five adjoining and facing Sub Lots, and be exercised by the written consent of the majority of the owners holding title to said five adjoining and facing Sub Lots.

6. No nuisance, and no gas or oil derrick, advertising sign, billboard or other advertising device shall be erected, placed or suffered to remain upon said premises, nor shall the premises be used in any way or for any purpose which may endanger the health or unreasonably disturb the quiet of any holder of adjoining land. No spirituous, vinous or fermented liquors shall be manufactured or sold, either at wholesale or retail upon said premises. No privy shall be maintained, placed or suffered to remain upon said premises, if sewer be accessible.

7. No heating apparatus in or for any building upon the premises hereby conveyed shall be operated with any but smoke-free fuel, unless such apparatus be equipped, operated and maintained with such devices as will prevent smoke.

8. No fence or wall of any kind or for any purpose shall be erected, placed or suffered to remain upon said premises nearer to any highway now existing or any hereafter established than the front building lines hereinbefore established, nor, in any event, unless nor until the written consent of the Grantor shall have been obtained therefor.

9. The premises hereby conveyed shall not be subdivided unless nor until the plat showing such proposed subdivision shall have been submitted to the Granter and the written consent of said Granter for such subdivision has been obtained. The Granter shall be the sole judge as to whether such subdivision shall or shall not be permitted, and in case of the subdivision of said premises, the restrictions, rights, reservations, limitations, agreements, covenants and conditions herein contained shall apply to each of the lots into which said premises shall be subdivided.

10. The Granter reserves the sole right to grant consents for the construction and operation of street railways, interurban, rapid transit or other public utility facilities, street railway, electric light, telephone and telegraph pole lines and conduits, and gas pipes in and upon any and all highways now existing or hereafter established upon which any portion of said premises may now or hereafter front or abut.

11. The grantor reserves the sole and exclusive right to establish grades and slopes on the premises hereby conveyed, and to fix the grade at which any building shall be hereafter erected or placed thereon, so that the same may conform to a general plan.

12. The Grantor reserves and is hereby granted the right in case of any violation or breach of any of the restrictions, rights, reservations, limitations, agreements, covenants and conditions in this Deed contained, to enter the property upon or as to which such violation or breach exists, and to summarily abate and remove, at the expense of the owner thereof, any erection, thing or condition that may be or exist thereon contrary to the intent and meaning of the provisions hereof as interpreted by the Grantor, and the Grantor shall not by reason thereof, be deemed guilty of any manner of trespass for such entry, abatement or removal. A failure of the Grantor to enforce any of the restrictions, rights, reservations, limitations, agreements, covenants and conditions contained in this Deed shall in no event be construed, taken or held to be a waiver thereof or acquiescence in or consent to any further or succeeding breach or violation thereof, and the Grantor shall at any and all times have the right to enforce the same.

13. The Grantor reserves and is hereby granted the exclusive right to grant consents and to petition the proper authorities for any and all street improvements, such as grading, seeding, tree planting, sidewalks, paving, sewer and water installation, whether it be on the surface or sub-surface, which in the opinion of the Grantor are necessary in the subdivision of which the premises hereby conveyed are a part, and the Grantee agree to and do hereby consent to and affirm any agreements that may be entered into between the Grantor and any public authorities with respect to the installation of said improvements and with respect to binding the Grantee and the premises hereby conveyed for the payment of the cost of said improvements, and the Grantee herein expressly agree to pay share of the cost chargeable to property, and the Grantee hereby waive all notice with reference to said petitions and hereby consent to all other acts and things that may be necessary in the matter and hereby authorize and agree to affirm and ratify all such agreements and acts on the part of the Grantor in regard thereto.

14. The Grantor reserves also *the* right to grant consents to and to petition the Gas Companies and Electric Light Companies for the extension of their respective service mains, which in the opinion of the Grantor are necessary in the highways upon which the premises hereby conveyed shall front or abut, and the Grantee agree to and do hereby consent to and affirm all agreements that may be entered into between the Grantor and the said Gas Companies and/or said Electric Light Companies with respect to binding the Grantee for the proportionate cost of said extensions as applied to said premises hereby conveyed.

15. The restrictions imposed by this instrument upon the use of the premises hereby conveyed shall not be held to prevent the use of adjoining and adjacent land by the Grantor or its successors or assigns, for *such other purposes* or in such other manner as will not, in its judgment adversely affect the premises hereby conveyed to a material degree, and such use of such other lands shall not be held as relieving the Grantee hereunder from the restrictions imposed upon the premises hereby conveyed.

16. The Grantor reserves the right to waive, change or cancel any and all of the restrictions contained in this Deed or in any other Deed given by the Grantor in respect to Sub Lots or parcels within The Van Sweringen Company's Subdivision, if in its judgment, the development or lack of development warrants the same, or if in its judgment the ends and purposes of said subdivision would be better served.

17. The herein enumerated restrictions, rights, reservations, limitations, agreements, covenants and conditions shall be deemed as covenants and not as conditions hereof and shall run with the land and shall bind the Grantee until the 1st day of May, 2026, in any event, and continuously thereafter, unless and until any proposed change shall have been approved in writing by the owners of the legal title to all of the land on both sides of the highway within the block in which is located the property, the use of which is sought to be altered by said proposed change, and the Grantee herein agree to require that these restrictions be recited at length in all future instruments conveying said premises or any portion thereof.

18. The Grantor reserves easements and rights-of-way in, over, under and across the strip of land $7\frac{1}{2}$ feet in width, comprising that portion of said premises which consists of the real $7\frac{1}{2}$ feet thereof, for the installation and maintenance of telephone and electric pole lines or conduits or for any other similar facility deemed convenient or necessary by the Granter for the service of the premises hereby conveyed and for adjoining and adjacent property."

APPENDIX E

VAN SWERINGEN DEMONSTRATION AND MASTER MODEL HOMES

Address	Year	Architect	Style
Van Sweringen Demonstration Homes			
19300 Shaker Boulevard	1922	Howell & Thomas	English Tudor Revival
2834 Courtland Boulevard	1922	Howell & Thomas	English Tudor Revival
2833 Courtland Boulevard	1922	Howell & Thomas	English Tudor Revival
19600 Shaker Boulevard	1922	Howell & Thomas	English Tudor Revival
19600 South Woodland Road / 3076 Kingsley Road	1924	Philip L. Small	English
19700 South Woodland Road	1924	Philip L. Small	French
19910 South Woodland Road	1924	Philip L. Small	English
20000 South Woodland Road	1924	Philip L. Small	English
3158 Morley Road	1924	Philip L. Small	English
3105 Van Aken Boulevard	1924	Bloodgood Tuttle	English
3113 Van Aken Boulevard	1924	Bloodgood Tuttle	Dutch Colonial
3125 Van Aken Boulevard	1924	Bloodgood Tuttle	French
3137 Van Aken Boulevard	1924	Bloodgood Tuttle	English
3149 Van Aken Boulevard	1924	Bloodgood Tuttle	English
18405 Van Aken Boulevard	1924	Bloodgood Tuttle	French
18419 Van Aken Boulevard	1924	Bloodgood Tuttle	French
18435 Van Aken Boulevard	1924	Bloodgood Tuttle	French
18513 Van Aken Boulevard	1924	Bloodgood Tuttle	French
18414 Parkland Drive	1924	Howell & Thomas	English
18428 Parkland Drive	1924	Howell & Thomas	French
18500 Parkland Drive	1924	Howell & Thomas	English
18524 Parkland Drive	1924	Howell & Thomas	English
3280 Maynard Road	1924	Howell & Thomas	French
18560 Parkland Drive	1924	Howell & Thomas	English
18580 Parkland Drive	1924	Howell & Thomas	English/French

Address	Year	Architect	Style
Master Model Homes			
17725 Scottsdale Boulevard	1928	Fox, Duthie & Foose	American Colonial
17732 Scottsdale Boulevard	1928	Fox, Duthie & Foose	Pennsylvania Farmhouse
18108 Scottsdale Boulevard	1928	Fox, Duthie & Foose	French
18302 Scottsdale Boulevard	1928	Fox, Duthie & Foose	Rural English Cottage
18305 Scottsdale Boulevard	1928	Fox, Duthie & Foose	English Studio
18320 Scottsdale Boulevard	1928	Fox, Duthie & Foose	French Country
18421 Scottsdale Boulevard	1929	Fox, Duthie & Foose	Colonial Revival
18716 Scottsdale Boulevard	1928	Fox, Duthie & Foose	Rural English Cottage

INDEX

Italic numbers indicate pages with art.

1893 Columbian Exposition, 19, 24; Chicago World's Fair, 20

African Americans, 85, 234
Albright, John Joseph, capitalist, 3, 158
Alleghany Corporation. *See* Van Sweringen railroad empire: holding companies
Allen, Frederick Lewis, *The Lords of Creation: The History of America's 1 Percent*, 4, 5n1
Ambler, Nathan Hardy, 53
Ambler, William Eglin, 53
Ambler Heights, 45, 49, 50, 53
American Revolution. *See* Revolutionary War
Ames, Richard and Ann, 225. *See also* Clanonderry
Anderson, Col. Henry W., attorney, 165–67
Andrews, Horace E., 49, 73
Anglo-Saxon Protestant, 78, 234
antislavery movement, 42, 25; abolitionists, 105
Appalachian Highlands, 35, 38; Appalachian Mountains, 125
Arcade, 24, 25, 212, 234
Atterbury, William Wallace, 162, 163, 169, 170

Bailey, Dr. Edward A. and Clara Hodgkins, 85
Bailie, Earle, investment banker, 193, 194
Baker, George F., capitalist, 3, 161
Baker, Newton D., attorney, mayor, and secretary of war, 81, 132, 135, 157, 158, 165, 168
Ball, George A., 3, 182, 191, 192, 194, 195, 201; Ball Brothers Company, 186
Baltimore & Ohio Railroad (B&O), 81, 137, 157, 161–65, 170, 174, 176, 177, 242
Barton R. Deming House, 58
Bauhaus school of design, 234
Baus, Louis, 66, 68, 70
Beaux Arts architecture, 24, 33, 127, 133
Beckwith, T. Sterling, 18, 19, 28
Bedford Township, 7
Beecher, Henry Ward, abolitionist, 105
Ben Brae, 111, *111*
Berkshire Hathaway, 242
Bernet, John J., 82, 97, 101, 135, 156, 158, 159, 162, 164, 168, 181
Bernstein, Nathan, architect, 226, 229
Bessemer & Lake Erie Railroad. *See* Van Sweringen railroad empire: operating companies

Bethlehem Steel, 199
Big Four (Cleveland, Cincinnati, Chicago, & St. Louis) Railroad, 137, 157
Big Four Systems (Pennsylvania, New York Central, Baltimore & Ohio, and the Van Sweringens), 174
Blosser, Raymond F., 2, 3, 166
Bohannon, James A. and Mary R., 212, 217
Bohnard & Parrson Architects, 55, *55*
Bond Clothing Company, 240
Boston & Maine Railroad, 164, 174, 175
Bowman, Robert J., 197, 199
Bradley, Charles L., 73, 81, 133, 135, 159, 182, 192–95
Bradley Chemical Company, 32; Bradley Fertilizer Company, 32
Breuer, Marcel, architect, 241
Brewer, Nelson J., judge, 185
Briggs, Charles, estate, 48, *48*
Brooke, George, railroad executive, 192–194
Brooke and Burrows, architects, 59, 103, 212
Brown, John Hartness, 45, 48, *48*
Brown, Marcus M., 51–53

259

Brown, M. M., Mayfield Heights, 45. *See also* Brown, Marcus M.
Brunner, Arnold W., architect, 19, 24
Brush, Charles, inventor, 24
Buckwell, Edward G., 55, *55*
Buffalo, Rochester & Pittsburgh Railroad, 157, 164, 170, 174
Buffalo Road, 7, 12, 16
Buffett, Warren, investor and philanthropist. *See* Berkshire Hathaway
Builders Exchange, 148; Builders Exchange Building, 148, *149*, 151
building standards, 62, 85, 103, 248
Burlington Northern Railroad, 175, 242
Burnham, Brunner, and Carrère, architects, 24
Burnham, Daniel H., architect, 19, 24, 129, 133, 151, 238
Burrows, George H., 59, 103, 212
Burton, J. Prescott, Jr., coal industry executive, 73, *74*

Cady, Asa and Teresa, 42, *44*
Calhoun, Patrick, attorney, 45, 47 48–50
Canfield, George, 24, 55, *55*
Cannon, John L., attorney, 78, 132, 157
Carrère, John M., architect, 19, 24
Carter, Lorenzo and Rebecca, 7, 12; replica cabin, *9*
Catholics, 85
Cedar Glen, 20, 45, 49, 53, 55, 79, 83
Cedar Heights, 45, 49, 50, *50*, *51*
Chapman, Caroline, 80, 81

Chase National Bank, 176, 197
Chesapeake & Ohio (C&O). *See* Van Sweringen railroad empire: operating companies
Chesapeake Corporation. *See* Van Sweringen railroad empire: holding companies
Chicago & Eastern Illinois Railroad. *See* Van Sweringen railroad empire: operating companies
Chicago Great Western Railroad, 174, 177
Chisholm, Henry, 16, 240
Cigliano, Jan, *Showplace of America: Cleveland's Euclid Avenue, 1850–1919*, 16, 33
Citizens Building, *179*, 181
City Beautiful movement, 19, 24, 82
Civil War, *x*, 2, 4, 28, 29, 66, 160
Clanonderry, 225, *221–24*
Clayton Antitrust Act, 81, 127, 198
Cleaveland, Gen. Moses, 7, 35, 133
Cleaveland, village of, *10*, city of, 32
Cleveland, city of, 5, 17, 20, 32, 33
Cleveland & Western Coal Company, 170
Cleveland City Council, 7, 20, 33, 80, 81, 132, 158
Cleveland City Hall, 19, 24
Cleveland Cliffs Iron Company, 90
Cleveland Clinic, 105, 116, 240
Cleveland Electric Illuminating Company, 20
Cleveland Group Plan, 24, 129; Group Plan Commission, 19, 24, 79; New Group Plan Commission, 241
Cleveland Heights, 35, 42, 44; village of, 45, 48, 62; city of, 103, 111, 150, 234
Cleveland Heights Board of Education, 42, 44

Cleveland Heights Methodist Episcopal Church, 44, *45*
Cleveland Mall, 19, 24, 79, 81, 132, 133
Cleveland Museum of Art, 38
Cleveland News, 186
Cleveland *Plain Dealer*. *See Plain Dealer*
Cleveland Press, 177
Cleveland Railway Company, 20, 21, 45, 49, 73, 78, 79, 82, 83, 133, 135, 150, 151, 162, 176
Cleveland Township, 7, 9, 12
Cleveland Transit System, 20, 110, 151, 162; Greater Cleveland Regional Transit Authority, 151, 162
Cleveland Trust Company, 51, 125, 174, 184, 193, 194, 240, 241
Cleveland Twist Drill Co., 16, 32, 55
Cleveland Union Terminal. *See* Van Sweringen real estate empire
Clover Leaf Company. *See* Van Sweringen railroad empire: holding companies
Clover Leaf Railroad. *See* Van Sweringen railroad empire: operating companies
coast-to-coast railroad system. *See* Van Sweringen railroad empire: operating companies
Collamer, village of, 35, 45
Collinwood, village of, 35, rail yard, 148
Colony Theater, 125
Colston, Col. William Ainslie, 101, 157, 165
Congregational Union of Cleveland, 105
Connecticut Land Company, 7, 65
Consolidated Rail Corporation (Conrail), 242
Corlett, Robert and Elizabeth, 41, 42

Corlett, William T., 20
Cosmopolitan magazine, 225
County, Albert John, 169
Cowles, J. G. W., 45
Cowse, G. E., attorney, 157
Cox, Jacob, 16
Crash of 1907, 51
Creech, Harris, banker, 193
Crowley, Patrick, 135, 162–64
Curtis-Preyer House, 42, 43
Cuyahoga Anti-Slavery Society, 42
Cuyahoga County, 38, 70; map of, 36; population of, 82
Cuyahoga County Administration Building, 241
Cuyahoga County Commissioners, 35
Cuyahoga County Soldiers' and Sailors' Monument, 1, 2
Cuyahoga River, 7, 9, 16, 133, 241

Daisy Hill. *See* Van Sweringen residences
Dalton-Dalton-Little-Newport, architects, 234
deed restrictions, 62, 85, 103, 116, 234, 252
Delaware & Hudson Railroad, 169, 182
Deming, Barton, 58, 61
Deming, Grant Roy, 56, 57, 59
demonstration homes. *See* Van Sweringen real estate empire
Denney, Charles E., 168, 181
Denver & Rio Grande Western. *See* Van Sweringen railroad empire: operating companies
Detroit & Toledo Shore. *See* Van Sweringen railroad empire: operating companies

Detroit, Toledo & Ironton Railroad, 174
D. H. Burnham and Company, 133
discrimination, 85, 170
Doan, Nathaniel, 7, 38
Doan Brook, 7, 29, 35–38, 65, 70, 103, 125
Doan's Corners, 9, 20
Doan Street, 7, 29, 32
Doctors' Hospital, 116
Doran, J. J., attorney, 197
Duncan, William McKinley, 157
Dodge, Samuel, 19
Dunham, Rufus and Jane Pratt, 12. *See also* Dunham Tavern Museum and Garden
Dunham House, 129; David Dunham, 129
Dunham Tavern Museum and Garden, 12, 13
Dyer, J. Milton, architect, 19, 111

Early Settlers Association of the Western Reserve, 12
East Cleveland, village of, 35, city of, 35, 83
East Cleveland Railway Company, 20
East Cleveland Township, 7, 24, 35, 42, 45, 51, 78
East Ohio Gas Company Building, 151
Eastman, Joseph Bartlett, 151, 159, 169, 185, 196
Eaton, Cyrus S., industrialist, 195, 199, 201
Eaton, Joseph Oriel, 55, 57; Eaton Axle Company, 57; Eaton Corporation, 57
Ellison, David H., architect, 225. *See also* Clanonderry
English Oak Room, 145, 148
Erie Railroad. *See* Van Sweringen railroad empire: operating companies
Erie Street Cemetery, 11, 12

escarpment, 29, 35, 38, 45
Euclid Avenue, 7, 12, 13, 16, *18*–20, 24, 25, 27–9, 35, 48, 79, 105, 110, 148, 150, 151, *179*, *180*, 181, 234, 240, 241. *See also* Euclid Street
Euclid Golf Allotment, Barton Deming's, 49, *58*, *59*, *59*, 61
Euclid Golf and Country Club, 49; Euclid Club, 49, 50, 61
Euclid Heights Allotment, 45, 48–51, 62, 85, 103
Euclid Street, 7, 16
Euclid Township, 7, 50
Everett, Peter R. and Lucy Hewitt, 51
Everett, Sylvester, 19

F. A. Pease Engineering Company, 73, 79, 82, 127. *See also* Pease, Fred Alwood
Farm Group. *See* Van Sweringen residences
Federal Aid Road Act of 1916, 243
Federal Highway Act of 1921, 243
Federal Reserve Bank, 173, 174
Federal Reserve Board, 173
fifth system, 170, 174, 176
First National Bank of the City of New York, 3
FitzGerald, William F., mayor, 157
Ford, Mrs. F. L., 19
Forest City House, 129
Forest Hill Allotment, Grant Deming's, 56, *57* 57
Fox, Duthie & Foose, architects, 103, 257
Fullerton, Harold Ott, architect, *114*, 116

G. C. Kuhlman Car Company, 82, 84
Gallagher, Michael, 73, 77

Gallimore, Harry C., civil engineer, 82
garden city, 82
Garfield, Abram, son, architect, 116
Garfield, Harry Augustus, 240
Garfield, James A., president, 45
Garfield, James Rudolph., son, architect 240
Garfield Apartments, 240
Garfield Building, 240
General Securities Corporation. *See* Van Sweringen railroad empire: holding companies
Geneva, Ashtabula County, Ohio, 29
George and Frances Ball Foundation, 192, 194–96
Gill, John, father, 48, 55
Gill, John T., son, 48, 49, 55
Gill, Kermode, son, 48, 54, 55
Gleason, William J., 2, 3
Glenville, 24, 35, 57, 125, 176
The Good Life in Shaker Heights, 225
Grand Trunk Railroad, 159, 160
Granger, Alfred H., architect, 45, 46, 47, 48, 48
Gray, A. Donald, landscape architect, 12
Gratwick, William Henry, Jr., 70, 73
Gratwick, William Henry, Sr., capitalist, 3, 70
Great Depression, x, 83, 151, 173, 175–7, 182, 185, 199, 242, 274
Gregory, Thomas W., attorney general, 81
Group Plan. *See* Cleveland Group Plan
Guidebook Of Better Homes, 103

Haberman, Ian. *The Van Sweringens of Cleveland: The Biography of an Empire*, viii, 1
Halle, Salmon, 85, 225

Halle Brothers' Shaker Square, 225, 226
Hamilton, James M., architect, 48, 49, 49, 73, 74, 76
Hanna, Marcus, 24
Hanna Building, 48, 150
Hanna House of Lakeside Hospital, 182
Hanrahan, William J. 185
Harcourt Manor, 54, 55
Harris, Albert Hall, 159, 162
Harris, Alfred W., architect, 117, 119, 120
Harkness, Steven V., merchant, 24
Harwood, Herbert H., Jr., *Invisible Giants: The Empires of Cleveland's Van Sweringen Brothers*, viii, 1
Hathaway Brown School, 105, 107, 110
Hayden, Warren, attorney, 81, 157, 159
Haymarket District, 79, 80
H. C. Van Sweringen residence. *See* Van Sweringen residences
Hecker, John A., 41
Hecker, Richard and Clarissa, 41
Hellmuth, Obata + Kassabaum, architects, 238
Henry, Frederick, A., judge, 194
Herrick, Myron T., attorney and diplomat, 49, 217
Herrick, Parmely, financier, 81
H. F. Bash House, 115, 116
Hickox, Martha and Wilson Beggs, 49, 49
Higbee Company, 151, 152, 194, 195, 234
Hillcrest Hospital, 116
Hilltop Realty Company, 184
Hinsdale, Reynold, architect, 90, 96
History of the Cuyahoga County Soldiers' and Sailors' Monument, Gleason, William, 2

Hocking Valley Railroad. *See* Van Sweringen railroad empire: operating companies
holding companies, 155, 159, 160, 166–70, 176, 177, 181, 185, 192–96, 242
Hollister, John B., 193, 194
Homestead Act of 1862, 35
House Interstate Commerce Committee, 177
Howard M. Metzenbaum US Courthouse, 24, 26
Howe, H. D., attorney, 82, 157
Howell & Thomas, architects, 61, 111, 256
Howells, Harry B., attorney, 194
Hunkin & Conkey Construction, 105
Hunting Valley, 79, 80, 90, 191, 203, 212, 217, 243
Huntington, Collis P., 160
Huntington, Henry and Arabella, 160
Huntington Bank, Huntington Bank Building, 240

Ingalls, A. S., 157
Ingalls, George Hoadley, 162
Inglewood, 45, 111, 116; Inglewood Historic District, *112–15*
International-Great Northern Railroad Company, 192
Interstate Commerce Act of 1887, 155, 198
Interstate Commerce Commission (ICC), 101, 155–65, 167–70, 174, 176, 185, 192, 196–201, 242, 243
Investment Bankers Association, 196
Invisible Giants: The Empires of Cleveland's Van Sweringen Brothers, viii
Isle of Man, 41, 48

J. P. Morgan & Co., 175, 185
Jackson, Kenneth, *Crabgrass Frontier*, ix
Jaffe House (Joseph and Virginia Jaffe), 227, 234
James, Arthur Curtiss, 175
Jeffrey, H. T., architect, 79, 86, 87
Jenks, Benjamin Lane, 2, 73, 79, 81, 90, 135, 173, 185, 191
Jenks, Daisy, 2, 73, 79, 80, 81, 90, 127, 182, 184, 185, 191, 243
Jenks, David, son, 2, 191
Jenks, Louis Clara Davidson. *See* Jenks, Daisy
Jews, 85
Johnson, Tom, mayor, 19, 79, 132
Jones, Paul, judge, 195
Joyce, Patrick, 177

K & D Group, developers, 241
Kansas City Southern. *See* Van Sweringen railroad empire: operating companies
Kewish, William and Jane, 41, *42*
Key Tower, 133, 238, *239*
Kingsbury Run, 79, 83
Kirby, Allan R., father, 192–96, 199, 242
Kirby, Fred, son, 242
Koellisch, Phillip W., landscape architect, 116
Kolbe, Frank F., 192, 193, 201
Kuhn, Loeb & Company, 196

Lake Erie, 35, 38
Lake Erie & Western (LE&W). *See* Van Sweringen railroad empire: operating companies
Lake Shore & Michigan Central, 81
Lake Shore & Michigan Southern, 81, 181
Lakeview & Collamer Railroad, 20
Lake View Cemetery, 12, 35, 45, 186, *187–189*
Lamb, Lawrence, 66, 70
Lamb, Thomas A, 70
Lamont, Thomas, banker, 176, 185
LAND Studio, 241
Land Ordinance of 1798, 35
Larick, Roy, PhD, 38
Laurel School, *109*, 110
Lee, Gen. Robert E., 29
Lee, Mother Ann, 65
Lehigh Valley Railroad (1932). *See* Van Sweringen railroad empire: operating companies
Leskosky, Vincent M., architect, 233, 234
Lincoln, James F., and Jane D. White, 203, 212
Little, Robert A., architect, 225, 226, 227, 234
Lock 38, Ohio and Erie Canal, 14, *15*, 16
Long Lake Company. *See* Van Sweringen real estate empire
Longwood estate, *110*, 111
Loree, Leonor F., 169, 182
LTV Steel Building, 151
Luce, Jesse H., 80

Marshall, John D., mayor, 135
Marshall Drug Building, 80
Marshall Field & Company, 151
Master Model Homes, 101, *102*, 103, 127, 257
Mather, Samuel, 28
May Company, 151, 234
Mayfield Country Club, 50, 103
Mayfield Township, 35
McAdoo, William Gibbs, 156
Meade, Frank B., architect, 47, 48, *48*, 49,*49*, 54, 55, 73, 103
Meade and Granger, architects, 47, 48, *48*
Meade and Hamilton, architects, 49, *49*, 55 57, 73
Medical Arts Building, 148, *149*, 150, 151
Midamerica Corporation, 182, 191, 192, 201
midcentury modern, 225, 228–32
Midland Bank, 148, 151, 176
Midland Building, 135, 148, *149*, 150, 151
Millennia Companies, 240, 241
Miller, Otto, 81, 159
Millikin, Benjamin and Julia (Ben Brae), 111, *111*
Millikin, Julia Wadsworth Severance, 111
Millionaires' Row, 16, 19, 24, 28, 45, 111
Missouri Pacific Railroad (Mo-Pac). *See* Van Sweringen railroad empire: operating companies
Missouri Public Service Commission, 174
Moreland Courts. *See* Van Sweringen real estate
Morgan, John Pierpont, 3
Morris, William B., architect, 234, 231
Morrow, Robert R. and Leah M., 203
most beautiful street in America, 12, 16, 28
Mowrey, Phinney, 129
Murchison, Clinton W., 200
Murphy, John, 175, 191, 193–95
Myers, John C., industrialist, 194
Myers, Rev. Charles H., 186

Nash, William Fowler and Anna, 73
Nathan Weisenberg House, *57, 59*
National Association Security Dealers, 196
National City Bank Building, 181, 240
National City Bank of New York, 173
National City Center, 240
National Railroad Passenger Corporation (Amtrak), 242
Native American Lake Shore Trail, 7
Nature Center at Shaker Lakes, 38
New England Building, 180, 240
New Group Plan Commission, 241
New Haven Railroad, 174
New Jersey Central Railroad, 163
Newport News Shipbuilding & Drydock Company, 195
New York, Chicago & St. Louis Railroad. *See* Van Sweringen railroad empire: operating companies
New York, Ontario & Western, 164
New York Central Railroad, 3, 81–83, 90, 137, 157–58, 160–65, 174, 176, 182, 196–200, 242, 243
New York State Supreme Court, 200
New York Stock Exchange, 171, 192, 193
New York Times, 19, 185
New York Trust Company, 176
Nickel Plate Securities Company. *See* Van Sweringen railroad empire: holding companies
Nickel Plate Road. *See* Van Sweringen railroad empire: operating companies
Norcross, M. A., architect, *225, 228*

Norfolk & Western, 160, 174, 241
North American Coal Company, 170
North Union (Shaker) Settlement, map of, *67*
Northern Ohio District Court, 195
Northern Ohio Interurban, 83
Northern Ohio Traction & Light Company, 162
Nutt, Joseph R., 73, 81, 157, 159, 193

Oaks, Joseph A. and Phillippina, 70
Ohio and Erie Canal, 16; Lock 38, *14*; Tinkers Creek Aqueduct, *15*
O'Neill, Francis J. "Steve" and Anne H., 217
O'Neill, Nancy Marsteller, 225
Ontario Street Cemetery, 12
Orange Avenue Freight Station, 82, 132, 151
Otis, Charles, 16
Otis & Company, 196
Pacific Railway Act of 1862, 155
Pack, Charles Lathrop, 111
Paine Webber, 176, 177
Painter, John Vickers and Lydia Ethel Farmer, 70
Painter, Kenyon Vickers (son) and Maude Wyethe, 70, *71, 72,* 85, 105
Panic of 1893, 45, 70
Parke-Bernet Galleries, 191
Pease, Fred Alwood, civil engineer, 70, 82. *See also* F. A. Pease Engineering Company
Pease, William, civil engineer, 79
Peerless Motor Car Company, 23, *24,* 212
Pegg, John and Dorothy, 85,
Pelli, César, architect, 238

Penn Central Railroad, 242
Pennroad Corporation, 170
Pennsylvania Coal Company. *See* Van Sweringen railroad empire: operating companies
Pennsylvania Railroad, 81, 90, 157–65, 169, 174, 176, 242
Pepper Pike Country Club, 125
Pere Marquette Railroad. *See* Van Sweringen railroad empire: operating companies
Perlman, Alfred E., 200
Perry, Nathan, 16
Phin Mowrey's Tavern, 129
Pittsburgh & West Virginia, *See* Van Sweringen railroad empire: operating companies
Pittsburgh Coal Company, 170
Pittsburgh Terminal Railroad & Coal Company, 170
Plain Dealer, 32, 50, 66, 70, 78, 86, 103, 116, 127, 129, 148, 151, 178, 181, 184, 186, 191, 193, 199–200, 212
Plymouth Church, 105, *106,* 186
Portage escarpment, 29, 35, 38, 45
Prentiss, Elisabeth Severance Allen, 111; Glen Allen, *111*
Prentiss, James, 38
Prentiss, Lucretia J, *113,* 116
Preyer, John Peter and Charlotte, 42, 43, 51
Prince, Frederick H., investment banker, 182
Prospekt Nevsky, 19
Public Square, 7, 12, 16, 19, 20, 28, 38, 70, 73, 79–82
Public Utility Holding Company Act, 177

Pugwash Conference of Nuclear Scientists, 199
pyramiding, 175

Quilliams, William T. and Nancy, *44*, 45

Rail Passenger Service Act of 1970, 175
Railway Executives Association, 175
rapid transit. See Van Sweringen railroad empire: operating companies
Reading Railroad, 163–65, 174
real estate standards, 248
Rea, Samuel, 162–65, 169
Reconstruction Finance Corporation, 177
Reed, Ronald A., architect, 233, 234
Reese, J. A., architect, 103
Renner, Dr. R. Richard, 116
Republic Building, 151
Republic Iron and Steel, 199
Republic Steel Corporation, 199
Revolutionary War, 7, 38, 65
Rice, William Lowe, attorney, 45, 70
Richardson, Sid W., 200
Richmond Terminal Railroad, 45
Ringle, Owen C., 70, 73
Ripley, William Zebina, 157, 167, 174
Robert V. Clapp Company, 103
Robinson, Philip E., architect, 59, 61
Rockefeller, John D., 16, 24, 32, 45, 49, 57, 61, 70, 73, 158, 170
Rockefeller Building, 181
Rockefeller Park, 29, 38, 57
Rockefeller Refinery No. 1, 79

Rockport Township, 12
Rocky River Railroad, 20
Rose Iron Works, 86
Rose, W. R., 129, 151
Ross, Walter L., 159, 160, 165, 168,
Rotary Club of Cleveland, 186
Roundwood Manor and garages. See Van Sweringen residences
Rowley, Charles Bacon, architect, 90, 225
Russell, Jacob, father, 65, *69*
Russell, Ralph, son, and Laura, 65, 66, 127
Russell, Return, son, and Jerusha, 65

Schneider, Charles S, architect, *106*, 116
Schofield Building, 2, 181
Schweinfurth, Charles F., architect, 48, *48*, 51, *51*, 111
Scofield, Levi Tucker, architect, sculptor, 1–3, 12, 20, 24, 137
Sears, Roebuck, & Company kit homes, *60*, *61*, *62*
Sedgewick Land Company. See Van Sweringen real estate empire
Severance, John Long (son), 111; Longwood, *110*
Severance, Louis (father), 24, 111
Shaker Farm Allotment. See Van Sweringen real estate empire
Shaker Heights, 4, 5, 41; city of, 78, 248, 252; village of, 78
Shaker Heights City Council, 41, 234
Shaker Heights Country Club, 38, 50, 103, *104*, 105

Shaker Heights Historical Society, 41
Shaker Heights Land Company, 70, 73, 86
Shaker Lakes Trolly, 79
Shakers, 38, 65, 66, *67–69*, 70
Shaker Square. See Van Sweringen real estate empire
Shaker Village, 78, 82, 85, 90, 101, 103, 105, 110, 116, 162
Sherwin Williams Co., 16, 80, 238
Sherwin, Henry, 16
Sixteenth Amendment, 20
Small, Philip L., architect, 73, 75, 86, 87, 88, 90, *91*, *92*, 101, 117. 121, 122, 212, 225, 256
Smith, Alfred Holland ("Mr. Smith") 3, 80–82, 156–58, 162, 163
Smith, J. Wentworth, 50, 51, *51*, 59, 61
Soldiers' and Sailors' Monument, 1; history of (Gleason, William J.), 2
Stager-Beckwith mansion, *18*, *19*, 28
Standard Oil Company, 16, 170
Statler Arms Apartments, 19
Stillman Hotel, 19
Stillman Theater, 19
Stockbridge Hotel, *27*, *28*, 55
Strong, Jacob, 41, *41*
Superior School House, *44*; Cleveland Heights Historical Society, 42
Superior Street Railway, 20

Taft, Frederick L., 32
Taplin, Frank Elijah, and Charkes Farrand Taplin, 169, 174, 195

Terminal & Shaker Heights Realty Company. *See* Van Sweringen real estate empire

Terminal Building Company. *See* Van Sweringen real estate empire

terminal complex. *See* Van Sweringen real estate empire

Terminal Realty & Securities Company. *See* Van Sweringen real estate empire

Terminal Shares, Incorporated. *See* Van Sweringen real estate empire

Texas & Pacific Railroad. *See* Van Sweringen railroad empire: operating companies

Thompson, Studer, 73, 75

Tinkers Creek Aqueduct. *See* Ohio and Erie Canal

Toguchi, Fred S., architect, 225, *230*

Toledo, St. Louis & Western (Clover Leaf Route). *See* Van Sweringen railroad empire: operating companies, Clover Leaf Railroad

Tomlinson, George Ashley, 181, 182, 191, 192, 194

Tonks, William, banker, *114*, 116

Tower East, 234, *236*

Transportation Act of 1920, 156, 159, 196

Transportation Building, 148

Tremaine, Henry A. 73

Triple Alliance, 164, 169

Truth-in-Securities Act, 177

Tuttle, Bloodgood, architect, 101–2, 116 156

underground railroad, 42

Underwood, Frederick, 168

Union Bank of Commerce, *180*, 181, 240

Union Properties Company, 181, 212

Union Terminal complex. *See* Van Sweringen real estate

Union Trust Company, 70, 73, 116, 133, 174, 176, 177, *180*, 181, 191, 203, 240, 241

United Society of Believers in Christ's Second Appearing. *See* Shakers

University Circle, 38, 53, 79, 182, 184

University School, 105, *108*, 110

Unter den Linden, 19

Upson, Asa and Chloe, 41, *41*

US Circuit Court of Appeals, 193

US Railroad Administration, 156

US Railroad Administration Act of 1920, 156

US Steel, 199, 240

US Supreme Court, 32, 85, 195

Van Aken, William J., 78, 82

Van Aken Boulevard, 78, 82, 84, 101, 103, 233, 234, 256

Van Aken Shopping Center (Van Aken District), 38

Van Sweringen business empire: organizational chart, 1922, *161*; organizational chart, 1925, *167*; organizational chart, 1934, *178*; organizational chart, 1935, *183*

Van Sweringen railroad empire:
holding companies: Alleghany Corporation, 171, 174, 177, 192–94, 196–201, 242, 243; Chesapeake Corporation, 169, 170, 176, 184, 192, 193, 194, 195; Cleveland Interurban Railroad Company, 80; Clover Leaf Company, 159; General Securities Corporation, 171; New York, Chicago & St. Louis Railway Company, 164, 165; Nickel Plate Securities Company, 156; United States Distributing Corporation, 171; Vaness Company, 159, 160, 166–169, 171, 174, 184, 185, 192; Van Sweringen Corporation, 175, 177, 185; Virginia Transportation Corporation, 168; Western Company, 159

operating companies: Bessemer & Lake Erie Railroad, 157, 164; Chesapeake & Ohio (C&O), 135, 160, 164–68, 170, 174, 176, 177, 181, 183–85, 191–201; Chicago and Eastern Illinois Railroad, 164, 174, 176, 177; Cleveland & Youngstown Railroad, 79, 80, 132; Clover Leaf Railroad, 156, 157, 159, 165, 166; coast-to-coast railroad system, 155, 175, 184, 199; Delaware, Lehigh Valley Railroad, 157, 160, 163, 164, 165, 174, 176; Denver & Rio Grande Western Railroad, 169, 175, 200; Detroit & Toledo Shore, 159; Erie Lackawanna, 242; Erie Railroad, 81, 83, 135, 137, 160–164, 167–68, 170, 174, 177, 185, 192, 201; Hocking Valley Railroad, 160, 164, 166, 168, 174; Kansas City Southern, 176, 177; Lackawanna & Western, 157, 160, 242; Lake Erie & Western (LE&W), 156–160, 166; Lehigh Valley Railroad, 157, 160, 163–65, 174, 176; Missouri Pacific Railroad (Mo-Pac), 169, 174, 175, 195, 199, 201, 241; new Nickel Plate, 159–161, 163–69, 174, 177, 181, 182, 184, 193–201, 242–43; New Orleans, Texas

& Mexico, 169; New York, Chicago & St. Louis Railroad (Nickel Plate Road), 81, 82, 101, 132 135, 137, 151, 156, 157, 159; Pennsylvania Coal Company, 161; Pere Marquette Railway, 135, 151, 157, 160, 161, 164, *167*, 169, 177, 192, 195, 196, 197, 199; Pittsburgh & West Virginia, 157, 164, 170, 174, 176; rapid transit, 79–83, 83, 84, 101, 105, 117, 132, 133, 137, 155, 161, 162, 175, 242, 243, 254; Texas & Pacific Railroad 169; Western Maryland, Monon & Ann Arbor, 164, 170, 174, 242; Western Pacific Railroad Company (Western Pacific Railroad Corporation), 175, 184; Wheeling & Lake Erie Railroad, 81, 83, 158, 164, 170, 176, 182, 195–98

Van Sweringen real estate empire: Cleveland Terminals Building Company, 175, 185; Cleveland Union Terminal Railway Bridge, 133; Daisy Hill, 80, 86, 90, *91–95*, 125, 137, 173, 176, 178, 184, 191, 203; Daisy Hill Company, 212, 217; Daisy Hill Farm, 191, 212; Daisy Hill gatehouse, *218–20*; Daisy Hill landowners, 191, 212; demonstration homes, 86, *97–100*, 101, 256; Long Lake Company, 80; Moreland Courts, 90, 117, *118–122*, 203; Sedgewick Land Company, 73, 80; Shaker Country Estates, 90, 125, *127*; Shaker Farm Allotment (Shaker Farm Historic District), 49, 73, *74–77*; Shaker Square 82, 83, 117, *118*, 123, 124; Terminal & Shaker Heights Realty Company, 194, 195; Terminal Building Company, 80; terminal complex, 129, 130, 132–34, 137, 151, 157, 158, 162, 203, 237, 239, 240, 241; Terminal Realty & Securities Company, 80; Terminal Shares, Incorporated, 175; Union Terminal complex, 129, 203, 241; Van Sweringen Company, 41, 70, 80, 83, 85, 157, 175, 184, 185, 194, 255

Van Sweringen residences: Hunting Valley: Daisy Hill farm, 191, 212; Daisy Hill farm group (Clanonderry), 95, 176, 191, 225, 221–24, 226; Daisy Hill gatehouse, *94*, 217; Roundwood garages, 90, 93, 191; Roundwood Manor, *91, 92*, 191; Shaker Heights: H. C. Van Sweringen residence, 90, *96*, 184, 191; South Park estate, 79, 86, *87, 88*, 184, 191, 203; South Park gatehouse, 86, *89*, 191, 203, *208–11*, 212; Swearingen residences Chippewa, 28, 29; Cleveland, 29, 32; Geneva, Ohio, 29, *30, 31*; Rogues Hollow, 29

Van Sweringens: brothers M. J. (Mantis James) and O. P. (Oris Paxton), viii, 1–4, 20; brothers' estate, 191, 192, 247; building the railroad empire, 156–59, 162, 165–67, 170, 174–77, 182; Carrie Blanche, 29–32, 79, 90, 105, 176, 191, 247; death of the brothers, 184–186, *187–89*; developing Public Square, 129, 132, 148, 151; developing Shaker Heights, 73, 78–80, 82, 85, 86, 90, 101, 103, 105, 110; early days, 28–32; early real estate, 45, 50, 62, 70, 73; Edith Elizabeth, 29–32, 73, 79, 90, 105, 176, 191, 247; genealogy, 246, 247; Herbert Curtiss, 29–32, 79, 90, 101, 191, 247; James Tower (Swearingen), 28–31, 33, 247; Jennie Curtis (Swearingen), 28–31, 247; Maude Alene, 29, 247

Wabash, 164, 174, 241
Wade Park Manor, 182
Wade, Jeptha, 19
Walker & Weeks, architects, 111
Wall Street Journal, 186
Walsh, Henry H., architect, 19
Walton, William and Edmund, Jr., 50
War of 1812, 16
Wardley, James and Jane, 65
Warner & Swasey Company, 16, 32
Warner, Worcester, 16
Warren, Daniel, son of Moses, 38
Warren, Margaret Prentiss, wife of Daniel, 38
Warren, Moses, 38, *40*
Warren, Priscilla Nourse, wife of Moses, 38
Warrensville Methodist Episcopal Church, 41
Warrensville Township, 7, 35, *39*, 41, 65
Warrensville West Cemetery, 41, *69*
Wayne County Courthouse, 28
Weddell, Peter M., 19
Wenneman, William H., 2, 175, 186
Western Air Express Airline, 243
Western Company. *See* Van Sweringen railroad empire: holding companies
Western Maryland, Monon & Ann Arbor Railroad. See Van Sweringen railroad empire: operating companies
Western Pacific Railroad Company; Western Pacific Railroad Corporation. *See* Van Sweringen railroad empire: operating companies

Western Reserve, 2, 12, 16, 38, 41; map of, 8; population of, 245
Western Reserve Historical Society, 1, 22, 23
Western Reserve University Medical School, 116
Wheeling & Lake Erie Railroad, 81, 83, 158, 164, 170, 176, 181, 196, 197, 198
Whitley, James M., architect, 232, 234
Willard, Daniel, 162,163, 164, 165, 167, 169
Willey, John W, mayor, 12
Williamson Building, 70, 80, 90, 238
Winton Motor Carriage Factory, 20, 22
Woodland Avenue Street Railroad Company, 20
Wooster, Wayne County, 28, 29, 183
Works Projects Administration (WPA), 12
World War I, 101, 156, 174, 243
World War II, 226, 243

Youghiogheny & Ohio Coal Company, 170
Young, Robert R., 192–201, 242

LAUREN R. PACINI is an architectural photographer and local history author whose work centers on the renovation, restoration, and repurposing of historic industrial, commercial, and residential properties throughout Ohio. His publications include *The Ever-Whirling Winds of Change: The Story of Saint Luke's Hospital, 1894–2014* (2014) (he was a recipient of the National Trust for Historic Preservation/HUD Secretary's Award for Excellence in Historic Preservation [2012] for the photography of the project that led to and was included in the book); *Honoring Their Memory: Levi T. Scofield, Cleveland's Monumental Architect and Sculptor* (2019), for which he was a recipient of the Ohio Local History Outreach Award (2019); *Cleveland A to Z: An Essential Compendium for Visitors and Residents Alike*, with John J. Grabowski, PhD (2019); and *Cleveland's Cultural Gardens: A Landscape of Diversity*, with John J. Grabowski, PhD (2022). He lives in Shaker Heights, Ohio.

For Indiana University Press

Tony Brewer *Artist and Book Designer*
Dan Crissman *Acquisitions Editor and Editorial Director*
Anna Francis *Assistant Acquisitions Editor*
Samantha Heffner *Marketing and Publicity Manager*
Brenna Hosman *Production Coordinator*
Katie Huggins *Production Manager*
David Miller *Lead Project Manager/Editor*
Dan Pyle *Online Publishing Manager*
Jennifer Witzke *Senior Artist and Book Designer*